D1521230

ENVY

Also By Victoria C.G. Greenleaf

A HANDFUL OF ASHES:
One Mother's Tragedy

FIGHTING THE GOOD FIGHT:
One Family's Struggle Against Adolescent Alcoholism

INTO A MIRROR AND THROUGH A LENS:
Forty Poems on the Mother/Child Relationship
From Conception to Marriage

INTERLINK
and Other Nature/Humankind Poems

ENVY

A Survey of Its
Psychology and History

Victoria C.G. Greenleaf, M.D., M.S.

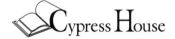

ENVY
A Survey of Its Psychology and History
Copyright ©2009 by Victoria C. G. Greenleaf

Cypress House
155 Cypress Street
Fort Bragg, CA 95437
(800) 773-7782
www.cypresshouse.com

Cover and book design by Michael Brechner/Cypress House
Cover art by Sandra Lindström

The ornament ✳ used in this book is the West African adinkra symbol for "fofo," a yellow flowered plant representing jealousy and envy.

Library of Congress Cataloging-in-Publication Data

Greenleaf, Victoria C. G., 1927-
  Envy : A Survey of Its Psychology and History /
Victoria C.G. Greenleaf. -- 1st ed.
    p. cm.
  Includes bibliographical references and index.
  ISBN 978-1-879384-75-0 (casebound : alk. paper)
  1. Envy. I. Title.

BF575.E65G74 2008
152.4'8--dc22   2007043086

Printed in the USA
9 8 7 6 5 4 3 2 1

Permissions

Dedication

This book is dedicated to the loving memory of my late husband,
Charles, companion of many years, father of my children,
and best friend, and to our grandchildren

Kristina Joanna

Madeleine Grace

Louis Alexandar

Charles Michael

Jackson Gilberto

and

Innominatus(a).

Acknowledgments

As I approach the end of this book task, I feel a glow of appreciation for those who have helped, far too many to mention them all individually.

Before I name those who have helped me with this project, however, I wish to acknowledge the unknown geniuses from millennia past, who have bequeathed us the tools for communicating with those in other places and times. After speech came language first printed as pictures, then in syllables, and finally in the letters of alphabets. Collections of written words followed in libraries in the desert sands, in monasteries, in homes of the wealthy, and in centers of learning. Recognition also goes to the unsung heroes who have made these works available to us by translating.

Libraries would be very difficult to use without reference books and systems, i.e., Library of Congress in most academic libraries, Dewey decimal in most public libraries, and more recently data bases and search engines. In an effort to help patrons, libraries are even set up to borrow from other libraries and other parts of the country. My late husband's nephew, from Ukraine but now naturalized here, expresses amazement at how our librarians put themselves out to find whatever we request.

Two librarians I wish to recognize individually. One is John Bellamy, who consistently found items for me before I even finished the sentence. The other librarian is Deborah Helfling, who generously contributed her time and expertise by teaching me to use the databases in the Cleveland Psychoanalytic Society's Library.

Several friends read an entire earlier draft: three daughters-in-law (Karen M. Hudson, Ph.D.; Patricia V. Denko; and Lisa C. Thomas, M.D.; my colleague and friend Sally Sherry; a retired librarian, book discussant, and critic Richard Gercken, to all of whom go my thanks, but particularly to William J. Cashman and James A. Walker, whose detailed criticisms and comments led to my rethinking and reorganizing the entire book.

Eschewing the standard advice to less experienced authors not to talk about work-in-progress lest they talk it out at the expense of writing it out, I have mentioned this work to many individuals and incorporated their responses. When Elizabeth Bott Spillius (a psychoanalyst I cite in chapter 13) was in town, she gave me an hour talking over with me my chapter on envy in psychoanalysis, and I am grateful for her encouragement. Similarly, I value the time spent on the phone with Sheila Rouslin Welt, reviewing her chapter and my plan.

I appreciate the help I received from John Kirk, who majored in philosophy before taking over his family business. He helped, logically enough, with references to philosophers. Blaise Levai, a clergyman, has found me several maxims, and we talked over the Apocrypha.

I am grateful for the efforts of Joe Shaw, my long-time editor at Cypress House; of Michael Brechner, our ingenious compositor; of Stephanie Rosencrans, my meticulous and parsimonious permissions gatherer; and of artist Sandra Lindstrom.

Finally, I must acknowledge the patience and willingness required in any family where a project like this commandeers hundreds of hours from ordinary family living. I appreciate my late husband's loving help, sacrifices, and encouragement throughout our long marriage to enable me to achieve my goals.

Foreword

There are words in the English language which occur quite frequently but whose meaning lacks significant general agreement. One such is *envy*. In some quarters it is considered a very negative quality or attitude, however transitory, and is even thought to be one of the Seven Deadly Sins. Elsewhere it is regarded as a spur to personal accomplishment, something to be tolerated for its usefulness despite the inner turmoil it may bring. After the 9–11 attacks and amid the ensuing confusion over what could have motivated such apparent hatred, this is a particularly apt moment for this book to appear. Perhaps one reason why more of us have not deduced that the rising disparity between various peoples makes such rage inevitable is that we are too used to not giving envy its due.

When one examines the contexts of its usages, as Dr. Greenleaf does in this comprehensive and revealing new book, one has to wonder if there is a single phenomenon being described by the term *envy*, if it is a convenient category-name for a variety of possibly associated mental states—with as broad a range as those collected under the term *love*. If the latter is the case, then one can speculate further why critical analysis that could differentiate the various subsumed strains has not been brought to bear on this subject. Are we lazy, or might this mental state incorporate elements of man's dark side, of which we are not proud and whose strength we seek to deny?

The possibility of the former being the case raises an equal number of questions. If it is a single phenomenon, as emotions are commonly thought to be, why is there such a range of interpretations of its cause and source? Is it one of our basic emotions? Is it primary, or secondary, perhaps composed of combinations of other mental-state colorations? In the paleontology of emotion, when did it arise—early or late? Has it changed over the decades and eons since it was first noted? To what extent does it depend on cultural, racial, or socioeconomic factors, or on the era, or time of life, in which it is experienced? Can various combinations of these factors give it differing forms?

Most people readily admit to having experienced envy but not all. Can we safely guess that those who don't simply won't confess this perceived weakness, or are they repressing their experience? Or are some immune—and if so, why? Many emotions persist long after their cause has been removed; does envy? Can there be *residual envy?* Can envy be a legitimate, logical response to an awareness of a general social imbalance even if it is triggered by specific instances? If so, can degrees of validity be assigned to its diverse eruptions?

Despite our accumulated insights about the dynamics of mental activity, we really know very little about the details of how the mind works, and yet it is still surprising that something so common should be so little understood. For we use the term all the time, as Dr. Greenleaf's fascinating chronological compendium makes clear. The term occurs in poetry and song, in historical analysis as well as popular fiction, and as requisite motivation for plotting many of our great dramas. In each instance it seems adequately grasped, if not understood—as if, like art, we can't quite explain it but certainly know what it is.

The occurrence of some emotions is accompanied by concomitant physical symptoms that help in their identification. But not envy; its detection is only possible through the admission of an individual caught in its thrall. We admit this tacitly by not challenging such a confession; if someone says, "I'm torn up inside with envy," the response is never, as it might be for love, "Are you sure?" Instead we sympathize, and even prescribe possible ameliorations—usually homespun folk remedies: "Focus on how God will judge them when they arrive at the Gate."

What dawns on readers of this book is a sense of surprise that something so common and yet so little understood has received so little critical attention. Dr. Greenleaf does not solve this puzzle so much as demonstrate its existence. By summarizing our shifting interpretations of this shadowy universal phenomenon, she has done us two fine services: challenged us to get serious about coming to terms with it, and provided us a starting point at which to begin. We can all learn something about ourselves—how we think and behave—from her book.

No doubt this book also has great heuristic value—not just stimulating us to think about envy, but spurring us to rethink our understanding of other emotions. As perhaps the most elusive emotion, a consideration of envy raises questions we can't help but apply to related factors we assumed were better known. Do they evolve? Mutate? Do they act singly, or in combinations? Is there a hierarchy, with those on top having more effect than those below? Which ones can be dominated by a rational mind? The flow of questions stemming from reading this book is endless. For that reason it should become a classic, the rare volume that leads to the creation of a new library shelf.

William J. Cashman
Writer and Publisher
Beaver Island, Michigan
2007

Preface

Thirty-some years ago, an article in *Harper's Magazine* by George P. Elliott, "BURIED ENVY: The Last Dirty Little Secret", attracted my attention. "The Last Dirty Little Secret"! This article reminded me of several uncomfortable experiences I had had, had not liked myself for having, had kept hidden ("buried") because of shame, and had pushed down out of consciousness as quickly as possible. With Elliott's help I identified the enemy. Its name is "Envy".

Thinking about this article, I began noticing not only situations that could be explained by my envying someone else, but also those in which I was probably the target of others' envy. The fact that this book includes my experiences with envy, some painful, some embarrassing, some ridiculous, shows the array of this problem that afflicts us all, ranging from trivial to devastating, from buried deep to written large in behavior, obviates the need to give examples here. As an only child, I am an example that it is not necessary to have siblings to learn to envy young, as some have believed.

My observations radiated outward, like waves from a stone skipped on the surface of a pond. As a recently fledged psychiatrist, I had heard many of the woes the flesh is heir to, but rarely would the patient identify envy as causal. Occasionally a patient well into treatment who had established what we call a good positive transference, feeling she could trust me to understand, would ask for help with her self-identified envy. Much more often I would hear from the patient a configuration that sounded as if it could be explained by envy, and by gentle probing I could usually lead the patient to recognize that phenomenon as the source of his pain, and I felt my way toward helping with it. I saved accounts of such incidents separate from my usual notes. And so I began my serious envy quest.

Heading toward the library for help, I found it strange that my own specialty of psychiatry had had little to say on the subject. Yet when I turned to the related specialty of psychoanalysis, I discovered that their specialists had generated a rather extensive envy literature. Although Freud himself suggested little beyond "penis envy" as an explanation for women, his follower Melanie Klein wrote extensively on envy, believing it originated very early in infancy. Whether it was "constitutional" as she believed or "reactive" to external stimuli has been debated by her followers for decades.

Soon I began recalling references to envy in literature, in modern fiction (e.g., Melville's *Billy Budd* and later Shaffer's *Amadeus*). A friend reminded me that de Tocqueville had found envy rife in our infant Federation. Whereas I had remembered Dante's *Divine Comedy* and Milton's *Paradise Lost,* an acquaintance in my husband's chemistry society sent me to a medievalist, who, noting that envy was very important in Renaissance literature and usually ranked as second of the "seven deadly sins", directed me to lesser known works of that era commenting on envy. I began thinking of examples from the Bible and from ancient literature and mythology. As a member and later leader of a Great Books Discussion Group, I returned to philosophers we had read and found several with extensive comments on my topic, specifically Francis Bacon, Schopenhauer, and Nietzsche. Friends began to look at my project as something of a treasure hunt and began sending me references from their specialties, such as church history, or from what they had found in their browsings. Responding to one friend's call, I thanked her and added, "Yes, Joseph and his brothers are in my chapter on envy in the ancient world."

As I pursued references and references of references, I found a tome (originally in German, but soon translated) by Helmut Schoeck, an Austrian sociologist, who drew attention to much of the above, to intentional stimulation of envy in the past century by third parties with their own agenda, and to positive effects of envy on the progress of civilization.

Schoeck's was one of four books I found early on, with title or subtitle the stark term "Envy". The others were a French novel, a Russian novella (both in translation), and a work published in French (never translated except for me by my French teacher friend) by a sociologist Raiga. More recently, I found a fifth book titled *Envy* by a psychoanalist. Later yet a sixth came out, one of a series from the New York Public Library, and another by a Protestant clergyman.

Besides examples of envy in myself, relatives, friends, and patients, I began noticing examples of envy on behalf of another person and termed this configuration "envy by proxy". And I found autobiographical and literary examples of the bitter envy of authors. For a time I thought I was the only one who had considered the discomfort of being on the receiving end of envy, but then I found that I had been anticipated six centuries by Petrarch, back in the fourteenth century. An ancient proverb advises us not to tell others of our joy, if we wish not to be envied.

Standing in the corner of my office, a box began to accumulate random "envy" notes on scraps of paper and backs of envelopes, as well as clippings, articles, and books.

As I kept my ear to the ground for references to envy, I found it in strange places ranging from a traveling olfactory art exhibit of the seven deadly sins as compounded by leading perfumieres and displayed in hanging gray cylinders at head level, entitled "7S: Instillation of the Seven Deadly Sins", to a performance by a female impersonator promising "A Guided Tour of the Seven Deadly Sins", in which (s)he represented envy by "His pickle is bigger than mine."

Over the centuries envy has been universally decried. Better, I decided, would be to find ways at least to detoxify it, or better yet, to turn it to our advantage, making it work for us. And so I looked for those.

When I queried people about their experiences with envy, their responses were almost universally what Sorge, the Protestant minister, also reported, a denial that they had a problem with this universal phenomenon, widespread as the human race. After readers have read this book, I would be astonished to learn that they still could claim immunity from envy but would at least admit that one or more of my examples reminded them, "That's much like the time when I..."

The organizational task remained. I soon noticed that envy virtually never appeared alone but mixed with others of the "seven deadly" such as pride and greed, yet other "sins" such as covetousness and *schadenfreude,* other reactions such as hostility and aggression, and some even positive, such as emulation or the pursuit of other advantages.

I began to conceptualize a large three-dimensional Venn diagram with envy deep in the center and intersecting many other emotions and reactions. Finally, I had to put it all down. Most importantly, my take-home message will be that despite all the downsides of envy, it can be seen as an opportunity, often missed, to reassess and redirect oneself and one's goals.

So let us have a look.

Contents

Envy is "a feeling of discontent and ill will at another's excellence or good fortune."

—Webster's Elementary School Dictionary

Maxims

Envy is the most universal passion.
—William Hazlitt

*Every other sin hath some pleasure annexed to it, or
will admit of some excuse, but envy wants both.—
We should strive against it, for if indulged in it
will be to us a foretaste of hell upon earth.*
—Burton

*Envy is a passion so full of cowardice and shame,
that nobody ever had the confidence to own it.*
—John Wilmot Rochester (English courtier)

Envy is more irreconcilable than hatred.
—La Rochefoucauld

*Other passions have objects to flatter them,
and which seem to content and satisfy
them for a while. There is power in ambition,
pleasure in luxury, and pelf in covetousness;
but envy can gain nothing but vexation.*
—Montaigne

*The truest mark of being born with great
qualities, is being born without envy.*
—La Rochefoucauld

*Envy feels not its own happiness but when it
may be compared with the misery of others.*
—Johnson

*As a moth gnaws a garment,
so doth envy consume a man.*
—St. Chrysostom

*Envy is a madness which cannot
endure the good of others.*
—La Rochefoucauld

*Our envy always outlives the
happiness of those we envy.*
—La Rochefoucauld

*We often make a parade of passions, even of the
most criminal; but envy is a timid and shameful
passion which we never dare to avow.*
—La Rochefoucauld

*Jealousy is in some sort just and reasonable,
since it only has for its object the preservation
of a good which belongs, or which we fancy
belongs to ourselves, while envy is a madness
which cannot endure the good of others.*
—La Rochefoucauld

*There are even more people without [self]
interest than without envy.*
—La Rochefoucauld

*Envy, among other ingredients, has a
love of justice in it. We are more angry at
undeserved than at deserved good fortune.*
—Hazlitt

*Those who are the most distrustful of themselves,
are the most envious of others; as the most
weak and cowardly are the most revengeful.*
—Hazlitt

*Envy is a littleness of soul, which cannot see beyond
a certain point, and if it does not occupy the
whole space, feels itself excluded.*
—Hazlitt

*To the envious person, again, nothing is more
pleasant than the misfortune of another, and nothing
more disagreeable than the prosperity of another.*
—Hazlitt

*Envy always implies conscious
inferiority wherever it resides.*
—Pliny the Elder

*Emulation admires and strives to imitate great
actions; envy is only moved to malice.*
—Balzac

*The very fact that a man is envied is
in itself testimony to his merit.*
—Cato

*Envy is like a fly that passes all a body's
sounder parts, and dwells upon the sores.*
—Chapman

*Fools may our scorn, not envy raise,
For envy is a kind of praise.*
—Gay

Envy is better than pity.
—Greek proverb

*Admiration is happy self-surrender,
envy is unhappy self-assertion.*
—Kierkegaard

*Emulation looks out for merits, that she may exalt
herself by a victory; envy spies out blemishes,
that she may have another by a defeat.*
—Caleb C. Colton (English clergyman)

*Base envy withers at another's joy, and
hates the excellence it cannot reach.*
—Thompson

Envy is punishing ourselves for being inferior. ...
He who envies admits his inferiority.
—Horace

The envious man grows lean at the
success of his neighbor.
—Horace

There is no man so wretched
That he is not envied by someone.
Nor is there anyone so fortunate
That he envies no one.
—Calderón, tr. by Cecilio Paniagua

He who would be without [being the target of]
envy must not tell of his joy.
—Ancient proverb

Men hate most what they envy most.
—H. L. Mencken

Envy is the basis of democracy.
—Bertrand Russell

Envy is one of the greatest sources of human misery.
—B. Russell

What separates us from the love of friends is envying or being envied, causing or receiving harm, insulting or being insulted, and suspicious thoughts.
—St. Maximos the Confessor

As for your own envy, you will be able to check it if you rejoice with the man whom you envy whenever he rejoices, and grieve whenever he grieves.
—St. Maximos

[Though the envy of contemporaries is shown by universal silence], there will come those who will judge without enmity or favour.
—Seneca

The envious will die, but envy never.
—Mme. Pernelle, a character in Moliere's *Tartuffe*

ENVY

Chapter 1

Vignettes

A number of years ago a young French major from an Ivy League university was referred to me for treatment. He had been studying for a few months in Paris, where external pressures from the family where he was boarding and internal pressures from his own perfectionistic striving to maintain his 4. average converged to produce something close to an old-fashioned "nervous break-down". He was triaged back from France and thence home, where he was referred to me.

Between removal of the pressures, appropriate medication, and (I do not hesitate to admit) good psychotherapy by me, he improved rapidly. Before we terminated, he gave me a beautiful print of tulips for the office wall and, an amateur chef, tried over and over to make a tricky, fancy *genoise à l'orange* cake, until his mother wouldn't give him any more eggs.

As his treatment progressed and he was improving, against all logic I found myself feeling worse and worse. I monitored myself, my reactions, and my interpretations more than we psychotherapists must always do, because early on I became aware of a confounding factor in his treatment.

Now we come to the crux of the matter: the young man's mother, a woman I never met face to face but talked to by phone a few times. The truth is that I was suffering envy of this woman whose son I was helping get well, because at the same time my eldest son, just two years younger, was behaving in antisocial ways at a sister institution and running roughshod over all the professionals who were putting themselves out to work with him and get him back on track because of his superior intellectual giftedness. Eventually the university was obliged to take him to court, and subsequently to expel him.[1]

"Why," I kept asking myself, "should I be able to help this talented, charming, intelligent student, while at the same time neither I nor my husband nor any of the professionals we have consulted over the past several years have been able to redirect our similarly intelligent but intransigent child? Why shouldn't I be the mother with a treatable one, to say nothing of a normal child, and reverse his malignant downhill course? I have been at least as good a mother as she. Not only had we welcomed and loved him after three failed pregnancies, but I have used every strategy of explanation, education, reward, punishment with no observable effect, to say nothing of all the professionals whose help we have enlisted."

What irony, I thought, that I should be able to help this French student so easily (I've had difficult cases, but this was not one of them) while other professionals have not been able to reverse my son's malignant course. "Why should that woman have a son back on track while mine is raising hell at a sister institution and getting himself taken to court twice and finally expelled?"[2]

My anger, even my humiliation, were intensified by our societal credo in those days maintaining that home environment, upbringing, and nurturance were overwhelmingly determinant in the outcome of the young (who were considered to be born a "tabula rasa", or blank slate, on which the world—read *mother*—wrote), and when anything went wrong with the child, the mantra was "Blame the mother!"[3]

It was an intolerable burden under which mothers like myself found ourselves in the latter half of the twentieth century. The ultimate irony was that my own profession of psychiatry only later began to loosen its hold on the idea that the responsibility of the mother for a child's outcome was carved in stone. Hence I was frantically scrutinizing myself for what I could possibly have done wrong, or not done right, or not done enough, for, with, or to this son. I had been at the good end of the large, hazy array of mothers, but the outcome had not matched the input. I had played by all the rules, but the game was somehow fixed.

As the young man's treatment progressed, I wanted it to end, but not, of course, before accomplishing its purpose. I looked forward to his return to school and the end of my constant reminder and shame over not being the envy-free person I would like to be.

Those several months were my most acute experience with envy relative to a patient. The patients I treat present a vast array of problems, and, happily for me, only rarely a configuration that elicits a feeling of envy and injustice that they have something I wanted, as in this case. However, a similar experience came close, but this one relative to a patient of my husband's, whose specialty spans a wide array of garden-variety disorders all the way to a few that are esoteric and difficult to diagnose and manage. One night a call came from his high school friend, Don, from whom he had not heard for several years.

Don described his grandson's symptoms, which had baffled all the physicians the family had consulted. "Put him on the plane. I think I can help," my husband told his friend. Having taken a detailed history from the child's mother and having performed a meticulous examination of the boy in the hospital, before putting pen to paper, my husband called the nurse to give the first injection. Almost miraculously the boy's condition began to respond within days. In a couple weeks he was discharged. In appreciation, the grandmother, who learned that I was collecting carnivorous plants, sent me some pitcher plants from Florida. She also sent for our younger boys, a baby cayman, which, when our nearsighted son held it up to study it, bit his nose. (How many of us have survived an alligator bite?) Over the years we have heard, not only from the grandfather but from the boy, gratitude for saving his life.

This example was not nearly so wrenching as the one with the French student, because I was not treating the sick child, and because the timing was earlier, when our son, while worrisome, had not yet progressed so far down the delinquency path. Still, I recognized the same surge of envy for that family with a child who was treatable and salvageable by the father of our disturbed child, who was not. I ventured to ask my husband whether he had not experienced a similar feeling relative to the two sons in question. "Doesn't it bother you that no one can do for Daniel what you just did for Don's grandson?"

He was shocked and replied only, "But that has nothing to do with it." He did not try to comfort me, as I had hoped. While this superawareness made me a better therapist, not mistaking or mis-attributing my emotions for something they were not, I decided that this was the downside of my having undergone a classical psy-choanalysis: no secrets from myself when I would rather that such uncomfortable, negative awareness about myself had remained hidden in my unconscious. My husband, never analyzed or requir-ing it, never recognized envy when he felt it himself, nor in his spe-cialty had he any need to.

My experience with the French student's mother illustrates some of the features of envy. First, envy always involves a comparison, with the envier coming out worse, denigrated, and humiliated. Second, envy is something we do not choose but are seized by, nor is there any moment of pleasure from it, as there is from other emotions or behaviors or sins (the "seven deadly" with which it is usually grouped) that are below our standard. Once identified, it can be a source of shame, adding insult to injury for someone with high personal principles. Third, it can be concealed from the envied one, as in this case, contained and never revealed by the behavior (including speech) of the envier. (Often the envier man-ages to hide it from himself by repression, and is unaware of the cause of his uncomfortable feelings.) Fourth, envy may be more apparent to outside observers, surmised by the envier's behavior, because people who envy admit it only in the most exceptional circumstances. (This behavior may be a sudden silence or avoidance, or any kind of hostile aggression, or even, sometimes, praise for the envied one, followed by a clause beginning with "but".) Fifth, envy may be felt for someone we love or like or are otherwise close to socially or emotionally or geographically, as, for example, at work, with the result that we cannot escape their presence on this and other occasions, as we might like. It is usually hard to flee from envy. Sixth, envy may result in behavior intended to harm or bring down the envied one, although it need not. In pure form, envy is internal, hurting only the envier. On the other hand, it virtually never appears alone, but is entangled in a welter of other emotions, almost all painful (such as covetousness, greed, anger, wounded pride, and resentment), but some positive, even in a context of love. A less common configuration is envy of someone to whom one gives something he cannot have himself, as in my helping the young man return to health, when no one could do this for my son.

My experience of envy in the juxtaposition of my son and my patient (and to a lesser extent the one with my husband's patient) is one of several confrontations with this enemy that put me on the path of writing about envy as I have experienced it, observed it (in family, friends, and patients), and read about it going back to the beginning of recorded literature.

As I was pursuing references for this study, I found a book on the subject, dating from 1933, in French and never translated. In fact I had to photocopy the entire book in duplicate from the one the library borrowed for me. My friend, a retired French teacher, agreed to translate it with me. He commented, "I guess I'm lucky—I've never had the problem of envy myself."[4]

"Well, maybe," I smiled to myself.

To give him an opportunity to preview what we would be working on, I dropped off his copy of Raiga's book one evening and went on to a concert with my husband. When we returned, the red light was blinking on my answering machine. My friend's voice said, "Where did you ever find this book? It hit me right between the eyes!"

Notes

1. The account of my life as mother of this son is told in *A Handful of Ashes*: *One Mother's Tragedy*.

2. The university told me that they had only five times taken a student to court, and mine was two of them.

3. I recall with shame how, several years earlier, as a psychiatric resident I had swallowed without question my teaching that to understand child patients, we had to scrutinize mainly the family environment for what had gone wrong, particularly the mother. I had been assigned first to a children's ward, and my very first patient was an eight-year-old autistic boy. There were stresses in the marriage, as often happens when a child is seriously ill. To this day I remember the look of anguish on the mother's face—and I know now that I should have comforted the parents instead of focusing on their marital problems. We had a visiting professor from Toronto, Dr. Ray Keeler, a man years ahead of his time whom I honor to this day for holding out alone for the biologic basis of childhood autism—"Look at him rock back and forth, look at that twirling motion, watch him bang his head! We may not understand how, but that behavior is somehow neurologic!"—while the rest of the staff covertly and overtly ridiculed Dr. Keeler. "Ray wouldn't know an id if he fell over it," said our chief.

4. This reaction about the possibility of envy in oneself is very typical. Not only have I encountered it a number of times, but Sorge, an author whom we shall discuss later, reported the same experience with those he queried. "Envy? No, not me, not that I'm aware of." The responder is not cognizant of how accurate is that latter qualification.

Chapter 2

What Is This Thing Called Envy?

In common parlance we hear the word occasionally, but when people toss off "envy" without giving it much thought, it is not with the genuine meaning we shall examine, but usually to compliment, with a meaning closer to "admire", as in "I envy him his gentle wit" or the Brits' frequently heard boast, "The NHS [National Health Service] is the envy of the world"[1] The word in its more basic, integral meaning does not roll off the tongue, because genuine envy is painful, wrenching, even humiliating, so we are ashamed to admit to envy. Yet it is, as the sociologist Schoeck maintains, a driving force in making not only personal but societal decisions.

Envy is a complex emotion (or awareness or attitude) that is difficult to come to grips with because it is, in the phrase of the psychoanalyst Rocher, an "exquisitely irrational phenomenon". Also, it is usually associated with other emotions (greed, anger) and behavior.

We have no test for envy such as litmus paper or an EEG, only the inference by the envied one or a bystander, since the envious person admits to envy only rarely and in very special circumstances, and, indeed, may himself be—often is—unaware of his feeling that is apparent to others. And therefore it behooves us to begin with a simple, rudimentary definition of envy. Throughout this book we shall consider observations and descriptions and characterizations of envy by commentators in many fields of thought, who view it through their own lenses and emphasize one or more of its many facets.

Webster's Elementary School Dictionary defines envy as "A feeling of discontent and ill will at another's excellence or good fortune."

Webster's Third International Dictionary lists, similarly, "painful or resentful awareness of an advantage enjoyed by another, accompanied by a desire to possess the same advantage".

The key word here is "advantage" possessed by another. Just behind it is "mortification and ill will". "Longing" for the advantage is the expression of the related mental state *covetousness.* The fourth feature of envy is its hiddenness. Epstein writes: "Of the essence of envy is its clandestinity, its surreptitiousness. Envy is above all the hidden emotion—so hidden that, often, one isn't aware oneself that it is, as it frequently can be, the motive for one's own conduct."

Elsewhere Epstein writes: "Envy being too ugly a feeling to admit to the world, the care one takes to camouflage it usually ends in disguising it from oneself."

Thus envy is harder to be aware of than other personal defects.

In an entirely different context (a discussion of punishment) Kant notes: "All terms which semiotically condense a whole process elude definition; only that which has no history can be defined."[2] In a later chapter we shall see why this particular word is more difficult than first appears. Nevertheless we shall try.

My opening definition for envy: Envy is a complex emotion resulting from comparison with another in some attribute or possession or accomplishment in a domain of importance to the envier, and finding oneself deficient, hence inferior, even humiliated, resentful, and ashamed. Thus the sequence is comparison, inferiority, resentment, and shame, first for the inferiority itself, then for being unworthy by being prey to the entire sequence. We are all subject to envy, whether consciously or unconsciously, but to widely varying degrees, those excessively competitive, proud, and narcissistic being more prone to envy. Envy is worldwide and universal, and, according to Schoeck, has a word or linguistic device in virtually all languages. Epstein writes: "Nobody can be ambitious and not envy others' successes." The proud person cannot avoid envy, but Dante claims that the truly proud man does not envy, and I believe he means because he is too proud. Someone who does not esteem a particular domain will ask, "Why would anyone envy *that*?"

Schoeck classifies envy as a "state of feeling" rather than an emotion, which can be pervasive and enslaving. My friend adds that a high discomfort from envy shackles the potential for *joie de vivre*.

Anger often accompanies envy, and it can range from the faintest whisper, like a cloud passing briefly over the sun, all the way up to galloping, malignant, towering rage. Other emotions, such as covetousness, greed, threatened self-love and self-esteem, and resentment are also often entangled with envy, and this combination can be fueled by ambition, competitiveness, and rivalry. (These are observed even in other species vying for their parents' attention and feeding.) Overt behavior in the form of retaliation, characterized by hostility and aggression, whether physical or social, is often provoked by envy but is not integral to envy and is a secondary problem of its own. Envy always involves someone else and can be thought of as a "directed emotion". It is, in Schoeck's words, "as much a constituent of social existence as it is generally concealed, repressed, and proscribed". My friend, who began by believing he was spared envy, now identifies envy as "a witness of vanity threatened". He adds the sequence: "Threatened self-love, self-esteem, and status produce resentment, which yields envy which goes on to reprisal." (I would reverse "resentment" and "envy" in his paradigm and consider "reprisal" as only a possibility.) Envy is rarely seen unalloyed but mixed with other emotions, mostly painful.

Envy always occurs in a dyadic relationship, the envier and the envied. However, more than two persons can be involved, but only when the envied compose a group or class, such as those who made the cut, the young and healthy, the rich, or the clique that excludes the envier. The envious can also be a group with similar hopes and resentment of another group with the wished-for advantage.

The primary and core feature of envy is that painful feeling of inferiority compared to the other with the advantage. Rivarol calls the ability to compare "the mother of envy". William R. Newell defines envy as "hate that arises in the heart toward one who is above us, who is what we are not, or possesses that which we cannot have or do not choose the path to attain". La Bruyère finds envy "as natural as a stone falling or fire rising." The Reverend David W. Hull states: "Envy is the one deadly sin to which no one readily confesses. It seems to be the nastiest, the most grim, the meanest. Sneering, sly, vicious. Therefore the face of envy is never lovely."

In this way, envy is predicated on comparison with another, regarding any advantage in the realm of human experience, anything tangible, such as wealth, or intangible, such as charisma. Aquaro is quoted as characterizing envy as "a manifestation of the belief that there is a limited supply of good".[3] This fact of limitedness is particularly appropriate in some cases, when we shall consider "positional goods", i.e., those advantages defined by there being just one, as in only one valedictorian per class. The value of one's advantage is lessened when someone else has it too, because that renders it less distinctive.

The envious individual is seized by (this is passive; he doesn't seek it out) a feeling of resentment ("Why does she have those classy cheekbones, and my face is lumpy like a potato?") and often a sense of outrageous unfairness ("I am just as good and worked as hard but didn't get the prize"). In other cases of resentment the envier may recognize the fact that the other had earned the advantage and was justified in receiving it. The "truly deserving", some say, are those who have cultivated the advantage, are modest about it, and wear it elegantly. Authorities disagree on whether envy is harder or easier to bear when the advantage is seen as legitimate.

Raiga, in his book *L'Envie: son role social*, which shall be discussed later (the source of the story about my French translator's belated recognition of envy in himself), describes all envy as "an explosive cry from the heart". He makes a distinction of the two extremes of envy: (1) *"l'envie vulgaire"* (common, everyday, resting on the natural differences in talents, life circumstances, etc., "he's just a better chess player than I", or "of course she got a better grade than I but she deserved it—she studied") and (2) *"l'envie d'indignation"* (envy with outrage over the unfairness and injustice of it all: "Why should I have to spend my life under the burden of racial discrimination when so many others of lower intelligence, worse values, cruel, etc., were born without this handicap?"). These two kinds of envy are easily distinguished at the extremes, but in real life they blend and merge over much of the continuum and are "called" according to the bias of the observer, whether envier or envied or outsider.

Because of the necessary comparison with another, envy by our definition cannot be experienced until a child has developed the ability to form a rudimentary differentiation between self and other. This is in contradistinction to the belief of Melanie Klein, a psychoanalyst whose work will be discussed later, who dates envy earlier in infancy, and thinks of it as an inchoate rage directed against the breast. For her, the most integral feature of envy is a wish to spoil what the other has, even though this in no way helps the envier. An example of such spoiling occurs in Genesis, where it is reported that the Canaanites, seeing the robust flocks and herds of the Israelites, threw dirt into their wells. We do not require the acknowledgment of the Canaanites that their motive was envy.

Sometimes we can envy someone for something we don't even want for ourselves, usually in areas close to where we are competing. As a young writer himself, Epstein learned that a poet had already had three poems published in the prestigious journal *Poetry*, at a younger age than his own at the time. Without any talent at writing poetry or wish to develop it in the future, he nevertheless felt a passing breath of envy of her success. This configuration of envying something we don't even want gives us the fable by Aesop and the metaphor "dog in the manger". Epstein was able to laugh at himself for this. This is a good strategy to develop for cases of relatively mild envy.[4] There are many irrational features in envy, but few that we find humorous.

Another noteworthy feature of envy is that it strikes most frequently persons who are close sociologically, geographically, or in kinship. The envier is constantly reminded of his relative deficiency, perhaps sitting at work beside the one he envies. Ironically, envy can be felt in an otherwise good, warm friendship. Still, to be envied is so uncomfortable in a friendship that it is wise not to acknowledge one's envy to this friend. Despite the many painful attributes of envy, at least the disparity is often small, not an order of magnitude placing the envied attribute beyond reach. In general, we do not envy persons at a distance. The British love Queen Elizabeth II, and do not seem to envy her wealth, although many resent her income-tax-free status.

Finally, as if the pain of inferiority were not bad enough, some who envy are ashamed of not living up to their own expectations. I had as a patient a young teacher with a hornets' nest of problems: being physically unattractive, entangled in an abusive relationship, and having lost a job in a triple play when her superintendent fired her to save his own neck. Her sister's situation was not much better, except for having a little son. One day, apropos of nothing, my patient just blurted out, "What low kind of person would envy the attention everybody showers on her three-year-old nephew?" That was my initiation in helping patients deal with this unwelcome emotion.

Epstein holds forth at length about our reasons for hiding envy: "People are least likely to want to own up to [envy]...probably ungenerous, mean, small-hearted...implicit pettiness." The subtitle of Elliott's article says it well: "The Last Dirty Little Secret".

Enviers who hold themselves to high personal standards feel

this added wrench when envy seizes them and they are forced to notice this gross disparity between their ego-alien feelings of envy and their self-defined ideal, as happened to my patient. They may think, *What low kind of person am I? I ought to be happy that my friend is expecting her third child. Her success has no bearing on my fertility problem. How can I be so petty? I ought to be—and am—ashamed. I would like to run and lick my wounds in private, but that would only give me away.*

Aquaro goes even further: "Envy is not a moral issue: no one can punish the envious more than they have already been punished at their own hands, nor has any society permitted unrestrained envy.... Morals have regulated the permissible expressions of envy, but envy somehow lies beyond the reach of ethics. Actions can be governed and eliminated, but base impulses can only be covered up and unacknowledged."

Enviers rarely if ever admit to envy, of course for the reason of shame we have examined. In fact, when someone uses the word "envy", says, for example, "I envy so-and-so for this or that", the meaning is trivialized, and often a joke or light banter is intended. One review of Epstein's book carried the teaser: "Envy readers who pick up this book." (I noticed Epstein's good review.)

Once my doctor asked what I was working on, and his response was "I envy you for writing a book about envy". He thought this witticism was original, but I must have heard that line a dozen times.

Another doctor said, half enviously, about my project, "Researching for that book must be like going back to college."

"Better than college these days. More like core curriculum or, better, the old sixteen-year Great Books format."

Often the envier has repressed his own envy to the extent that he is unaware of the source of his uncomfortable feeling around a certain person or in certain circumstances. In such cases it can often be surmised by onlookers, who often mislabel the problem "jealousy" (a differentiation we shall make presently). One clue is a sudden silence in the normal give-and-take of conversation, on the part of the person who envies. My mother, who was not given to criticizing anyone, once drew my attention to the fact that her elder sister, who displayed a delightful, chatty persona and who had traveled widely, would suddenly fall silent when someone mentioned traveling somewhere that she had not visited.

Envy is not necessarily wanting what the other has. That comes under the rubric of covetousness, a state of mind closely related to envy. The two more often than not are encountered together, and wish for the other's advantage is part of the envy constellation. Sometimes, however, envy consists in just wishing the other would not have it, even to destroy or to spoil what the other has. (Melanie Klein considers wanting to spoil more integral to envy than wanting to have, even though the other's advantage in no concrete way harms or takes from the envier.) Many things about envy are irrational.

Frequently confused with envy is jealousy. This emotion is also other-related, but it occurs in a triadic setting, the jealous one believing that something that is or should be his has been or is about to be taken by a third party. He finds himself robbed or cheated of love or esteem or attention that he perceives is rightfully his. Jealousy is often sexual and it is more easily understood and accepted by others than is envy. In France it has been considered a perfectly understandable reason for murder in a love triangle, and such murder was formerly legal in Italy. Raiga believes that envy occurs in a situation where someone is still in competition for something, whereas with jealousy he has already lost. This is not my read on envy: there are opportunities for envy where no possibility exists to have the advantage. As a friend points out, it is possible to be envious of another's sexual prowess without being jealous of its object(s).

Epstein says, "[O]ne is jealous of what one has, envious of what other people have." I disagree because often the favor has been definitely usurped, according to the jealous person, whose loved one has shifted affections. Raiga's formulation is almost opposite.

He asserts that jealousy drives the battle for love, but he finds envy in the defeated. Epstein holds that whereas jealousy is not always bad (we are legitimately jealous of our good name), envy (in the personal relationship we are discussing, but not necessarily in larger groups) is always, with one small exception, negative and something to be ashamed of. That one non-pejorative exception is envy of a true religious feeling by someone who cannot share it, as Epstein himself would like to do, noting the added dimension religious fervor gives to magnificent baroque music.

Not covetousness, not jealousy, envy is also not something else, although it comes close to this emotional state, and the two often march together. I refer to a kind of pleasure in contemplating another's pain, sorrow, or discomfort, without having caused it, and without it doing the observer a particle of good. For this sister emotion of envy we do not even have an English word but use the German schadenfreude, from the roots meaning "to harm" and "joy, pleasure, and feeling good". My dictionary's definition is "glee at another's misfortune". I believe schadenfreude is a poor compound noun because it suggests that pleasure comes from the act of harming (thus a kind of sadism) or from being harmed (which would be masochism), whereas schadenfreude is neither. I have tried to coin a better noun from two English terms, but I have been able to come up only with a kind of multiply hyphenated monstrosity such as pleasure-in-beholding-another's-grief. Since schadenfreude is generally understood, it is probably best to leave it at that. This is the obverse of a coin of which the reverse is sadness over another's happiness, again at no cost to the sufferer. Schadenfreude may be the motive for many who turn first to the obituary page, who favor sad stories and current events for their own sake, who rush to be the bearer of bad news, and who gossip about others' illnesses. Such people make good friends when things are not going well for the other but are unable to share and rejoice in good times. Gore Vidal, an author not lacking in recognition, is reported to have said that it wasn't enough that he succeed; his friends had to fail.

In the *New York Times* of August 24, 2002, Warren St. John wrote an article about schadenfreude entitled "Sorrow So Sweet: A Guilty Pleasure in Another's Woe". At that time many highly paid executives had recently been arraigned on various kinds of financial fraud charges, and many people who envied their high income felt satisfaction over their downfall. St. John cites persons willing to be quoted ("It serves them right") and also psychologic studies on the topic.

A *New Yorker* magazine cartoon about the same time showed a newspaper entitled *Schadenfreude Monthly* with headlines about bankruptcies in the rich, a short-run Broadway play, cosmetic surgery failing in an obnoxious heiress, and other bad outcomes for readers to enjoy.

Schoeck notes that one feature of envy is that the envious one may fail to warn of a danger, when that would be the decent thing to do, and he would do so for a stranger. This is a first cousin to schadenfreude. An example that comes to mind is watching a rival photographer back off a pier into deep water.

Harry Stack Sullivan, a psychiatrist who wrote for the popular market, offered a systematic list of features of envy some of which we have been discussing: (1) envy is automatic (unintended); (2) envy cannot be relieved or fixed through misguided person's kindness; (3) envy endures, sits there ready to spring forth; (4) envy provokes the envier to "act despicably" toward the one with the advantage; (5) envy makes the envier a good friend only when things are not going well for the other; (6) the envious person's self-worth is boosted by the other's misfortune (schadenfreude); (7) envy works without thought of consequences; and (8) envy sets the stage for jealousy. Sullivan sees the following sequence: (1) feeling deficient; (2) feeling envy; and (3) feeling jealousy. Two important features Sullivan left out: (1) the wish to spoil whatever advantage the other enjoys, and (2) the fact (as we shall examine later) that even getting "it" often does not relieve envy ("too little and too late").

It is apparent that envy rarely if ever appears alone, but is accompanied by one or more of an assortment of other emotions, never other than painful, most commonly covetousness, often greed, anger (against the innocent envied one, nature, God, or society), sometimes schadenfreude, on top of the basic inferiority and diminished self-esteem that characterize the primary state of envy, while the frosting on the cake is shame over being, in the words of my patient, "that low kind of person" in the first place. Sometimes stabs of envy are accompanied by feelings of a positive nature, e.g., grudging admiration and determination to emulate the envied person, to work to excel in that domain, perhaps even outstrip the other, or to look for another arena in which to take pride, all known to be healthy ways to deal with envy. Physical beauty holds no high rank in my catalogue, and so I am comfortable admiring my friend's large green eyes. In my practice over the years I have treated three women of stunning beauty and have found no envy to overcome in working with them regarding the special problems this attribute presents for those on the receiving end of envy.

Envy is certainly something we never court, but a feeling that slips in and seizes us against our will. It springs up unbidden and is there before we realize what has happened. Unlike all others of the seven "deadly sins" or negative mindsets, such as gluttony and greed and lust, that we may be ashamed of and regret later but enjoy at the time, perhaps indulge in on impulse, envy never rewards us with even an instant of pleasure. If we consider it a sin, as centuries of theologians did, it is a sin against the self.

When the fact that we are lacking in a domain of importance to us by comparison with someone near us is somehow displayed to others or even just brought to our attention, we feel belittled and humiliated, feelings identified as the most basic and universal features of envy. In an acute envy attack, these emotions are accompanied by physiologic manifestations related to the autonomic nervous system, consisting of quickened heartbeat, faster breathing, tightened muscles, dry mouth, and gritted teeth, and these are only partially under our control. Strangely, the individual who feels these sometimes does not recognize their source or identify their cause. He may suddenly become silent with a forced smile, and this itself may signal onlookers of his predicament.

Reactions by the envious person may range over the spectrum including: (1) dislike of the envied person with no inkling why; (2) unidentified discomfort (depression and chagrin); (3) awareness of the cause of resentment with a wish to escape but fear of betrayal of something that our pride demands be hidden; and (4) anger all the way up to fury with no effort to conceal it (sometimes associated with physical violence).

In the latter case the envier may try however possible to tip the balance back in his favor, plan revenge, plot sabotage, overt or covert, anything to bring down the envied one, hurt him, somehow take away her advantage. While we are not responsible for envy, we are responsible for what we do about our envy, and that is responsibility enough. Tactics we consider may range from gossip, lies, and slander ("who steals my name", etc.), backbiting, irony, scorn, damning with faint praise, sarcasm, joining others who oppose the envied person for whatever reason ("The enemies of my enemy are my friends" as Raiga reminds us), and covert attempts to bring down the object of our pain, all the way up to overt aggression. While it is true that these may actually hurt the envied one, the backlash to the envier can be even worse, in terms of damaged relationships and damaged self-esteem. However, if we realize that these tactics are unworthy of us[5] and control our aggressiveness, we might wish at least to distance ourselves from the situation with its painful connotations, but, ashamed as we are, we realize that to run would serve to let others surmise our shameful predicament, so we do our best to conceal an emotion we did not ask for in the first place and are ashamed to be burdened with in the second. We may try to hide behind pretended increased friendliness, but this may be recognized as overcompensation. In the longer range, we may try to work with our deficit, redoubling our efforts to outperform the object of our envy, trying to obtain the advantage we lack or a different one, perhaps even outdistancing in the future the person we envy. Sooner or later we must realize that there will always be someone with more or better whatever it is we long for, and it behooves us to come to terms with this fact. Frequent and intense envy and how we handle it is determined by—and determines—that part of our character. As Raiga and others have noted, character traits are somewhat modifiable.

With all the grueling minuses inherent in the fact of envy (including the fact that most cases are in persons near socially and geographically and therefore a daily reminder), a soupçon of solace may be taken in the fact that the envied advantage is often close enough to be within reach, either in its original form or in a derivative, not an order of magnitude away.

Despite the many unwelcome and painful features of envy, my take-home message is that envy, properly handled, is an opportunity to learn, to reevaluate our strengths and weaknesses, to reassess priorities, and to redirect our efforts.

Targets can range from an acquaintance with a son covering himself with glory at a prestigious university to a classmate with apparent facility in translating Xenophon's *Anabasis*.

Notes

1. Ask the patients who wait six months for a biopsy.

2. Kant makes this observation regarding difficulty of definition in connection with punishment, since there have been so many different kinds, administered for so many different reasons, over history, e.g., an attempt to discourage repetition, an attempt to recompense the injured party, an attempt to make the guilty party suffer as he has done to someone else, and many others.

   My example of an object that has changed use, if not definition, over time is the telephone, originally an instrument to enable communication over a distance, now a device to avoid talking to objectionable callers.

3. The anthropologist Foster promulgates "the Image of Limited Good", held in peasant societies. See Anthropologic Index.

4. I have spotted an analogous experience at classical concerts. I will subtract the composers' birth dates from their death dates and note that they died younger than I and compare my paltry output in a different field with their musical legacy, even while appreciating what their genius has left us. This habit is silly but harmless, and I don't fight it. As Schoeck notes, we admit to envy only (with few exceptions) when it is mild and nondestructive. You have to pick your battles. This comparison helps send me back to work on a current project.

5. They are "infra dig" (beneath our dignity), as the boys' prep school jargon used to have it.

Chapter 3

Advantages We Envy

What do I mean about ability to translate Xenophon?

I refer to one of my experiences with envy, in this case with me on the receiving end, which led to my writing this book.

As a college freshman I signed up for Greek because I wanted more background in classical languages and literature than just high school Latin. I realized that I would never again have as convenient a time, whereas I knew there would be other opportunities to study modern languages. My friend Minerva and I were the only women in the Greek class, the other students being pre-seminarians pursuing their requirements for admission. The men struggled with the language, largely because they had not had prior exposure to a highly inflected language. The professor was impatient with their unfamiliarity with declensions and conjugations, so Minerva and I helped them.

Fast-forward to a class reunion forty years later, at which I happened to be seated beside one of the ministers, by then highly respected and retired, and leading tours to the Holy Land. Apropos of nothing, he blurted out, "I never could understand why you could translate Greek so easily and it was so hard for me, when I was the one who needed it. It wasn't fair. Why didn't God help me instead of you?"

I was, for once, at a loss for words and could only mumble, "I'm sorry." I should have said, "He did—He sent Minerva and me." I hoped that this man's confrontation with his old wound would help him, but I was too stunned to draw him out. At the subsequent reunion, to my astonishment he repeated the same observation. By then I was able to explain about my background in Latin and help him ventilate a little.

In an era when professors had no compunctions about handing out failing grades, this young man envied Minerva's and my apparent facility when Greek was the door that opened a professional life to those with a religious calling, while for us it was little more than a frivolity.[1] This added, in the old cliché, insult to his injury. Note that the minister never used the word "envy", and the emotion had to be surmised by the observer, in this case myself. This feature of envy, that it is too shameful to name, is usually observed in those rare circumstances in which a sufferer even admits to this emotion, in the pre-seminarian's case envy that had gone underground for decades. Of help to the minister was that he had not been reminded by seeing me (or, probably, Minerva) in the interim. Envy is harder to bear and to acknowledge when you are in daily contact with the object of your painful emotion.

This incident illustrates how uncomfortable envy can be for the envied individual too, once the latter is aware of it. It illustrates, also, how efforts to equilibrate the advantage (our helping the pre-seminarians) do not alleviate envy. Such efforts to share may increase the envier's pain, even while helping the envier in ways extremely important to him.

The resentment that this man carried half a lifetime was one of my determinants to start this study.

What are all these advantages, the good things of life that others have that we lack, that cause us to envy? They are as all-inclusive as human values. Philosophers and others have prepared lists of broad classifications that subsume almost an infinite number of specifics.

Boethius, a sixth century Roman philosopher, listed the five categories we expect will bring us happiness: money, power, prestige (i.e., respect), fame, and joy. But he warns against expecting too much: "Wealth cannot ensure sufficiency, nor kingship power, nor high offices due respect, nor glory fair fame, nor pleasure joy." He was in a position to know, as he wrote his *chef-d'oeuvre The Consolation of Philosophy* while imprisoned awaiting an unjust execution.

Not surprisingly, male observers lean more heavily on the domains of importance to men, while I shall more often give female examples, as in the upcoming area of reproductive envy.

George P. Elliott, whose short article in *Harper's* was another incentive for this book, lists specifics as well as broader categories in his piece poignantly subtitled "The Last Dirty Little Secret":

> You have something I want and lack—riches, beauty, acclaim, new sneakers, enough to eat, children who love you, a reputation for goodness, goodness itself, top billing, a mother's sympathy, a Stutz Bearcat, the Presidency, a penis. You do something I would like to do and can't—bear a child, win the race, get your picture in the paper, command, catch a husband, stay married, star in a movie, vote, make love, sing beautifully, ask for your share, get your share, heal the sick, see. [2]

Once you have life's basics and are not hanging on by your fingernails, special skills and traits are the most painful things to envy. Abstract, inborn qualities, including musical, mathematical, and linguistic, physical prowess and dexterity, as well as general intelligence, and the physical attributes that produce what in any culture is considered beauty are among the envied traits I have observed, experienced, and find interesting. Some authors, such as Schoeck, rank property and tangible goods, wealth and possessions, at the top of the heap. Those seem to me more like targets for greed and covetousness. What is most envied by any individual depends on what is his most important domain.

Schoeck, an Austrian sociologist whose ideas we shall examine under the politics of envy, has reviewed anthropologic accounts of preliterate peoples and found them as prone to envy as are we in technologic societies. This contradicts our (in the West) almost romantic belief, even among anthropologists, going back to the Enlightenment, that in primitive societies people live together without much of this world's goods but in loving harmony—a remnant of our erstwhile belief in a Golden Age in the early history of mankind. Actually, envy has been a problem in all societies as far back in time and as far-flung in space as we know. It is mentioned in some versions of the Gilgamesh Epic, the world's oldest recorded literature, as we shall see.

Wealth and its tangible expressions are so commonly a subject of envy that many think of money as the target of envy par excellence. Even without a money economy, however, another person's good luck in the hunt or a good crop can arouse not only covetousness ("I'm hungry and want his kill") but also envy ("Why didn't my garden produce as much as hers?"). One of the devices for coping with envy that evolved in many primitive societies is belief in the "evil eye", as the ability to harm or be harmed by those we envy or hate for other reasons. To deal with this, other counterphobic charms and devices evolved. Without protection from the envy of others, inventive and analytic persons in any culture may be afraid to try innovations.

A friend from Lithuania relates how his father, a landed farmer, planted trees to serve as windbreaks. His neighbors could not understand why his crops suffered less wind damage than did theirs, and apparently envied him for it.

Envy of wealth in our own time and place is apparent on all sides. The old expression "keeping up with the Joneses" refers to the well-known struggle to "get ahead" in such arenas as clothing, houses and furnishings, automobiles, boats, airplanes, vacations, and private schools for our children. Sometimes these material possessions are employed for their ability to provoke envy more than for their primary function. Envy may lead to imitation, "the sincerest form of flattery".

Money in itself and as a proxy for all good material possessions can be a source of gnawing envy. While unequal distribution of wealth may result from unfairness and injustice, money also may be acquired legitimately by lawful, fair, honest, and honorable labor. Even when such wealth is deployed in socially valuable ways, creating work and/or helping others help themselves, wealth-envious persons focus on what they perceive as unfair: "Why was she born to all that money instead of me? I have better uses for it."

Envy seemingly based on money may really be envy of the flexibility that a little more money permits. And such envy-invoking comparisons may result from choices made decades earlier in life. Young idealistic persons may choose a career oriented to social good, environmental protection, or education, none noted for high salaries, which is not an obstacle to the insouciant youth at this crossroads. Several years later, however, with the ever-escalating needs of a young family, a salary at the lower end requires constant balancing, compromise, regrets over lost opportunities, and envy of companions who made more lucrative choices.

A young friend of my son's talked with me about his career direction. He would have preferred teaching, like his father, but he admitted to anger over the fact that both parents (his mother not holding a paid job) were working evenings cleaning office buildings, to get their four children educated. The young man complained, "My mother shouldn't have to do that," skirting close to admitting what I call "envy by proxy" of me on behalf of his mother. (On another occasion his teacher/father explained the night job as the reason he and his wife could not accept our invitation to attend a Baker Street Irregulars meeting with us, since I had heard he was a Sherlock Holmes aficionado.) I commended the young man for weighing the more idealistic choice against the needs of a possible future family. He eventually entered accounting.

Epstein noted similarly that academics (particularly in the less-well-paid humanities) had often chosen that route because their self-esteem in early life came in the classroom. However, when, as teachers, they followed the careers of mediocre students who had followed better-paid lines of work, they could see that those students were living more pleasantly. One Renaissance specialist noted that his former student became a mediocre lawyer with a villa in Tuscany. These professors' envy and resentment are understandable, and they can be attributed to changes in values over the years.

I have observed that couples of retirement age who have agreed to spend their lifetime with one wage earner, the other providing creature comforts for the entire family, sometimes envy the more comfortable retirement income of two-earner couples, with its perquisites, and see this as unjust.

Possessions can be symbolic in their significance, by their rarity or their mode of acquisition. I feel a twinge of envy for a colleague who did not win but inherited a Nobel medallion from his grandfather. I own a fossil dinosaur tooth I found myself, given to me by a paleontologist at a dig where my husband and I spent an afternoon troweling, dusting off, carting away rubble, and talking and learning about the allosaurus. I was shocked when they said I could have the tooth and asked "But don't you need it for the skeleton?" "No," they said, "we always find more teeth than anything else." My sons would all like to inherit that tooth. Garage-sale junkies often flaunt their "finds" to others who may feel bested in that competition.

Attractive appearance is an attribute close to wealth as a value that women and girls—always younger and younger girls—envy. For reasons of its own, society doesn't make life easy, bombarding us constantly with messages about feminine beauty and ways to enhance it. Of course these advertising messages are not intended to increase female self-esteem; they are aimed, in advertising, to slake another thirst: greed of the purveyors. Epstein notes that the entire advertising industry can be considered an envy-promoting machine, driving our economy.

Although in thrall to appearance, women don't usually compare themselves unfavorably to the beauty goddesses of the day, film stars or models, because they are farther removed emotionally and geographically. We do not envy Helen of Troy.[3]

Women are more prone to emulate such celebrities (a recommended way to deal with envy, in any case), spending a lot of money for a few cents' worth of chemicals and pigments. We are much more likely to envy a marginally more attractive sister, cousin, friend, or fellow worker, for a particular feature. The silky hair of this one, the massive (perhaps fake) bosom of that, the slim body of someone else—these and other physical attributes elicit a childish pout as we think "Why can't I be pretty like that" or "I'm so plain" or "I'm ugly" or "I can't stand how she acts superior over those 'good legs'" and finally, "I hate her." Then we feel cheated and angry over the unfairness of life. The closer the attractive one is in time and space, the more painful the envy, partly because of the constant reminder, what we used to call "having our noses rubbed in it", and seeing the dividends it pays in male attention. When we go home alone and lonely, we feel the bite of this particular form of envy.

Sisters often experience difficulty in dealing with their differences in attractiveness, if not actual beauty. This we shall examine in the Inge play, *Picnic*.

"Venus envy" this has been called, and the original, Venus herself, inspired envy in the goddesses in the Greek pantheon. The cosmetics industry, health spas, fat farms, fashion industry, plastic surgery—all aim to exploit this widespread manifestation of envy, promising or implying more than they can deliver in relieving it.

Stunning beauty does make problems for the woman so endowed, problems that many other women would be willing to work with. It brings with it not only the possibility of attraction from males with no other criteria than the beauty, but also the possibility of frequent envy and all kinds of sabotage. A friend of mine is blessed with not only striking and unusual beauty but also Mensa-level intelligence, which enabled her to graduate with a high school teaching certificate at twenty. She has always loved teaching and used many creative devices, and I made sure that my sons benefited from her French classes. However, at the age of fifty, she was kicked by a girl in her class, inflicting injuries that caused even the doctor of the board of education to declare her permanently disabled and requiring ongoing physical therapy. Because of her early start as a teacher, she had worked the requisite minimum of thirty years, to receive a disability pension and ongoing rehabilitation. The older, more average-appearing women on the board fought this determination and finally lost to my friend. She and I believe that their stand was affected by the fact that they would have preferred to retire and hated to see a beautiful woman younger than themselves retired, even with an orthopedic handicap, and even though she would have preferred to go on teaching. As in most examples of envy, this one had to be inferred by the onlookers, and I believe we were right.

Men also are not unconcerned with male appearance. They pay less attention to countenance, more to body build—height, powerful shoulders, massive genitalia. By these the male ego judges itself and often finds itself deficient. Epstein, again, reflecting that nobody has everything, comments from this perspective of male vanity, "Unless this is the voice of envy, most outstandingly handsome men turn out to be rather lunkheads." We tend to think also of beautiful women as deficient in this regard (the dumb blonde chorus-girl stereotype), and this, too, is not true, and this also may be the voice of envy.

Envy of appearance, like most others, is a mixed bag, not all bad. It can inspire a healthy effort to correct, improve, or make the most of what nature gave us. But corrective action can become a consuming obsession, and we may spend more on it than it is worth or we can afford in time, money, focus, and distraction from other values. I worry when I see my little granddaughters giving more than passing attention to their appearance. Snow White and the wicked queen ought to teach that there will always be someone more beautiful (or endowed with any other attribute we envy), so forget it.

An enormous arena for envy is prerogatives. Those who can snap their fingers, literally or figuratively, and make people jump are the objects of envy. Status (elected official), position (CEO), rank (military), and authority (judge) are targets of envy for those sent to fetch the coffee. Often those employed in satisfying work, at good salary, with regular hours, envy the self-employed, even though they must work longer and harder, with less assurance of success—because of the cachet of "owning your own business". Whether or not the envied one has earned these perquisites by years of hard work and climbing the ladder is often lost on the envious upstart who wants it all right away. Our veterinarian took early retirement because she encountered problems in recruiting younger vets to work with her. "They wanted the same hourly rate, no calls, and backup from me. What they demanded I call 'the instant finish'," she complained.

In Britain, class is marked by speech, the so-called "R.P.", or "received pronunciation", identifying those who have attended "public school" (i.e., expensive private school). Wishing to get ahead in such areas as announcing on the BBC is sometimes enough to send applicants to speech tutors to acquire this proxy for upper-class status. This is slowly breaking down, and the BBC is questionably the bastion of good diction it once was. A recent review of a biography by Teal on the life of Stanley indicated that one enduring feature of emotional life in Britain is envy, and he blamed the rigid class system. I have noticed that persons thinking about envy often attribute it to a group they belong to.

Prerogatives that are envied by women—worldwide and throughout recorded history[4]—are men's privileges. At the end of the nineteenth century, Freud, starting to open up the subject, and, insensitive and a little naive as a male, called this phenomenon "penis envy". But his followers and others soon recognized that what women really envied and/or coveted in their husbands, brothers, fathers, and sons was not so much a few grams of flesh as the prerogatives that went with it: opportunity to come and go ad lib, enjoy sexual freedom (free or for pay) without consequences (except for a lot of syphilis, which they often received via their husbands from the brothel and, similarly, gonorrhea, which often sterilized them), emancipation from the kitchen, equal pay for equal work, even suffrage.

This repudiation of the idea that what females envy in males is genitalia is not entirely true, but it would seem to affect mostly children, who grow out of it. A colleague of mine quoted a little girl patient as saying "'Ladies have more "things" than men, but they're all inside.'" And I distinctly remember as a child envying my cousin's equipment when he flaunted it, and thinking, "What's going on here anyway? Why don't I have one of those?", but I somehow sensed that this was not a welcome question. (I handled the problem by inventing a contest to see who could urinate farther from the branch of a tree, thereby leveling that playing field, and I always won.)

Envy of prerogatives is an equal-opportunity emotion, for men and women, boys and girls. It can be directed from child to adult, or adult to child. In primitive societies, their often painful and sometimes cruel initiation rites of passage for young boys often reflect the elders' envy of the upcoming generation.

My mother used to look at a newborn asleep in a crib and imagine the infant comfortable in the assurance "You have to take care of me", as she yearned to be cared for. Neglect and abuse of infants and children were not commonly acknowledged in those days, and my mother saw only infants basking in the love, compassion, conscientiousness, and intuition of their mothers. Then, as now, some infants were helpless in the hands of uncaring, incompetent, even abusive caregivers.

Nor is envy precluded by love. My mother and I were very close. She made sure I received the education she had not had, and she loved my husband and children. She also enjoyed visiting and attending university functions with us. Only after her death and while working on this project did I surmise that she had probably envied my good life. If so, she handled it very well.

I know of an example in science (but they must be found also in other groups working as units) in which the individual with higher status and more power envies the accomplishments of someone beneath him, whose work, nevertheless, reflects positively on the entire operation. Such a superior must decide whether to suppress the output of the member he envies (perhaps cut funding), thereby diminishing the recognition due the entire department and himself as chief. He, of course, would say he spent the money on something more urgent. He might be worrying about the threat to his position offered by the lower member.

The big brother of prerogatives is power, and this also is a target of envy for both sexes and all ages. To the toddler, the parent is perceived as not only all-powerful, but arbitrary in decision-making. Hence children envy their parents' ability to give or withhold, and they nurse resentment—but soon learn to fight back with tantrums, manipulation, and accusations of "You don't love me." Too often these have the desired effect of evoking feelings of guilt in the beleaguered parent for not being the all-giving adult we have been brainwashed into believing we owe it to our children to be.

Thomas Jefferson and the Declaration of Independence notwithstanding, it is immediately apparent that not only are all persons not equal, but no two persons (not even identical twins at birth, who can have had different qualities of placental intrauterine nourishment) are equal, nor, in our imperfect society, are all persons even, as Jefferson meant, equal before the law. Understandably, parents may envy others whose sons were not killed in war, or, perhaps even worse, missing in action, or others whose loved ones did not succumb to cancer or another tragic illness early in life. Some, with one form of Epstein's "extraordinary good luck", were born to two loving parents expecting and planning for them, while others have just one parent, and some no real parent at all, but a sullen teenaged babysitter held hostage to a squalling infant she didn't foresee, or a foster family in it for the money. Such children languishing in foster care are usually hoping, yearning for adoption into a real family, if they haven't already given up hope.[5]

Some children born with fetal alcohol syndrome or neonatal drug addiction, if they understand the cause of their difference from other children, with some justification hate the mother whose disorder caused their handicap. Is it any wonder that the handicapped envy their contemporaries with normal endowment? I worked with one such young woman whose mantra that she kept repeating to me and to her grandmother who was bringing her up was "I want to find my mother and knock her on her ass". I could only understand, stand by, support her in her anger, and work with her, looking for strengths and areas of self-esteem and satisfaction.

We know that Life offers no guarantees, and Nature is monumentally indifferent, although we would like to believe otherwise.

Possessions are different from, sometimes more significant than, and do not equilibrate with wealth for potential to incite envy. They can be one-of-a-kind art objects that collectors bid for and use to inflict envy on the losers. They can have symbolic value, such as trophies that are won, sometimes by cheating. They can be objects from the natural world that are more or less rare and can be obtained, sometimes, by purchase or found sometimes by an informed searcher. I went once with my cousin on a kind of treasure hunt for Michigan's state stone, the Petoskey. Knowing on which spit of land they washed up, she took me there, and we each found a bagful. In this case there was no cause for envy, but if I had not found my own, even if she had shared her largesse, I would nevertheless have envied her because in that case I was playing at being a prospector and would have failed. It has been noted that well-intentioned efforts to share with an envious person do not alleviate but usually exacerbate the envy. You will note that certain foci of envy appear ridiculous, like my Petoskey stones, to anyone to whose heart they are not dear.

I went on another similar expedition to look for trilobite fossils on Corps of Engineers' property, where they invite visitors to prospect, hoping to find one such to leave to each of my grandchildren. My nephew found a broken one and gave it to me. I did not envy him, although I would prefer to have found it myself. I plan to return on another search.

We have deviated from envy for possessions to envy for accomplishment, success, recognition, respect, or fame. Raiga relates that in academic circles and professional societies, envy runs rampant, as the members jostle for position. Members of unions suffer the same problem because of competing in the same arena. As physicians, many of us enjoy esteem (and maybe envy) from our professional colleagues for our professional successes, including, sometimes, the social status of our patients, as well as in the prestige of our academic connections, publications, grants, and awards. Practitioners climb over one another to rise in the pecking order. Appointment at certain prestigious medical institutions requires family subsidy for their newly fledged offspring because such institutions are not pinched to pay living wages. Most authors agree that they and their colleagues are especially prone to envy because their work is more intimately bound up with their self-esteem than almost any other. They will have their own chapter in this book.

All these show the intimate association between ambition, pride, competition, and envy.

It has been said that some of the best acting coming out of Hollywood is witnessed at the Oscar presentations, as the losers pretend joy for their winning competitors. Similarly, Epstein points out that if you want to see the pinnacle of raw, rampant envy, visit Harvard, Princeton, Stanford, or another prestigious campus on the day the McArthur Genius [so-called] Awards are announced.

Several years ago I attended a breakfast honoring a woman Nobel laureate visiting our institution. As she related her experiences, she sat fingering her medallion, which she wore as a small pendant on a chain. I was painfully conscious of envy in myself, and when I discussed it later with a colleague who had attended, she ruefully admitted to the same feeling. We agreed that probably we were not the only breakfasters so afflicted. If I had thought I could have escaped without betraying my shameful feeling, I would have been "outa' there".

Intelligence and learning are objects of envy, in academic and other settings. When I was planning an intervention for my alcoholic adolescent son, I invited his best friend, a basketball teammate, to help my child redirect his life by addressing his addiction.[6] His friend declined, saying, "He couldn't be alcoholic and play such great basketball!" Years later, after my son had undergone hospital treatment twice and begun to "recover", that young man had the honesty and dignity (rarely seen in those who envy) to apologize to both my son and me, on separate occasions, admitting that he regretted not having come to the intervention and that he envied my son's intellectual giftedness.

Somewhere between envy of the old for the young and schadenfreude (or pleasure in preventing the young from having life any better than the old had it), is an example I heard from a friend and mentor who followed the state legislature's voting record. A bill intended to protect and help abused children was defeated, and some of the nay vote came from members who themselves had been abused as children.

Similarly, when the matter of medical training is discussed, and the backbreaking hours that residents are expected to work are criticized, older physicians insist that being available for whatever happens is the only way to learn the practice of medicine. Probably closer to the truth is the rationalization "We had to work thirty-six-hour shifts, so why shouldn't they?"

Attention is another arena for envy, and (counterintuitively) it doesn't even have to be good attention. This sought attention is represented by the familiar "sibling rivalry". The multichild family is sometimes seen as the school for envy (and even more for jealousy), as siblings jockey for position vis-à-vis the parents. But opportunities for these unpleasant emotions abound without siblings—with parents, cousins, and neighborhood children. If it were not so, we could pick adult only children out of a crowd. Children who rightly or wrongly believe that a sibling is being favored can find ways to force parental attention, and bad attention is better than none at all. Having been an only child, I was unprepared for the ingenious attention-getting devices of our eldest son after the birth of his next brother. He had been ousted from his only-child position at four, the worst possible age because he was old enough to remember life as the king of the hill but too inexperienced to develop good compensatory devices. He easily diverted attention from his brother by urinating into a wastebasket, tearing pages from books, puncturing slides, overturning a heavy chair, and blaming it all on his baby brother. My husband, who had grown up with siblings, asked the toddler to show us all how he could overturn the chair, thereby putting the lie to his brother's accusation.

Not only can attention be commandeered by bad behavior, but envy-provoked attention can be sought for reasons both ridiculous and irrational to an outside observer. A woman I treated had two daughters, one with cystic fibrosis (a condition that limits life expectancy), which required innumerable unplanned trips to the doctor, the emergency room, and the hospital, and aborted other promises, pleasures, and excursions. The healthy sister acknowledged to both her mother and me that she wished she had been the one with the terrible disease, for all the attention it brought.

Attention-hungry envy is not limited to children, as in the blatant example of the out-of-work teacher who blushed to admit she envied her three-year-old nephew, already described. She demonstrated not only envy but also the shame with which we punish ourselves for not living up to our own standards.

I encountered another admission of envy in another patient, a woman of fifty, whom I saw just once before she was transferred to another therapist in the clinic where I was working. Remarkably, in her only encounter with a new doctor, this woman ventilated her lifelong envy of a younger brother and resentment of and anger toward her father, who, after a series of daughters, finally acquired a son. In an age when favoritism was not considered as opprobrious as it is now, this man, at mealtimes, would hold the boy on his lap, feeding him choice tidbits of chicken, while our patient, and perhaps her sisters, smoldered. This example may come closer to jealousy, in that the younger brother had received what the sister felt was her due, or should at least have been shared.

When I was already an adult, my mother once confided to me her bitter pain over the fact that one Christmas her mother had given an older sister a hope chest, but her gift to my mother was only a handkerchief. Years later, after my mother's death, I related this story to my aunt, the older sister. Shocked, she replied, "That isn't true. Your mother got that wrong. Your grandmother would never have done a thing like that to Marian. I was already working and bought that chest. I wish I had heard this before she died, so I could have set her straight."

Even pets have been observed to react with envy and/or jealousy when a new baby is brought home.

As long as we are healthy, most of us go through life accepting our good health as our due. But the good health in everyone around us grabs our attention as soon as our own health is threatened by serious illness. In the recent best-selling *Tuesdays with*

Morrie, the warm, elderly, truly professional teacher with limited life expectancy acknowledged envy for those without a terminal illness (and for the young with time on their side, "time yet to write an impressive record" as Epstein admits). This teacher was too wise and self-disciplined to be profligate with time, his commodity in shortest supply,[7] nor did he let his feelings impede living life to the fullest as long as he was able—and to continue to teach others, like his former student, as you would expect from a dedicated teacher.

Persons with disabilities, sometimes lifelong, are wise to surmount envy and use whatever friendship and help are offered. I had a blind friend who enjoyed movies and particularly liked to go with me because, as she said, while she could follow about 75 percent of the story from the voices, having trained other capacities (hearing, memory, and imagination) to substitute wherever possible for vision, she found me good at whispering precisely those parts of the plot with no alternative to vision. This blind woman had long since memorized much of what the rest of us can look up, e.g., her own telephone book. When I expressed amazement over this, she replied, "You could do it too, if you had to." She was wise enough not to give in to envy of the sighted but to cultivate us who would complement her visual handicap.

My husband spent his life with a disabled leg from before the days of polio vaccines. His leg did not prevent him from living a full, contributing, rewarding, and happy life. And I never heard anything from him suggesting envy of those with, as he put it, "two good legs", until he was being treated for Parkinson's disease. He had a marvelously empathic physical therapist whom we all loved, who happened to be black. I heard him tell this man how as a ten-year-old he would always be chosen last for a baseball team because of not being able to run fast around the bases. Later he explained that he believed the man would understand because of his own "handicap". Although I never thought of my husband as envying those with perfect legs (we hiked together in the mountains), I had considered that perhaps his disability had served as a prod to achieve more, as Bacon commented about persons with other handicaps to overcome. Fortunately, my husband also loved chemistry and academe.

In a chapter trenchantly titled "The Young, God Damn Them", Epstein comments on envy the old feel for the young, the years ahead in which to make their own mistakes. It does not help that they are observed often to be squandering their time. One of Dawn Powell's (a mid-twentieth-century novelist) characters, Professor Walter Kellsey, envies his students who don't have to listen to him or even bother coming to class, and he even envies our president's free rent. Elders' envy is often associated with regrets over past mistakes, lost opportunities. I have a son who acknowledges envy for his beloved little daughter's future, with the opportunities he plans for her.

The random distribution of talents and abilities among the population cannot escape the attention of persons who long for a particular gift. The stay-at-home housewife/mother may envy her violinist sister. Her ongoing envy may have a long history, dating to their early years when their parents had to choose how to allocate limited resources among these two daughters and perhaps other brothers and sisters. Should scarce funds go to expensive music lessons for the child with the special gift, perhaps to the exclusion of Girl Scout camp for the other? If the violinist's talents had not been nourished, might she have felt embittered for a lifetime over a musical career that never materialized? Being a parent can be a years-long juggling act.

Persons with inequities at work, real or imagined, unfair or deserved, can envy and be envied. Advancements and special opportunities, such as work-related travel, can hamper or vitiate the friendship of coworkers. Those who envy may live with smoldering resentment or they may work harder to earn comparable opportunities, or they may retaliate by sabotaging the efforts of the one they observe as favored, legitimately or not, or they may change jobs. None of this is ever pleasant for the envied one as soon as he or she becomes aware of the chilling relationship. As various authors have pointed out, an envier may feel victimized, but the envied one may become the real victim.

Dawn Powell, the novelist just mentioned, used an expression to describe one of her characters: "conscious of privilege". I recall her phrase in two situations because I am similarly and unpleasantly "conscious of privilege". One of these I notice when traveling in impoverished Africa, where the children smile and are curious about us, but their elders glare at the "rich Americans" coming through, despite the fact that one of their main sources of income is ecotourism, and we are importing the dollars they so desperately need. However, transfer of assets does not eradicate felt envy; indeed it can fan the flames. While many of my fellow travelers are rude, arrogant, and obnoxious, generating the "ugly American" phrase, others are respectful visitors in a foreign land, but this makes little difference to the locals. I have been amazed that often my fellow travelers, when I inquire about this privilege matter, seem oblivious to it.

I have also been astonished to note that people who are otherwise sensitive are often heedless of the special constraints I believe such privilege should place on those with a good mind, education, a supportive family, a modicum of this world's goods, and opportunities. All these should carry with them the obligation to deploy them for the benefit of others as well as oneself. I have tried to instill this idea in my children.

At yet another level, without persons with privilege, like the Rockefellers and the Gateses of this world, none of us would be able to enjoy museums, libraries, art, concerts, and other cultural opportunities that we cannot buy, one by one.

Another area where I am affected by this "consciousness of privilege" is in the case of certain patients, who display the double anger that I have a travel opportunity that they would like and that I am "abandoning" them for my own pleasure. As a young therapist,

I tried to mollify them, virtually apologizing by letting them know that these trips served a dual purpose—not only to visit other lands but to attend medical meetings at which my husband presented his research findings. As I became a more seasoned therapist, I realized that the patients and I both had to deal with their envious feelings, for them to move forward, despite this being one of the more unpleasant tasks of psychotherapy. We shall return to this in the chapter on psychoanalysis.

Another patient was able to examine with me her basis for envy, the fact that she too had been accepted to medical school many years earlier, but when they learned of her juvenile diabetes she was rejected retroactively (which could not occur now). She had made her peace with her disappointment by becoming a highly respected dietician.

Charisma, or personal charm, is another target for envy. I have a friend who admits envying his son's "easy way with people". "The most popular student", "the girl on the cheerleading squad", "the best dancer" all come in for this kind of envy, being close enough for daily comparison. (I have seen examples of bad mistakes resulting from using criteria like these for picking mates, e.g., my friend who eloped with the high school quarterback and another who ran off with her ski instructor.) Because of social and geographic distance, "celebrities", so-called, don't seem to evoke envy in most people, although St. John makes the point that the schadenfreude many of us experience when they "fall" — e.g., are arrested or succumb to addiction—stems from our latent envy.

A young post-doc I met at a party honoring my son's new appointment, on learning of my envy project, immediately ventilated her example of envy for charisma. She volunteered that she and her friends envied a colleague at a former institution, who, when he lectured or spoke informally, projected such charm that his hearers did not, for the most part, notice the mediocre nature of his data and imputed value to his work that did not bear up on close scrutiny. "Why can't I have that magnetism?" they would ask, and add,

"And how unfair that he gets all that credit for his uninspired work."

Another arena for envy to consider here is personal and family relationships that through the lens of outward appearances seem more gratifying than our own. We may envy others their "perfect" spouse, parent, kindly old Uncle Drosselmeyer, their children whom all the world admires, our classmates with a whole "real" family, not, like us, in foster care, a friend with an intact family when we have suffered an unexpected and devastating death in ours, someone whose sex life we imagine (often from their lying braggadocio) to be better than our own.

Bion, a psychiatrist, points out that we may even envy someone else's freedom from something negative, e.g., frustration, anxiety, anger, even conscious envy, which can be chronic issues for persons who long for contentment, serenity, and tranquillity.

A number of years ago, when homosexuality was closeted much more than it is now, a well-known politician, enjoying political success and recognition, a man from a rich family, wealthy in his own name and in no way dependent on politics for his living, struggled against his homosexual longings. A patient of mine related that a homosexual friend of his, waiting table at a resort hotel on Cape Cod, was called to this politician's room, who, though nude, would not consummate the act over which he was so conflicted. As he fought desires, he envied the straight community because he could not share the simple pleasures of hearth and home like 'everyone else'. He eventually committed suicide.

Thus persons with these and innumerable other conceivable or imagined bits of good fortune are the innocent objects of our envy. We, the enviers, feel inadequate by comparison, although we know intellectually that their advantages in no way took life's plums away from us. We know further that it is our challenge to play the cards we were dealt, although we wish we could have been dealt a better hand. We even know that we have other advantages that others lack. Nevertheless our envy is hard to control. And so we are ashamed, shame being the outgrowth of envy for those of us who are proud of our otherwise high standards and goodwill toward our fellows.

Notes

1. Thorstein Veblen, in *The Theory of the Leisure Class,* indicated that when young men from well-to-do families were given a traditional classical education with Greek and Hebrew, with no plans to teach or to enter the ministry, it demonstrated wealth that permitted them to spend several years not working to support themselves. In his famous phrase, "conspicuous consumption", Veblen underscored flaunting wealth in new fashions of clothing, household furnishings, leisure, etc., as a way to evoke envy.

2. You will notice later in the book that I identify envy in myself for things just as ridiculous and others just as poignant.

3. When our sons were in junior high, one brought home an assignment to collect as many units of measure as he could (ångstroms, watts, lumens, pascals, light years, etc.), so we sat around the dining table thinking them up. Finally my husband, with a twinkle in his eye, suggested, "Ask your teacher if he knows what a millihelen is." I bit: "A millihelen? I never heard of that. What's a millihelen?" My husband jostled me in the ribs and said, "Like you—beauty sufficient to launch one ship, mine."

4. Before written language, it is believed that women were held in higher esteem relative to men than later, due to their magical-appearing reproductive abilities, since the relation between sex and reproduction was not recognized. Priestesses enjoyed status and respect as they served, among others, the universal Earth Mother, Gaia.

5. I saw a heart-rending segment on television about efforts to find adoptive homes for older children in foster care. Desperate to place children of an age when adoption becomes harder, the authorities tried "adoption parties" at which children and prospective parents met and looked for a match. One girl related that the "mother" she wanted had hoped for a girl with green eyes, but our prospective proband failed as this designer child. Later the adoption worker found her a family without such specifications. I suffer vicariously the pain of those who didn't make a match at the "party". Nevertheless, if

others were lucky, those who didn't come away with an adoptive family were no worse off than before, except for the incremental pain of another disappointment.

6. Greenleaf, *Fighting the Good Fight,* Cypress House, 2002.

7. In line with one of the Greenleaf Rules of Living, "Always maximize the commodity in shortest supply". While this may be money when we are young, it often becomes time (and energy) as we age.

Chapter 4

Reproductive Envy

D ifferences in the reproductive functions of the sexes produce more areas for potential envy and more serious problems from envy for females than for males.

But males are not exempt from reproductive envy. Sometimes a man experiences nausea and an expanding abdomen during his wife's pregnancy and contractions during her labor, a phenomenon known as couvade, which is psychologic and sometimes attributed to envy of his wife's generative powers. After the birth, particularly the first, some men experience envy for the new interloper, who has commandeered their wives' attention, time, and energy as the father's playmate. This configuration may take on the features of a jealous love triangle. Years ago (I cannot remember the source) I saw figures to the effect that one in twenty-four (about 4%) men would prefer to have been female, whereas one in six women (16%) would prefer to have been male with its possibilities and perks. The reasons for the latter were discussed earlier.

Small children of both sexes are said to envy the parent of the other sex, including little boys wishing to take on the role of birthgiver, as will be discussed in the chapter on psychoanalytic beliefs about envy.

Sterility in men is most frequently caused by mumps orchitis or undescended testes. Such men may grieve for their loss of reproductive powers and envy their peers able to father a family. If recognized early enough in childhood, this can be corrected with relatively uncomplicated surgery. A young man came to consult me for several problems, including the fact that his surgery for crypt-orchidism had been performed in his teen years, due to parental procrastination, too late to prevent sterility, and leaving him with pain. His story was that year after year, the school doctor had sent home a note advising his parents to attend to this problem, but they did nothing. He and I surmised that the reason was that he was the one of five children sired by "Uncle Harry", and his mother probably thought that taking him to the doctor would somehow bring this to light. My patient was considering suing his parents.

In the First World, this condition is routinely treated. But in places like India, such males grow up sterile. Since this makes them unacceptable as husbands, they cannot expect a normal adult life. Therefore they band together and support themselves by gatecrashing parties and weddings and blackmailing the hosts by threatening to embarrass the guests unless paid off. In a news-paper in New Delhi, I read about two such gangs warring, and later I met a physician who confirmed this bizarre practice.

In Papua New Guinea, initiation rites for the young men have features in which, among other rituals, they imitate women before being admitted to adult male society. Their fascinating customs are recorded in Herdt's *People of the Flute*.

Examples of male reproductive envy in our time and place fre-quently include men disappointed in their hopes for their sons, in contrast to the sons of their friends. "Why does mine want a cello instead of a baseball mitt?" The birdwatcher who leads groups in our park complains that none of his children will take up the hobby, as he leads other whole families of birders. Family busi-nesses must often be sold for lack of interest by the offspring, especially with our smaller families, to the regret of the retiring generation. The husband of a woman I treated had a competent and skilled employee of many years and a son with little interest and less aptitude for the machine shop business. The owner faced the prospect of the business failing if left to the son but could not bear to see it pass to someone outside his bloodline.

Males' reproductive envy, however, is spared one feature that women with this kind of envy can hardly avoid: in the workplace, and in the neighborhood, women's incessant discussion of motherhood or lack thereof. At work, men discuss the big three: sex, sports, and automobiles, rarely children.

Since women are responsible for almost all the reproductive work before a new and separate person emerges, and since women usually do more than half of the care after birth, it is not surprising that they also experience most of the envy in the area of pregnancy, "that state between health and disease", as my obstetrical text acknowledged. It is also not surprising that envy in the area of reproductive functions is most severe in women who place less value on work, career, and other extra-familial pursuits, and the highest value on their maternal hopes, longings, and family feelings. Throughout most of the life span, from the early years of conceiving their first pregnancy to the end of their own life, such women may feel not only the joys of motherhood but the frustration due to the never-ending possibility of disappointment in reproductive functions and in children themselves.

Problems with infertility causing envy are described in the Old Testament. Rachel, envying her sister and co-wife Leah for having children, adopted the method of having children by sending her handmaid in to her husband as a surrogate wife.

When two young women friends eagerly anticipate starting families and the pregnancy test for one turns positive quickly but her friend cries through dozens of menstrual periods, while trying hard to be happy for her friend as she watches her expand at the waist—this is a fertile field for envy. The birth of her friend's baby does not make it easier for the woman yearning to conceive a pregnancy of her own when she finds herself two years and, if she chooses the fertility clinic route, thousands of dollars behind her friend. One such woman described sitting in the waiting room of the clinic and asking herself which of the patients she had seen on other visits were now carrying an early pregnancy and which, like herself, were on the verge of giving up. As with other occasions, envy is not an acceptable admission here, but its presence can be surmised, mixed with other emotions, primarily discouragement and sadness, sometimes anger, even rage. "Why was it so easy for her, but impossible for me?" At the same time a woman in this situation must work constantly to conceal these feelings from her friend, lest they jeopardize the friendship.

Once her friend and others in their coterie have begun their families, social groupings usually shift, as young families face a new set of problems (sleepless nights, babysitter requirements, tight finances, etc.) different from those of childfree couples who can pick up and run off at a moment's notice to enjoy themselves. This relative freedom is bittersweet for the still-trying young woman.

Our newspaper recently carried an account of a woman so desperate to have a child that she killed a woman at term and quickly performed an amateur section to kidnap the infant.

One way to address this congeries of problems is through adoption, with all its emotional, legal, and financial complications, including the sometimes search for the birth mother.

Another method of dealing with these issues is through the burgeoning artificial conception industry (while enormous numbers of children go unadopted).[1]

Other women working toward a family may have difficulty maintaining a pregnancy. I knew one woman who gave up after her seventh miscarriage, grieving after each loss of the child, suffering a blow to her self-esteem as a woman, and envying women who carried pregnancies easily and naturally. Having suffered three failed pregnancies myself before carrying one to term, I understand how such a woman would feel recurrent disappointment, frustration, injury to her self-esteem in the area of femininity, and envy of her friends and their easy accomplishment, for whom the whole process had been as natural and normal as we had all been taught that it would be. With my first pregnancy, I thought how I would enjoy going to a young woman obstetrician for prenatal care and then be delivered by my friend who had been in her obstetrical residency while I was an intern. I had narcissistically visualized going to parties showing off my bulge, in my black kangaroo skirt and American-beauty-rose flowered tunic, but it was not to be. Soon it became apparent that even with the help of her mentor/obstetrics professor and chief, she could not save my child. No one could have. Her successful pregnancy a few months behind mine served as my introduction to reproductive envy. I can empathize with women with similar experiences, since I spent seven years trying, before finally carrying our eldest son to term at the cost of eight months at bed rest.[2]

For women unable to achieve or to maintain a viable pregnancy, the sight of an infant's rosy skull as it sleeps in its mother's arms, even the arms of a stranger in a grocery store, is almost unbearable. This phenomenon, rarely admitted even to the best of friends, is envy at its cruelest. I have seen it mentioned by an occasional psychotherapist, always a female, such as Sheila Rouslin Welt, whose work will be discussed, but never in men's writings on envy.

The next stage rife with opportunities for envy of other mothers comes after the birth of the infant. "I'm so tired—why can't mine sleep like hers?" is an example of the envy possibilities we face as a result of the constant comparisons we make with our peers as mothers and with our children compared to theirs.

Another configuration abounding in opportunities for an older woman's reproductive envy occurs in a woman's first marriage, when it is the second marriage of her husband, who has already had a family by his first wife. When his second wife hopes for her marriage to be procreative but fertility problems ensue, she may feel—and have difficulty concealing—envy for her husband's prior success. Similarly, if such a woman has a child who suffers serious medical or other problems, again the mother is set up to envy her husband whose "eggs are not all in one basket". Years ago, my mother had a friend who was younger than she, about halfway between my mother's age and mine. This woman was a second wife and, approaching the end of her childbearing years, had a beautiful little boy, with "skin like alabaster". Tragically, the reason for this was leukemia, in an age when that diagnosis was a death sentence. The bereaved mother was so depressed by her only child's death that, when she found a lump in her breast, she did not seek treatment but committed suicide by neglect. I never met this woman, but her case was set up for envy both of her husband for his prior family and of my mother for her surviving only child.

Life presents us all with many medical problems well within the broad, hazy range of small and treatable (allergies, nearsightedness, recurrent earache, and the like), but other disorders in childhood are long-term physical and emotional conditions that present challenges to the entire family (worst are retardation, autism, generalized developmental disorder, defiant/conduct disorder, malignancies, muscular dystrophy, juvenile diabetes). Problems like these usually require that the family's entire life center around the disadvantaged child, while the parents cannot help but compare their life to that of families close to normal. Besides envy, they often suffer conflict about how to juggle the problems raised by one child's disability to allow a close-to-normal life for the other child or children.

One of my patients was a single[3] mother, already mentioned, with one daughter with cystic fibrosis and another closer to normal, although with morbid obesity. She related trying to share her experiences with other mothers, but after many futile attempts learned that they could not comprehend how she had to live always on the edge of tragedy, under the dire prediction of her daughter's shortened life expectancy, with literally hundreds of trips to the emergency room and the hospital, and with drastic curtailment of the normal experiences and pleasures of family life. Much of my therapy consisted of support for her life that had to be held hostage to much that could have been joyful had medical necessity not preempted time. My patient could not help envying mothers with an easier, more normal family life. Since they could not even imagine themselves into her situation, she felt no communality that would have made true friendship possible.

That woman was a single mother with one child with cystic fibrosis. I know a couple who had two C.F. children (deceased in early adolescence and early twenties, respectively), who daily, with her husband, for several years, prepared for the day by freeing the children of mucus in their airways by working with them on a tilt table. None of this, of course, is what we expect when we paint the nursery.

As our children grow and either achieve or do not achieve the fantasies we have for them, the goals we set for them, intentionally or not, we may experience the kind of envy I felt for the mother of the French major. Even a bumper sticker HONOR STUDENT raises the envious question, "Why can't my child live up to his potential?"

At the funeral of my aunt, my cousin's husband (whose daughters were doing well at an Ivy League university) inquired about my son, having no way to know he had just been expelled.

"I never discuss my children," I told him.

"Oh, come on. You don't have to be modest with me," he said.

I excused myself to greet another relative. From then on, until mine settled down as adults, I have never inquired about anyone else's child, both because the parent might not want to tell me and because she might then ask about mine.

Mothers who consciously made every effort to do everything "right" and to be "perfect" mothers are especially subject to the disappointment/frustration/envy of other, more casual, mothers whose children seem to be "making it" with no apparent struggle on the family's part. I treated a journalist/mother of a sixteen-year-old adopted daughter who was giving her and her husband all the adolescent horrors. The girl was starting ninth grade for the third time because of no passing grades, not to mention truancy that exceeded the limits for passing. She had been attracted to an undesirable gang with whom she ran in the parks. One night, at thirteen, she had climbed out of her second-story window, crossed the roof, taken her mother's car, totaled it, and returned home streaming blood. The mother lamented, "This is my punishment for teaching her to be democratic and not judge people by their families. So she runs to the druggies. This is not what I sewed Halloween costumes for!"

Another couple, a lawyer and his wife, thinking their daughter was enjoying a sleepover with a classmate down the street, heard a thump on the porch. There they saw their unconscious daughter slumped against the door, as a car squealed around the corner. "Why should our daughter be living this way? She didn't learn it here." This is a frequent question with parents these days.

One answer is suggested by Judith Rich Harris, who studied children in different communities. She found that they tended to model themselves after peers two years older than themselves.

Many out-of-control adolescents later calm down, and we mercifully forget the worst of it.

I had a friend of many years, an elementary and remedial reading teacher, a good parent, as was her husband, to their two sons, one of whom led the family down the delinquency path and committed suicide as a young adult. Reflecting on how we had been programmed to believe that if parents followed certain principles, they could expect an acceptable outcome in their children, my friend told me bitterly, "I feel ripped off!"

I heard by the grapevine about the problems my children's sixth grade teacher was facing with her two teenaged children, and, struggling with similar problems with my eldest son, I asked her about how she found it possible to work with other people's children while living with such envy-provoking disappointment of her own. This woman comforted me and, a devoted teacher, explained how while doing her best with her own children, used her successful teaching experiences as a form of self-therapy.[4]

Envy can raise its ugly head and be recognized and admitted to themselves by women who have consciously and from the start spared no effort and, in the old cliché, left no stone unturned to do what current thinking requires of a "good" mother, and it has been unavailing, while other average, carefree or careless mothers seem to have children up to the mark. Why, in an age when we had been taught that the role of the mother is critical and determining of the child's outcome, do we see these exceptions to the rule? Envy for neglectful or abusive mothers who seem to have been rewarded for no apparent reason with praiseworthy children produces envy akin to Raiga's *"l'envie d'indignation"* —envy of outrage—not over societal injustice, but the injustice of nature, i.e., Raiga's *"l'envie vulgaire."* As I have said, the two kinds of envy come together.

And it need not be children with behavioral disappointments. The woman I treated, whose acceptance to medical school was revoked because of juvenile diabetes since the age of seven, was one of four children, only one of whom was healthy. Although neither parent had diabetes, another sister had diabetes, although of less severity than my patient's, and moved out of the state. The youngest child, a son, suffered generalized developmental disorder, and finally the aging parents had to find a group home for him. The parents had traveled with these four children, even though the process of setting out each morning would take a couple hours. My patient quoted her father as lamenting, "How was I to know that I should never have had children?" Some months after she and I terminated her therapy, I learned that she had been found dead of sudden cardiac failure, as diabetics sometimes suffer. Her father lived with one of the worst kinds of reproductive envy, that of having nature turned on its head from the death of an adult child (the one to whom he was closest), instead of the usual march of generations down the slope.

Mothers whose children who do not live to grow up are positioned to envy the more fortunate mothers of the survivors. All such losses are tragic, especially for older mothers whose biologic clocks have stopped. Worst are the cases where the child's death seemed senseless by occurring in the context of one of the "preventable" adolescent horrors—deaths by automobile accident, by suicide, by drugs, by self-destructive behavior such as the practice of enhancement of masturbatory response by "temporary" hanging. I knew a woman whose son died by the last mentioned. We can empathize with her grief and surmise her envy for mothers whose children either avoided such risky behavior or survived it. My acquaintance coped with her sorrow mixed with anger, envy, and shame by lecturing in states where she wasn't known, about the hazards of this practice.

George McGovern's daughter died an alcoholic death in her forties. Her father may have felt envy for the other residents who were able to use the help and begin lasting "recovery", when he visited in her numerous treatment facilities. (One of these was a halfway house where my son was a resident. After McGovern's daughter's death was reported in the media and no longer a confidentiality issue, our son told us about meeting him.) Her father tried to let her death serve a social purpose by writing a cautionary tale, *Terry*, about her life and death, for the lessons it had for other parents about his perceived errors. He has also established a foundation to address the alcoholism epidemic.

Years ago I observed that we rarely hear about the lives or accomplishments of the children of historic figures, although expecting such offspring to be outstanding because of their parents is both unfair and unrealistic. One might ask, for example, whether any descendants of Shakespeare are living and, if so, what they are doing. It is true that we don't see many scientific or literary families, although a great-granddaughter of Charles Dickens, Monica Dickens, writes children's novels popular in the erstwhile Empire, especially Australia. Music may be an exception with a few families with surnames like Bach. On the other hand, politics seems to run in families, and we observe the Holmes legal family. Having raised this question in my mind, I began noticing in biographies that the subjects' children may be a disappointment, like anyone else's.[5]

Women of grandmotherly age sometimes re-enter the envy/competitive cycle with their friends who are enjoying the (less diluted) joys of grandparenthood. "*She* has *one* child and *five* grandchildren. Wouldn't you think *one* of my five would have children?"[6]

These women may need to find other children to whom to be surrogate grandmothers.

With sorrows like all these, is it remarkable that well-intentioned parents struggle to find ways to deal with the cauldron of grief, self-blame, guilt (real or imagined), and, sometimes, envy of seemingly casual, even careless, parents not so afflicted?

I recall that a number of years ago Anne Landers asked her readers whether, knowing what they had learned as parents, they would do it again. I was both astonished and shocked that 70% of her respondents said they would not. But we know that the angry or disappointed ones would be more likely to respond and skew the figures.

Another insight into this question comes from the Terman study (begun in the 1920s) of the lives of children identified with very high IQ's. He studied these people with annual questionnaires and in-depth follow-ups at five-year intervals, and passed his enormous data files on to Robert and Pauline Sears to study them until death. As the women subjects approached retirement age, the researchers found that those with the best adjustment and greatest contentment were the women who had pursued a career but had not had children. Many of those with children were at that late date still trying to help solve their children's problems.

I have sometimes considered the question of why certain personalities in the right place at the right time are able to make their contribution, even in the most adverse of circumstances.

Recently I had a friendly argument with an astrophysicist who took the position that Einstein was the leading scientist of all times.

"In judging people I factor in where they began and the help they were given, or not given," I told him. "Of course Einstein was great, but he had the advantage of a well-to-do middle-class Jewish background and education. Compare him to the posthumous child of a farmer, whose mother, a few years later, was offered marriage on condition that she leave her child with his grandmother. Before even getting to the country school, this boy was marking on the farmhouse walls where the sun hit on different days of the year. As an adult this man was still praying to be forgiven for wishing his mother and stepfather dead. When the math he needed was not there, he invented it. I nominate Isaac Newton."

In the context of envy we replay the old "nature-nurture controversy" about the role of what is innate and inherited from ancestors in the person we become, and what is shaped by experiences in the environment. For much of the twentieth century the pendulum swung widely toward "nurture", and "nurture" was considered the critical and determinative role of the mother in a child's development. This placed an intolerable burden on the mother, who, if conscientious, weighed every word and deed for its effect on her child. The converse was that if anything went wrong with the child, it must have been the mother's fault, and mothers of children who did not measure up were considered and considered themselves to blame. Now we have become more aware that parents may pass along ancestral traits they do not themselves express, which may be traits of temperament and personality as well as physical traits.

Current estimates hold that nature and nurture each contribute about 50% to the developing child, but we must remember that "nurture" is far from the exclusive province of the mother, or even of the family. Children spend much more time with each other, with day care, "play dates", activities of all kinds, unlike earlier times when most children grew up on farms and spent long hours helping in the family endeavor. Furthermore, while the environment's input used to come mostly from the family and the church, now this is becoming less so as children raise each other. Judith Rich Harris, one researcher already mentioned, presents evidence that the strongest nurturing influence on the growing child comes from admired "peers" about two years older. Schools are moving toward teaching less formal subject matter, more in the area of "values". Families that consider this a preempting of their prerogative sometimes go so far as to circumvent the school by home schooling to regain some of this lost influence. The conclusion I draw from all this is that when we have children, we should look at it as a new adventure, trying to accept what our children bring rather than setting up our hopes[7] and dreams for our children, to maximize and enjoy what is good, trying to redirect what is undesirable, but not to blame ourselves when this is unsuccessful, to try not to envy those whose luck was better, and to diversify, pursuing other areas for joy in life. At the same time we should try to help our children learn to enjoy but not envy the advantages of others and to make the most of their own assets.

Notes

1. If I were making the decision, I would eliminate this solution, because while helping the privileged few well-to-do prospective parents, it does nothing for the disadvantaged masses of children in need of families. I believe that more potential parents would make homes for some of these children if the artificial conception door were closed.

2. Told in Greenleaf, *A Handful of Ashes,* Cypress House, 2001.

3. Many marriages cannot survive a child with a severe abnormality.

4. For this episode, see Greenleaf, *A Handful of Ashes.*

5. I remember when one of my children brought home a children's biography of Galileo, in which it was noted that one son was a gambler and a wastrel who would come to his father to cover his debts. Even when he married, his father supported him for several years. (As a middle-aged man, however, he helped the blind Galileo by building for him a model of Galileo's invention.) Galileo's daughter, on the other hand, was a professional woman of her time, who compounded remedies from herbs and plants, but died before her father, while she was still the child to whom he was closest. Having read this biography, I felt sorry for the scientist father for his griefs from his children.

   Recently, however I happened upon a biography of Galileo's daughter Virginia, quoting from an abundant and rich correspondence with her father (his responses have never been found). This confirmed her love for him and his for her, after the fashion of the time. He never married the children's mother (professors were expected to remain bachelors, and he was tenured at the University of Padua), although later he got the Church to "legitimatize" the son, but not the two daughters. Under this stigma, they could not expect to marry at their father's social status, and so he put them into a convent, whose grounds they could never leave for life. Sister Maria Celeste (formerly Virginia) worked in the convent pharmacy. She copied for the printer her father's manuscript of *Dialogue of the Two World Systems,* the book that got him into trouble with the church. She continued preparing medicinal treatments for her father and others. While her father was detained in Rome for ongoing questioning, she even ran his local household for him, from the convent. And she died of some kind of ulcerative colitis before her father was allowed home to live out his house arrest. By then I felt sorry for the daughter, not the father.

I learned of a child/father disappointment on a trip with my husband and other physicians around Central Europe, comparing ideas of medical ethics in several countries. In Prague, our bus pulled up in front of an apartment building, and the guide asked whether we could guess who lived there. No one had a clue. "Einstein's son," she told us, "who is also a physicist but will not let his father's name be mentioned," apparently because of his failure to assume the fatherly role. It seems that what this father gave his son was only the genetics for high intelligence.

Apparently being in the public eye does not necessarily help family relationships, maybe just the opposite.

6. Delays and refusals by young women to have children are producing a decline in populations of European origin and, some predict, their eventual takeover and/or assimilation with the other populations of the world.

7. Because disappointed hope is such a devastating emotion.

Chapter 5

Envy by Proxy

When I considered the welter of emotions, particularly the longing for superiority that surfaces when comparing the relative advantages of two persons, I came to recognize a variant of envy. I realized that the dark face of envy need not be limited to the disadvantaged individual. It could be a third person, usually, but not necessarily, someone I loved, whose relative disadvantage caused me pain, especially when injustice or unfairness was a prominent component. And so I evolved the concept of envy one step removed, i.e., envy on behalf of someone else, who might or might not envy on her own behalf. In most cases this was the envy where Nature was the culprit, but not necessarily. There may be cases of birth handicaps, where I envied, for example, a normal twenty-year-old on behalf of a twenty-year-old "savant"[1] from the neighborhood, who visited me to "play school", so he could choose to be a teacher, when my sons and other neighborhood children were afraid to associate with him for fear of ridicule by other children. Mine was Raiga's "*l'envie vulgaire*", but by proxy. It related to an advantage that nature had given to others, which they had done nothing to earn, any more than he had done something to "deserve"[2] his disorder. I have come to call envy of either type on behalf of another "envy by proxy". The term was suggested to me by the term for the psychiatric disorder "Münchausen's syndrome by proxy".

As has been mentioned, envy often is felt between friends and colleagues in similar endeavors. A number of years ago my husband was nominated for an award in an international competition in his specialty. I helped prepare his documentation for submission, even having to locate European standard paper on which to present his credentials, and typing the letter-perfect description of his work, at a time before I had access to a word processor. He came in second, edged out narrowly. He knew and respected the winner and his work and acknowledged that the other man also deserved the honor. While understandably disappointed, my husband, who is blessed with suffering or recognizing little in the way of overt envy, was not conscious of envy, which I perceived went underground in him—envy for the cascade of respect, fame, academic advantage, and financial award that went to his colleague. His relative freedom from envy is a fortunate advantage, and I envy him for it, as well as envying the winner on his behalf. When the award was offered four years later, my husband was not nominated.[3]

This envy by proxy is not a stranger to parents who see their children passed over in favor of their contemporaries, when it comes to the good things of life. My precious granddaughter, born out of wedlock to a loving, single mother, is without a meaningful father. This lovely child certainly did nothing to deserve such a social handicap that might lead to psychologic damage in later years, any more than other children did to earn two parents to love and care for them. I suffer envy on her behalf, although she is strong and is thriving.

Even more, I know envy[4] on behalf of countless children born to no genuine parents at all, and languishing without prospect of adoptive homes. When my son and daughter-in-law went to Ukraine to adopt a child, the method was to visit Ukrainian "babyhouses" and pick one out, with bribes along the way. (My son said that "Ben" helped him. "Ben?" "Benjamin Franklin's portrait on the hundred-dollar bills we were told to carry.")

It all sounded like going to a farmer's market and thumping a watermelon. They, understandably, chose the youngest child. This was possible when the infant was six months, but only with a few shenanigans about a fake "medical condition". He was in good health, though underweight. "How could you stand to see all the ones you had to leave," I asked, "and the ones with greater physical and psychologic needs than his?"

"Not having adopted him would have in no way helped the rest," said my analytic son. "In fact, his being taken to America left a little more of the scarce resources for the others. The people we met were caring, and struggling to do the best they could with what little they had. They loved him enough to be delighted that we took him and will give him a chance in life that he could never have had there."

I find myself envying on behalf of all the unadoptable children left in the Ukrainian "babyhouses".

While many crimes have resulted from jealousy, as in love triangles, some have also been traceable to envy and even to envy by proxy. Schoeck relates a case of a disadvantaged late adolescent boy whose friend came from a well-to-do middle-class family, all of whom treated him kindly and included him in family events. However, he resented the fact that the other mother had the good things of life that his own mother lacked. And so he killed his friend's mother.

In *Amahl and the Night Visitors*, a one-act opera by Gian Carlo Menotti, the dirt-poor widowed mother envies on behalf of her lame son the baby Jesus, to whom the wise men are carrying precious gifts. She rationalizes that that infant king doesn't need those riches, but her son does, and so she tries to steal a gold jewel. Although she is apprehended, the miraculous gift to the son is cure of his crippled leg.

An example in the opposite direction (envy on behalf of a parent by an adult child) is found in the work of John Wideman, an African-American English professor and author of the memoir he entitled by his portmanteau coinage *Fatheralong*. He and his father traveled to seek out their roots in a tiny town in South Carolina. By inquiring at the church, they found cousins and other relatives.

The proprietor of a small bookstore put Wideman in touch with a friend of hers, a white retired history professor from the community college, whose specialty was local history going back to slave times. This man generously spent several hours on different days, graciously took Wideman to the courthouse to go through deeds and land records, saved him a great deal of time, and was a valuable help in his task. But Wideman writes:

> I'd enjoyed his company, benefited incalculably from his patient tutelage, his stores of information as he conveyed to me the mysteries and mechanics of using Platt books, indexes, cartridge-case-like boxes of wills that had recorded property transactions in the county since before the Revolutionary War. I was grateful, even fond of this elderly man who shared himself, his insights and craft, so unreservedly with a stranger, and that's why I was surprised, shocked even, by the ice-cold wave of anger, the fury compressed into one of those if-looks-could-kill looks I found myself flashing down at the back of his thin, freckled bald skull.
>
> From my perch on a ladder as Bowie Lomax read their serial numbers from a king-sized ledger, I was passing down metal boxes stuffed with ancient wills, letters, bills of sale, itemized appraisals of real estate and personal property that were required to legally convey wealth from the dead hand to the living. While the professor led me through the process of unearthing our shared past, my father sat outside the courthouse, basking in the sun on a bench in the restored square of Abbeville. The unanticipated glare of pure animosity had a lot to do with my father, I'm sure. He was about the same age as Bowie Lomax, as smart, as curious and engaging. Yet, because of his color, my father had been denied the prospects, the possibilities that had enriched the career and life of the white man below me.
>
> Quickly, I realized I felt no desire to actually harm Bowie

Lomax, but damage had been done. A silent apology issued from me almost simultaneous with the explosion of hostility. Nothing personal. Nothing about you, my new friend. However, the urge to strike, to destroy, wasn't totally abstract, either. It was Professor Lomax's skull I had envisioned shattering, spilling all its learning, its intimate knowledge of these deeds that transferred in the same 'livestock' column as cows, horses, and mules, the bodies of my ancestors from one white owner to another. Hadn't the historian's career been one more mode of appropriation and exploitation of my father's bones, the pearls that were his eyes. Didn't mastery of Abbeville's history, the power and privilege to tell my father's story, follow from the original sin of slavery that stole, then silenced, my father's voice. The professor was a bona fide expert. He'd earned a living studying, passing on, institutionalizing what he knew about us, including how we were bought and sold, how a region flourished based upon trafficking in human souls. Not only flourished, but attempted to legitimize and preserve its prerogatives for all the world to see with these crumbling pieces of paper we were disinterring.

I wanted the room to disappear, the hardy, vital old man to disappear, every vestige of the complacent, unrepentant reality of slavery to be scoured from the earth. My rage was not meant for my companion in that musty room crammed wall to wall, floor to ceiling, with decaying documents. What I wanted was another chance for my father.[5] I wanted this air cleared for a different world, not so my father would be Bowie Lomax, not so Bowie Lomax would be struck down and made to suffer for the crimes of his fathers. I didn't know what kind of world, what kind of life I wished for my father or the professor or what they might wish for themselves. What should come next is always imponderable, always problematic, but I knew in that moment my anger flashed we had not severed ourselves from a version of history that had made the lives of my black father and this white man so separate, so distant, yet so intimately intertwined.

Upon a stepladder in the probate-office storage vault in Abbeville, South Carolina, I had experienced with unprecedented immediacy the fact of slavery. A grave full of chained skeletons wouldn't have been more convincing. In this room there was no denying the solid, banal, everyday business-as-usual role slavery played in America's past. Meticulously, unashamedly, the perpetrators had preserved evidence of their crimes. Given their practice the official stamp of approval. Not only did a world that once had been, shove its reality into my face, these documents also confirmed how much the present, my father's life, mine, yours, are still being determined by the presumption of white over black inscribed in them.

Neither Wideman nor I can conjecture what the father's and son's lives would have been if a world without slavery had left them in Africa, nor would they have been likely to be the descendants.

Envy by proxy for those deprived of what we think of as basic human rights—this envy lies on the borderline with abstract desire for social justice, and blends and merges with it. Fairness is a value that meets envy in the center of a continuum and becomes mixed and muddied with it, when we believe that others have been undeservedly given something that we or those we empathize with deserve and cannot have. If we could, we would take it from them and give it to the deserving ones who would appreciate it and use it wisely. This kind of envy/justice confusion spills over into the area of politics, and persons who register this sympathetic feeling often address it by joining organizations such as abolitionist societies to correct it, either politically or socially.

Notes

1. Formerly called "idiot savant".

2. "Deserve" is a slippery word, having been commandeered by advertising moguls, as in "You deserve a Lexus", meaning not "You have earned it" but "We'll get the bank to buy one for you". Meanings of words often change over time, usually becoming less specific and precise, more sloppy. An example is "cooperate". Whereas formerly it meant "to work together toward a common end", now it has come to be used to signify "to do what I want you to do", usually "for your own good". I noticed it when nurses would report "He won't cooperate; he won't take his medication."

3. Fortunately, not all disappointments are envy-related. Years earlier, my husband was offered lifetime support (i.e., his salary paid at any institution with which he could negotiate an appointment and laboratory facilities, which would be much to the institution's advantage and give him wider choice). Later the offer was withdrawn because "the money ran out" (why didn't they know?). At least we didn't know who made the final cut.

4. One of my critics suggests that what I am describing here is really sympathy, which may be the side of envy by proxy that we show to the one whom we perceive disadvantaged. This is another example of the fact that many emotions are not sharply delineated from one another.

5. In this instance we see the relationship between envy and resentment. "Resentment" subsumes the greater anger Wideman felt for the advantage of Bowie Lomax's white heritage. The stronger French form "*ressentiment*" is an ongoing, recurring, perpetual reminder of old injustice.

Chapter 6

Envy in the Ancient World

The occurrence of envy is documented in the world's oldest extant recorded literature, the myth of Gilgamesh. This is the account of humankind's first efforts to search for answers to life's enduring quandaries, e.g., why our loved ones and we ourselves must die. It appeared first in Sumeria. Later versions were recounted in Babylonia, Akkadia, and Assyria, all employing Sumerian as the lingua franca. Preserved in cuneiform script on clay tablets, many broken, in various libraries in the sands of the desert, no single complete version has yet been found intact, and various translators and retellers have had to cobble segments together. Some fragments of the story have not been found yet, such as the explanation of the magical power of a certain door, touching which led to Enkidu's death, and the nature of certain stone "things" that were critical for passage into the underworld. One such retelling relates how Gilgamesh's dear friend, Enkidu, wished his young temple priestess prostitute friend a life so successful and happy that even young maidens and mothers of seven sons would envy her. Later in the odyssey the god Shamach advised Gilgamesh (a hero/king/god, considered ⅓ human and ⅔ god by his mixed ancestry) that when entering the underworld in search of Enkidu, he should take off his fine clean clothes and change into dirty old rags so as not to incite the envy of the dead.

✳

The Judeo-Christian Old Testament relates many tales with envy as the motive for hostile behavior. The Garden of Eden story was later amplified, in the Catholic Scriptures (Wisdom of Solomon),[1] into an account in which the serpent was identified as Satan, and envy invoked as the reason for his temptation of God's "new favorite", leading to mankind's fall and eviction from Eden: "Death came into the world only through the Devil's envy, as those who belong to him find to their cost." In Ecclesiasticus we read, "The eye of the envious is wicked; and he turneth away his face, and despiseth his own soul." In his *Paradise Lost*, Milton used Satan's envy of God to explain his rebellion and subsequent eviction from Paradise, and Satan's envy of Adam and Eve's blissful state as his reason to tempt them to sin.

The oldest recorded crime, Cain's murder of his brother Abel, was occasioned by Cain's envy of his brother for the fact that Abel's offering from his fat flocks found favor with God, while Cain's offering of vegetable harvest of the field was rejected. And so Cain killed Abel. (Schimmel explains God's seeming favoritism by the fact that Abel offered the "choicest" of his increase, whereas Cain brought any old weeds. Another explanation is that agriculture was considered "women's work", as it is in all primitive societies, and therefore not suitable for a man.)

We recall that when the Israelites were having better success with their flocks and herds than their surrounding neighbors were, the Canaanites responded by throwing dirt into their wells.

Abraham, having been promised by God to be the head of an entire nation, questioned how this could come about since his wife Sara was already postmenopausal. Loving her husband and wanting to give him a son, Sara used the old method of sending her handmaiden Hagar to Abraham to serve as surrogate wife, and Hagar subsequently bore Ishmael. Against all expectation, Sara finally also had a son, whom they named Isaac. Then, with Isaac's patrimony established, out of envy for Hagar and Ishmael, Sara drove them into the wilderness with the intention that they would die in the desert. They survived, and Ishmael came to be considered the forerunner of other Semitic peoples.

Like Cain and Abel, the twin brothers Jacob and Esau illustrate envy in sibling rivalry. In this case, Jacob determined to circumvent the established practice of primogeniture, with his mother's help, by deceiving his father so as to receive his irreversible blessing and succeed his father as patriarch. (Some believe that the father knew what was going on but recognized Jacob as the better choice and went along with the deception.) One would expect primogeniture to evoke envy worldwide in non-firstborns, but counterintuitively to us in a fluid society, some observers (Raiga, de Tocqueville) believe that birth order as a given basis for status is easier to accept in rigidly class-stratified societies.)

One sympathizes with Joseph's brothers for their father's blatant partiality to Joseph in admiring his interpretation of dreams and therefore giving him a beautiful coat. Joseph's flaunting of his talent for dream interpretation and his coat of many colors did not help his popularity with his brothers. Therefore the older brothers were led to retaliate by selling Joseph into slavery. Throughout history until recently, there has been no onus on a father's right to favor a child or children in whatever way the parent wished, for any or no reason whatsoever. One way our civilization has crept forward is to expect fair treatment for all one's children. This is more honored in principle than in practice and is often difficult because of differences in children.

Saul, the king, portrayed as envying the youthful David who was more popular with the people, tried unsuccessfully to arrange for David's death, even though David played his harp for Saul as music therapy to alleviate Saul's black depression. David even passed up opportunities to kill Saul. (Envy of the healthy by the sick and of the young by the old is rife throughout history. Efforts by the envied to dispel the envier's resentment by kindness or gifts are notoriously unsuccessful, although one of my critics points out that successful efforts pass without notice.)

Solomon, who has become prototypic for wisdom, had to judge between two women, both claiming to be mother of a particular baby, when one mother's infant had died. In a move that has been touted as evidence of his wisdom, Solomon offered to split the baby between them, thereby identifying the envious impostor mother as the one willing to have the baby killed so the other woman couldn't have it if she couldn't have it herself, while its true mother agreed to surrender the child she loved rather than sacrifice the infant.

In the New Testament, the story of the Prodigal Son illustrates sibling rivalry producing envy in the breast of the diligent, faithful, stay-at-home brother left to toil in the fields, for the preferential attention showered on his delinquent brother when he finally had had enough of "partying" and decided to shape up and come home. (This story illustrates, also, a parent's understandable relief and rejoicing when a child finally requites his fatherly love. It shows too the perennial problems when parents are caught in the crossfire of trying to do right by all the children, who can vary in their needs and wishes.)

Envy is one motivation to which various behaviors are attributed, such as the high priests handing Jesus over to the authorities to be executed on charges of blasphemy (although the more common explanation is political), or the apostles' squabbling over their rank-order and favoritism of Jesus.

Throughout the Bible, Old and New Testaments, are found a number of prohibitions against envy, often with figurative warnings (such as "envy rots the bones"). But nowhere are we given any practical help in dealing with this unasked-for, unwelcome emotion, except to cultivate love, a remedy that is at once simplistic and frighteningly profound, and it takes a lifetime to accomplish as a remedy for envy.

✳

Envy is found also in Greek mythology.

Throughout history, beauty contests have been a prime occasion for the incendiary combination of competition and Venus envy. Animosity between winners and losers often results in efforts to bring down the winners. It was no exception when Paris awarded the golden apple to Aphrodite in Greek mythology. The envious goddesses subsequently took sides in the Trojan War.

In the many skirmishes on Olympus, the gods and goddesses jockeyed for superior position and resented each other's assets and superiorities.[2] Mercury's (Hermes') two-snake caduceus was considered first as a protection against envy.

In Ovid's *Metamorphoses,* one tale illustrates the entanglement of jealousy and envy in a love triangle, using the personification of Envy. In this convoluted tale, Mercury, swift in matters of the heart as he was in flight, beheld the beautiful Herse, one of three human sisters, and determined to make her his own, to the jealous rage of Minerva (called Pallas in Greek). He seeks and buys the cooperation of Herse's sister Aglauros.

> Determined to prevent this new liaison,
> At once Minerva went to Envy's cave,
> A hovel, dark with blood, in a deep valley,
> Hidden where no sun ventures, no wind stirs,
> And night air falling with continual cold;
> No fires were lit to temper rain and fog.
> War's virgin stood aside, nor would she enter
> That fouled dwelling, but clanged her spear against
> Its sagging doors, which, swaying inward, showed
> Envy at feast, eating great snakes and vipers,
> A perfect diet for increase of venom.
> The goddess, sick at the unholy sight,
> Turned eyes away, while Envy, leaving scraps

Of half-chewed meats upon the floor, lunged
To her feet and shambled toward Minerva
Who stately stood in armour. Envy moaned,
Changing her face to suit Minerva's sigh,
Grew death-pale, and her body seemed to shrink,
Eyes wild, teeth thick with mold, gall dripping green
To breast, green from her tongue, for Envy never
Smiles unless she sees another's misery;
Envy is sleepless, her heart anxiety,
And at the sight of any man's success
She withers, is bitten, eats herself away.
Although Minerva hated what she saw
In the foul creature's face, she gave instructions,
Clipping her speech: 'Make it your duty, woman,
To infect Aglauros, one of Cecrops' daughters,
So that your poison streams within her veins.'
And with this said, she thrust her spear to earth,
And swiftly, lightly vaulted back to heaven.

Squint-eyed old Envy saw the goddess vanish,
Nor could she bear to think of so much glory
Without inward whines and tears. She gathered
Up her stick grown thick with thorns, her dark cloak
As cloud on her shoulders, and sped straightly
Her errand. And where she walked all flowers died,
Grass perished, and blight ran over tops of
Highest trees, and as she breathed she tainted
The streets of peopled towns, even in homes.
At last Tritonia's city came to view,
City of art and peace and joy; since Envy
Did not find tears in others' eyes, hardly
Did she hold back her own. But when she came
Into Aglauros' chamber, she set to work
And did Minerva's will: with festered hands

She stroked Aglauros' breast, then placed within
Her heart a nest of thorns, then filled her nostrils,
Until it reached down bone and tissue, with black
Venomous breath. Then to make cause for grief,
Envy placed deep within Aglauros' mind
An image of the marriage yet to come,
As though it shone in magnifying mirrors—
Her sister and the naked god in bed;
At this Aglauros ate at her own heart,
Haggard by day, in misery by night;
As ice is glanced by stray beams of the sun,
Slowly she tasted hate to waste away;
As fire smoulders in hidden heat beneath
Dank grasses, creeping to soot-blackened ashes
And self-devouring flames, so when she thought
Of Herse's happy hour, so she was eaten.
Rather than know the measure of Herse's joy,
She longed to die....
At last she sat herself
Across the threshold of her sister's room
As if to bar the door against the god.
When he arrived, soft words poured over her,
He begged, he pleaded, yet she answered, "No,
I will sit here until you go away."
"Then we shall keep our pact," said Mercury.

In this example one member, Minerva, of a love triangle—Mercury, Herse, Minerva—tries to break up the triangle by setting up envy of one sister by another—Aglauros of Herse.

And Mercury turns Aglauros into a marble statue.

Zeus is portrayed as the envier par excellence. Specifically, he resented sharing knowledge with humankind because he anticipated

competition. Therefore, when Prometheus brought the arts of civilization to humankind (written language,[3] fire, architecture, agriculture, music, mathematics, etc.), Zeus punished him by having
him tied to a rock, where a vulture pecked away at his liver daily
for eons, although it regrew nightly, because of wanting to keep
knowledge to himself, or at least to the pantheon. This is drama-
tized in Aeschylus' *Prometheus Bound*.

In Robert Whitelaw's poetic translation, we read Prometheus'
explanation for why his liver is eaten away daily by the vulture and
regrown for the next day's feast:

> Deem not that I of stubbornness and pride
> Am silent: with my thoughts my heart is wrung,
> Seeing myself with insult overborne.
> Yet to these upstart gods who if not I
> Made absolute partition of their sway?...
> The miseries of men
> I will recount you, how, mere babes before,
> With reason I endowed them and with mind
> And not in their disparagement I speak,
> But of my gifts to memorize the love:
> Who, firstly, seeing, knew not what they saw,
> And hearing did not hear; confusedly passed
> Their life-days, lingeringly, like shapes in dreams,
> Without an aim ; and neither sunward homes,
> Brick-woven, nor skill of carpentry, they knew;
> But lived, like small ants shaken with a breath,
> In sunless caves a burrowing buried life...
> And took no thought, till that the hidden lore
> Of rising stars and setting I unveiled.
> I taught them Number, first of sciences....
> I first put harness on dumb patient beasts,
> Obedient to the yoke; and, with their bodies
> That they might lighten men of heavy toil,

I taught to draw the car and love the rein
Horses, crown of the luxury of wealth.
And who but I invented the white-winged
Sea-roving chariot of the mariner?
For mortals such contrivances I found,
But for myself alas no wit have I,
Whereby to rid me of my present pain....
More is behind, more wonderful to hear:
Skill and resource, contrived by me for men.
This first and foremost: did a man fall sick,
Deliverance was there none, or 'twixt the teeth,
Or smeared, or drunken; but for very lack
Of healing drugs they wasted, till that I
Showed them to mix each virtuous remedy,
Wherewith they shield them now from all disease.

Prometheus takes credit for teaching humans the superstitious arts of prophecy and haruspicy. All of this Zeus preferred to withhold from humankind, because of envy.

This story has some similarities to the Garden of Eden story in that both deities wanted to retain superiority over humankind by refusing to impart knowledge. Jehovah focused on "knowledge of good and evil", while Zeus wanted to withhold all kinds of practical knowledge, such as agriculture, which Adam and Eve were portrayed as already practicing. Jehovah apparently wished to retain superiority over humans by keeping to Himself more philosophical and ethical kinds of knowledge. When our ancestral mother was tempted by the serpent, Eve was not just curious; she also wished for education in the belief that it would make her and Adam "like gods".

✳

In ancient times and in preliterate societies, there has been little occupational specialization, except by sex. The same individual, however, might combine, as shaman, the roles of priest and doctor, sometimes also tribal leader. The advent of written language was a giant leap, and a powerful tool became available for those who mastered it. It even opened up a new profession for record keepers and scribes. This device of the written word extended the functions of all professions and made life richer and more complicated for them and succeeding generations. The advantage for us is that across the millennia we can learn what they thought at the dawn of civilization about law, for example, in the Code of Hammurabi, about medicine in the Ebers Papyrus, and about religion in the *Egyptian Book of the Dead.*[4]

In this almost magical way, ideas have passed from one mind to others across time and space. As gradually people became specialized, their thoughts about envy found their way into written records. Since this topic has been of interest to priests and philosophers, psychologists and sociologists, writers of fiction and mental health personnel, we shall look at the beliefs of these specialists on this topic, beginning with religious thinkers.

Notes

1. This and the Ecclesiasticus reference are found in the Catholic Apocrypha, which were not retained in the Protestant Old Testament.

2. We use the phrase "the envy of the gods", as something to avoid by not parading our advantage. When I heard this expression as a child, I questioned why the gods should envy anyone, since I assumed that their divinity was "all-powerful", so gods and goddesses could presumably have anything they wanted. Only later I learned that in classical times members of the pantheon were considered powerful, but within limits, with the result that they maneuvered for position and power at a higher level than humans. Thus envy drove behavior intended to maintain a relative superiority, just as with humans.

3. In some versions of the Gilgamesh epic, Enkidu is credited with bringing civilization to humankind, including written language. It is true that cuneiform writing on clay tablets antedated the Greek alphabet, as well as Egyptian writing.

4. I have read recently someone's regret that we can never know our ancestors' thoughts and fears over the advancing Big Ice because it antedated written language.

Chapter 7

Envy as Viewed by Early Christian Church Fathers

Over hundreds of years Roman Catholic theologians debated which seven sins to group (seven being a magical/religious number from prehistoric times and in many cultures). This collection was called, variously, "capital" or "mortal" or "deadly" sins. They were often matched to seven metals or to the seven visible "planets", meaning "wanderers" (sun, moon, Mercury, Venus, Mars, Jupiter, and Saturn). Over the centuries the list of sins firmed up, depending on the influence of the theologian. Soon envy was included in all lists, and it was considered second only to pride (hubris), from which sprang some of the others (e.g., if you think too highly of yourself in some particular parameter, then you are likely to envy those who have an edge in that regard). The final list consists of pride, envy, wrath, gluttony, greed, lust, and sloth (meaning not just laziness but amotivation or anomie, a frequent problem for persons with religious vocations). Bloomfield, an author and specialist in the "deadly sins" in Renaissance literature, notes that the term "deadly" is a misnomer in that these seven are considered forgivable and do not lead to eternal damnation.[1] Hence "capital" would be Bloomfield's accurate, preferred term, but he goes along with common usage in the phrase "seven deadly sins". Bloomfield cites many works dealing with the seven but never singles out one or other, such as envy, for discussion.

✳

In the early years of the Christian Church, at the same time that theologians were debating just which texts to include in the Old and New Testaments, they were also writing their interpretations of dogmatic theology. They were not averse to commenting on envy, which they considered a sin in its own right, even when the envier keeps it strictly internalized and under wraps, and does not give vent to any overt expression of hostility directed against the envied one. This is analogous to how Christ considered thoughts of murder and thoughts of adultery as sins within the heart.[2]

The Catholic Catechism credits Origen in the second century as the first to number envy as a capital sin, because from it spring hatred, calumny, detraction, and other types of malevolent behavior.

Schimmel, in his review of Christian and Jewish bases for morality, has collected comments from the following ancient theologians.

In the third century St. Cyprian of Carthage wrote:

> Whoever thou might be, O envious and malicious one, look at how wicked thou art with regard to those whom thou hatest, how noxious and unpleasant. Thou art the enemy of no one else but thine own salvation. Everyone whom thou persuest with envy can run and slip away from thee, but thou canst not run away from thyself. Wherever thou might be, thine adversary is with thee, the enemy is always in thy heart, perdition is contained within. Thou art entangled in and bound by unbreakable chains, thou hast become a captive of the jealousy that has prevailed over thee, and no consolation whatever will come to thine aid.... It is not permitted for a disciple of Christ to be jealous and to envy.

In the fourth century, combining envy and schadenfreude, St. Basil the Great wrote:

There is no other passion engendered in human souls more pernicious than envy. It does less harm to strangers, but is the chief homegrown evil for whoever possesses it. As rust eats away at iron, so envy eats away at the soul in which it lives. To say it better just as they say of vipers, that they are born by gnawing through the belly that gives them birth, so also envy usually devours the soul which is tormented by it. Envy is grief over a neighbor's wellbeing. Therefore, the envious man never has a lack of sorrows and afflictions. What can be more pernicious than this disease? This is a corruption of life, a profanation of nature, enmity against what is given to us by God, opposition to God.

In his Catechism, St. Augustine (fourth to fifth centuries) of Hippo (modern town of Bone in eastern Algeria), calls envy "the diabolical sin". He saw envy in Christians who vied to be God's favorite. "The mistake is…in not rejoicing with their fellowmen, but grudging [Y]our grace to others."

In *The City of God,* Augustine attributes Satan's temptation of Eve to envy, but he doesn't make much of it.

St. Gregory the Great (second half of sixth century) lists the consequences of envy: "From envy are born hatred, detraction, calumny, joy caused by the misfortune of a neighbor, and displeasure caused by his prosperity."

The only recommended antidotes to envy include developing charity and goodwill toward others, and combating pride, because pride leads us to hold too high an opinion of ourselves and envy those whose advantages threaten it.

Moving forward seven centuries, in St. Thomas Aquinas' massive *Summa Theologica* we find several pages of the author's views on envy, in which he includes schadenfreude. Citing many of the earlier theologians, his observations include virtually everything that has been attributed to envy by later, as well as earlier, writers. He states:

> We grieve over a man's good, in so far as his good surpasses ours; this is envy properly speaking, and is always sinful ... because to do so is to grieve over what should make us rejoice, viz. over our neighbor's good. ... We may grieve over another's good, not because he has it, but because the good which he has, we have not. ... [T]he envious grieves over the good of those who are deserving of it.

Elsewhere:

> But this does not apply to people who are far removed from one another: for no man, unless he be out of his mind, endeavors to rival or surpass in reputation those who are far above him. Thus a commoner does not envy the king, nor does the king envy a commoner whom he is far above. Wherefore a man envies not those who are far removed from him, whether in place, time, or station, but those who are near him, and whom he strives to rival or surpass. For it is against our will that these should be in greater glory than we are, and that gives rise to sorrow.

St. Thomas comments on the relation between envy and pride and relative reputation:

> A man does not strive for mastery in matters where he is very deficient; so that he does not envy one who surpasses him in such matters, unless he surpass him by little, for then it seems to him that this is not beyond him, and so he makes an effort; wherefore, if his effort fails through the other's glory surpassing his, he grieves. And thus it is

those who love to be honored are more envious; and in like manner the faint-hearted are envious, because all things are great to them, and whatever good may befall another, they reckon that they themselves have been bested in something great.

He notes further that if we have lost something, we envy those who have it. His examples are the old envying the young, and those who have struggled to acquire something envying those who got it for little money or effort. He observes that high status does not protect from envy, and pride even contributes to it:

Those who lack little, and who love honors, and who are considered wise, are envious. ...
[A]nother's good may be reckoned as being one's own evil, in so far as it conduces to the lessening of one's own good name or excellence. It is in this way that envy grieves for another's good: and consequently men are envious of those goods in which a good name consists, and about which men like to be honored and esteemed.

Nor does this author neglect the expressions of envy:

The number of envy's daughters may be understood for the reason that in the struggle aroused by envy there is something by way of beginning, something by way of middle, and something by way of term. The beginning is that a man strives to lower another's reputation, and this either secretly, and then we have 'tale-bearing,' or openly, and then we have 'detraction.' The middle consists in the fact that when a man aims at defaming another, he is either able to do so, and then we have 'joy at another's misfortune,' or he is unable, and then we have 'grief at another's prosperity.'...Grief at another's prosperity is in one way the very same as envy, when, to wit, a man grieves over another's prosperity, in so far as it gives the latter a good name, but in another way it is a daughter of envy, in so far as the envious man sees his neighbor prosper notwithstanding his efforts to prevent it. On the other hand, 'joy at another's misfortune' is not directly the same as envy, but is a result thereof, because grief over our neighbor's good which is envy, gives rise to joy in his evil.[3]

Soon after Aquinas (thirteenth century), we see the beginning of the Renaissance, with its flourishing of literature which, while still concerned with religious motifs, begins to assume the form of secular fiction and poetry. We shall examine these in a later chapter.

Notes

1. Indeed, Dante places the envious not with the other eternally damned in his Inferno but in his Purgatorio where they must spend untold eons in expiation before admission to Paradiso.

2. With my Protestant upbringing, I had always conceived of sins as overt behaviors of a proscribed nature, and there were plenty of them. I am advised by several Protestant theologians that I have missed the more sophisticated meaning of sin, which is being out of harmony with God. From this would stem both the overt bad behavior of the Ten Commandments and the negative ways of being a person of the Seven Deadly.

   On more mature consideration, I rather approve of the idea of looking upon envy as a sin, not for what it might do to others, but rather as a sin against the self, for the pain it causes and the harm it does the individual who envies. Better yet, since envy is not "committed", but afflicts one, we might think of it as not a "sin" unless we let it vitiate us. Persons who try to treat others with fairness and kindness often need help in treating themselves with the same consideration. Persons who envy need help in dealing with this extremely painful emotion, which, as we have reiterated, they never sought out. The problem is that help is rarely sought, and the envious person usually does not know how to help himself.

3. As I see it, neither joy in another's misfortune nor grief over his good fortune need to have resulted from any behavior by the envious, such as his efforts to prevent his neighbor's good fortune, but rather just his observations of the good things that either good luck or hard work and planning have brought to the envied one.

Chapter 8

Envy as Understood by Philosophers

Since philosophy has the deepest roots in our culture after religion, it seems fitting to look next at some of the philosophers' beliefs about envy over the millennia.

The Greek philosopher Aristotle, when a guest at a drinking party, is quoted in Plato's *Symposium* as referring to literary offspring surviving long after the author is dust, when he opines:

> Everyone would prefer to have children like that rather than human ones. People look enviously at Homer and Hesiod and other good poets, because of the kind of children they have left behind them, which provide them with immortal fame and remembrance by being immortal themselves.

Literary recognition and lasting fame are certainly one of the top-ranking venues for envy, as we shall explore in the chapter on authors' envy of each other.

In his *Nichomachaean Ethics*, Aristotle describes a continuum:

> Righteous indignation is a mean between envy and spite, and these states are concerned with the pain and pleasure that are felt at the fortunes of our neighbours; the man who is characterized by righteous indignation is pained at

undeserved good fortune, the envious man, going beyond
him, is pained at all good fortune, and the spiteful man falls
so far short of being pained that he even rejoices.

My conceptualization is that righteous indignation is an appeal to
fairness on behalf of someone unjustly deprived of what good fortune should have been his and is therefore not the mean between
the other two, but one extreme. Envy occurs when the envier is or
feels outclassed by the one he envies. The person who rejoices over
another's bad fortune is feeling schadenfreude, not the same as
Aristotle's "spite". Thus we have semantic differences. Like other
observers, I see the validity of the continuum between envy and
"righteous indignation" over injustice, the slope between the two
being slippery indeed.

The references to envy in the *Nichomachaean Ethics* describe
envy as always bad, unlike some emotions that are wrong if excessive, sometimes right in the right circumstances.

The Greeks recognized and treated envy in a way we do not, and
unabashedly provided a forthright way to address it: ostracism. If
a citizen appeared too well favored, his fellow citizens could vote
to exile him for a period of ten years, and against this the envied
one had no defense. I see such a solution outrageous, particularly
since there did not seem to be any judgment relating to how the
advantages (wealth) had been acquired or used.

Francis Bacon,[1] a sixteenth/seventeenth-century philosopher,
essayist, and statesman, in his essay "On Envy" calls it "a state like
to an infection.... It tainteth even that which is sound." Later he
adds, "It goeth in the modern languages by the name of discontent."
Perhaps it did so in his day, but I question even this because there
are so many causes for discontent other than envy.

Bacon makes the observation common to envy-watchers that

the persons we envy are likely to be kinsfolk and coworkers, peers with whom we rub elbows constantly. Only kings envy kings, he noted.[2] From his own vantage in the English court, he suffered envy for "those in high places" and feared it from others in the jockeyings for position in the workings of the patronage system of the English court of his day.

He observed, as have others, that we envy unworthy persons when they receive undeserved advancement, because that is like a gift, whereas when someone has worked for a good end and is rewarded accordingly, it seems to the observer more like payment of a debt and even holds out the hope, if not a guarantee, that we shall likewise be rewarded justly. Thus when persons of merit get their just deserts, we are comfortable with it at first, but Bacon believes that after a time it lasts too long and wears thin, and our envy increases.

It was Bacon's belief that persons of noble birth are envious of the newly arrived, because this reduces their relative superiority.[3]

If honors come at the cost of great perils, such as difficult travel (which could be a challenge in Bacon's day), we are more likely to be sympathetic and less likely to envy. Cognizant of this, persons recently returned from distant parts may stress the obstacles they surmounted in order to minimize being the target of envy. Also, if an individual who has been promoted makes a point to preserve the rights of underlings and treat them fairly, that mitigates the envy of those left behind.

On the other hand, those who flaunt their greatness in a proud and insolent fashion induce envy. Bacon finds it advisable to walk a middle path because if one goes to the opposite extreme of hiding his success in a sly and crafty manner, this behavior, when it surfaces, also elicits envy in the observer.

Bacon notes that most persons with uncorrectable flaws (he lists physical deformities, eunuchs, bastards, old men) are envious, although a few such persons may be brave and heroic. They may even find ways to capitalize on having succeeded despite their disadvantage. This is true also of those in the broad category of normal who fight their way back after a major setback or calamity.

Persons who are ambitious in several domains also may feel the bite of envy for those who devote all their efforts to pursuing just one endeavor, thereby enhancing their likelihood of success. Bacon cites the Emperor Adrian who yearned to be not only political but recognized also in the arts. Therefore he envied successful poets and painters.[4]

Bacon believes that those without virtue envy the virtuous. Maybe in Bacon's time, but my observation is that virtue these days buys little respect.

He relates envy to inquisitiveness, what we might call "nosiness" in contrast to more wholesome curiosity. He asserts that those who mind their own business are less likely to suffer envy, for "envy is a gadding passion, and walketh the streets, and doth not keep home".

He refers to "public envy", a phenomenon occurring when someone gets out of bounds and is envied by many, who then tend to ostracize the envied one, though not in the ancient Greek way. This serves the socially useful function of keeping the envied person bridled. This is the kind of envy that he believes spreads "like an infection", which he dubs a "discontentment".

Bacon believes that of all the emotions, only two can "fascinate or bewitch", that is, love and envy, because they are both associated with vehement wishes translatable into imagination and "come easily into the eye". He subscribes to the medieval view that the envious can irradiate evil by staring. It is just one step to equate envy with the "evil eye". He even attributes the association of envy and the "evil eye" to the Scriptures (I have seen this in one older translation). Astrologers of Bacon's time attributed the experiencing of envy to "evil influences of the stars". Bacon believes that the "percussion" of the evil eye is worst when the envied one is in a state of glory or triumph. (It must have been a terrible burden to live with the fear that every success rendered you vulnerable to someone's stare.)

His association of envy and witchcraft led him to the conclusion that the cure is also witchcraft, i.e., somehow magically switching the envy directed to oneself to someone else with an advantage, who would be an unsuspecting target.

Bacon sums up by calling envy the most importune and continual of the "affections" and "the vilest and most depraved", hence "an attribute of the devil". "The envious man ... soweth tares amongst the wheat by night." (Just as the Canaanites, observing the health and vigor of the Israelites' flocks and herds, threw dirt into their wells.)

I credit Bacon for his scrutiny and honesty.[5]

Descartes,[6] a seventeenth-century philosopher and mathematician, in *The Passions of the Soul*, wrote:

> What we usually call envy is a vice which consists in a perversion of nature which causes certain people to be annoyed with the good which they see coming to others, but I here use the word to signify a passion which is not always vicious. Envy, then, insofar as it is a passion, is a kind of sadness mingled with hatred, which proceeds from our seeing good coming to those whom we consider unworthy of it; then envy is not excited in us except for loving justice naturally. We are angered that it be not observed in the distribution of good things.

Elsewhere:

> But when it is (i.e., the good things of life are) represented to us as pertaining to other men, we may esteem them either as worthy or unworthy of it; and when we esteem them worthy, that does not excite in us any other

passion but joy, inasmuch as it is some satisfaction to us to see that things happen as they should. There is only this difference, that the joy that comes from what is good is serious, while what comes from evil is accompanied by laughter and mockery. But if we esteem them unworthy of it, the good excites envy and the evil pity, which are species of sadness.

Descartes does us more credit than we have earned when he believes we envy only those we esteem less worthy of the good than ourselves, or that we necessarily pity those visited by undeserved evil.

Spinoza, a seventeenth-century Dutch Jewish philosopher, commented on envy in "On the Origin and Nature of the Affects", the third section of his *Ethics*. He felt that "no one so far as I know has determined the nature and strength of the affects, and what the mind is able to do towards controlling them" including the "celebrated Descartes"[7]. He indicated that it was the style to "prefer to detest and scoff at human affects and actions than understand them", which he proposed to rectify. He intended "to endeavour to treat by a geometrical method the vices and follies of men ... and vanities, absurdities, and monstrosities. ... The affects, therefore, of hatred, anger, envy, considered in themselves, follow from the same necessity and virtue of nature ... have therefore certain causes through which they are to be understood, and certain properties which are just as worthy of being known as the properties of any other thing[8] in the contemplation alone of which we delight. ... I shall consider human actions and appetites just as if I were considering lines, planes, or bodies."

The nature of man is generally constituted so as to pity those who are in adversity and envy those who are in prosperity, and (Prop. 32, pt. 39)[9] he [mankind] envies with a hatred which is the greater in proportion as he loves what he imagines another possesses. We see also that from the same property of human nature from which it follows that men pity one another it also follows that they are envious and ambitious.

Men are by nature inclined to hatred and envy, and we must add that their education assists them in this propensity, for parents are accustomed to excite their children to follow virtue by the stimulus of honour and envy alone....

Corol. No one envies the virtue of a person who is not his equal.

Demonst. Envy is nothing but hatred (Schol. Prop. 24, pt. 3).... [H]e cannot feel any sorrow because he contemplates a virtue in another person altogether unlike himself, and consequently he cannot envy that person, but will only envy one who is his own equal, and who is supposed to possess the same nature.

Schol. Since, therefore, we have said in Schol. Prop. 52, pt. 3, that we venerate a man because we are astonished at his wisdom and bravery, &c., this happens because (as is evident from the proposition itself) we imagine that he specially possesses these virtues, and that they are not common to our nature. We therefore envy them no more than we envy trees their height or lions their bravery.

In so far as men are carried away by envy, ... so far they are contrary to one another, and consequently so much the more are they to be feared, as they have more power than other individuals of nature.

Spinoza recognizes the related schadenfreude: "[E]nvy is hatred in so far as it affects a man so that he is sad at the good fortune of another person and is glad when any evil happens to him."

He believes that envy is usually connected with emulation. As we noted, Spinoza believed that we envy virtue only in our peers. (Spinoza is the third philosopher who regarded virtue in relation to envy.) He felt that other intangibles were not to be envied. "When we admire wisdom, talents, merits, we recognize them as exclusively their property and do not envy."

Good for Spinoza! I see just the opposite: a combination of admiration and envy of these intangibles, whereas I don't see much concern for virtue at all in our times.

Several prominent philosophers, regardless of their main area of interest, included comments on envy, and there is a remarkable similarity in what they have to say. The eighteenth century Scottish skeptic David Hume, after studying law, developed what he called "an insurmountable aversion to everything but the pursuit of philosophy and general learning" and was twice turned down for university teaching positions for his alleged atheism.

His analysis of envy rests on comparisons. "[A]s we seldom judge of objects from their intrinsic value, but form our notions of them from a comparison with other objects; it follows, that according as we observe a greater or less share of happiness or misery in others, we must make an estimate of our own, and feel a consequent pain or pleasure. The misery of another gives us a more lively idea of our happiness, and his happiness of our misery. The former, therefore, produces delight; and the latter uneasiness. ... The direct survey of another's pleasure naturally gives us pleasure, and therefore produces pain when compared with our own. His pain, considered in itself, is painful to us, but augments the idea of our own happiness, and gives us pleasure.

"This reasoning will account for the origin of *envy* as well as of malice. The only difference betwixt these passions lies in this, that envy is excited by some present enjoyment of another, which by comparison diminishes our idea of our own: Whereas malice is the unprovoked desire of producing evil to another, in order to reap a pleasure from the comparison. The enjoyment, which is the object of envy, is commonly superior to our own. A superiority naturally seems to overshade us, and presents a disagreeable comparison. But even in the case of an inferiority, we still desire a greater distance, in order to augment still more the idea of ourselves. When this distance diminishes, the comparison is less to our advantage; and consequently gives us less pleasure, and is even disagreeable. Hence arises that species of envy, which men feel, when they perceive their inferiors approaching or overtaking them in the pursuits of glory or happiness. In this envy we may see the effects of comparison twice repeated. A man, who compares himself to his inferior, receives a pleasure from the comparison: And when the inferiority decreases by the elevation of the inferior, what should only have been a decrease of pleasure, becomes a real pain, by a new comparison with its preceding condition…. [E]nvy, which arises from a superiority in others … 'tis not the great disproportion betwixt oneself and another … but on the contrary, our proximity…. [N]or does an eminent writer meet with so great jealousy in common hackney scribblers, as in authors, that more nearly approach him…. [T]he great disproportion cuts off the relation, and either keeps us from comparing ourselves with what is remote from us, or diminishes the effects of the comparison."

"[P]roximity in the degree of merit is not alone sufficient to give rise to envy, but must be assisted by other relations. A poet is not apt to envy a philosopher, or a poet of a different kind, or a different nation, or of a different age."

What saves us, Hume writes in a section on "Justice and Injustice" is "[A]s to *envy* and *revenge*, though pernicious, they operate only by intervals, and are directed against particular persons whom we consider as our superiors or enemies…. There scarce is any one who is not actuated by it; and there is no one who has not reason to fear from it, when it acts without any restraint and gives way to its first and most natural movements. So that, upon the whole, we are to esteem the difficulties in the establishment of society to be greater or less, according to those we encounter in regulating and restraining this passion."

Kant, in the late eighteenth century, is another philosopher with a few observations on envy in his work on virtue.

> The Vices of Hating Mankind...make up the detestable family of envy, ingratitude, and malice. The hatred involved in these is not open and violent but secret and veiled, which adds meanness to one's unmindfulness of his duty to his neighbor, and in this way violates one's duty to himself as well. (a) Envy (*livor*) is a propensity to view the welfare of others grudgingly, although their welfare does not damage one's own. When it breaks out in action (by impairing another's welfare), it is a special kind of envy.... Envy is only indirectly a vicious disposition, namely, vexation at seeing our own welfare overshadowed by another's, because we prize our welfare and make it tangible not according to its inner worth but only by comparing it with that of other people.... Thus the agitations of envy lie in the nature of mankind, and only their eruption makes them into the abominable vice of a sullen passion that is self-tormenting and, at least in wish, destructive of the happiness of others. There, this vice is opposed to a man's duty to himself as well as his duty to others.

✳

Schopenhauer, a nineteenth-century philosopher, has thought and written about fame, reputation, position, and, by implication, envy. One such chapter is entitled "On Reputation". He quotes classical authors (Cicero, Seneca, and Hobbes), whose observations are included with the maxims.

Since much of Schopenhauer's work pertains to envy as experienced by authors, he will be considered in the chapter devoted to envy in authors.

The Danish philosopher and theologian of the mid-nineteenth century, Søren Kierkegaard, observed that envy "strangles, inhibits, levels...stifles, impedes".

Writing in the latter half of the nineteenth century, the German philosopher Friedrich Nietzsche has been blamed for inspiring Hitler by lauding the Übermensch, or Superman, the person who "has it all", i.e., intelligence, power, and drive, which Hitler (but not Nietzsche) seized on as prototypic of the Aryan "race". In *Also Sprach Zarathustra*, in a remarkable seven-page essay entitled "Flies in the Marketplace", Nietzsche writes in his pithy aphoristic style, without once using any word for "envy", of the insufferable comparison felt by those of inferior talents, and their urge to revenge. "Thy neighbours will always be poisonous flies. That which is great in thee — that itself must make them still more poisonous and ever more like flies."

"Because thou art tender and of a just mind thou sayest: 'Their small existence is not their fault.' But their narrow soul thinketh: 'Guilty is all great existence. ... They feel themselves to be small before thee, and their lowness glimmereth and gloweth in invisible revenge against thee."

In *Beyond Good and Evil,* Nietzsche credits social control to our desire for equality and justice, and hence envy. In his view, as well as Feuerbach's and others, Christianity owes its immense and lasting success to offering promises of true equality and perpetual bliss in the afterlife as compensation for and a way to tolerate the injustice experienced in this one, beside which all tribulations in the here-and-now are trivial.

Schopenhauer (considered with "essayists"), Kierkegaard, and Nietzsche all recognized the function of envy in society, as we shall discuss in an upcoming chapter on politics.

Notes

1. A man four hundred years ahead of his time. I was astonished to discover in his writing a formula for a simple controlled experiment, an idea that was largely ignored until rethought of early in the twentieth century.

2. This is in contrast to Raiga, who has observed masters envying their servants' good traits, such as nobility of character.

3. My husband's father is an example of this kind of resentment for those who rise above their erstwhile station. Forty years after arriving in New York as a callow youth of nineteen and being robbed of his paltry handful of rubles, he attended an ethnic picnic and was astonished to encounter the wife of the landowner, by then dispossessed by the Soviets, on whose farm his ancestors had worked as serfs. She bragged how well her two sons had done in business in this country. Then my late father-in-law related that his two sons were doctors. Shocked, she responded, "How can that be when your family used to work on our estate?"

4. A modern example is women who try to be "supermoms" while pursuing a career. Having taken on the time- and energy-consuming assignment of motherhood, they may envy the success of childless career women devoting all their energy to their professional ambition. This kind of double jeopardy in which nature places women, along with lack of opportunity for women through the ages, may account for the fact of appreciably less name recognition of women throughout history.

5. I credit him also for being the only author I ever heard of to dedicate a book to his amanuensis. I credit Loren Eiseley for bringing this to our attention.

6. Descartes has recently come under criticism in mental science circles for what has been called "Cartesian body-mind dualism". While there is no doubt that the mind works through the nervous system (and other organs and chemicals), I believe that this division is a not

unreasonable, but convenient way to look at these processes, and a good operational distinction. Where Descartes and I parted company was in his culpable insistence that animals can feel no pain because "they have no soul". Soul or no soul, I am outraged that in the seventeenth century anyone with a nanogram of sympathy was able to deny the sounds and behavior of animals in pain. Remarkably, in the twenty-first century we encounter the same denial of the death agony in fish taken out of water, the only vehicle in which they can breathe.

7. He was being sarcastic.

8. Both Spinoza and I are unaware of any earlier interest in the study of psychology, and we could not agree more that it is a suitable subject for study.

9. With this kind of notation, Spinoza reasoned in a way analogous to theorems and corollaries.

Chapter 9

Treatment of Envy in Renaissance Literature

With the coming of the Renaissance we find a gradual shift in the direction of literature, toward more secular tales, some even intended to entertain (e.g., Boccaccio's *Decameron*), but much of it retaining its erstwhile function of moral, uplifting stories and allegories supporting the teachings of the Church.

Since the Renaissance began in Italy in the fourteenth century and then spread northward, it is fitting that our consideration of Renaissance literature should begin with Dante's poetic odyssey, *The Divine Comedy*, written in the first quarter of the fourteenth century.

Dante followed in the tradition of classical convention, in which no self-respecting hero (Gilgamesh, Odysseus, Aeneas) would return home from a quest without detouring to the underworld/afterlife for help and advice.[1] In his epic poem Dante himself as hero seeks an understanding of sin and redemption, as he travels through the geography of the Roman Catholic afterlife (Inferno, Purgatorio, and Paradiso) with Vergil as guide. Everywhere he encounters those he had known personally or by reputation on earth. He finds them willing to explain their sins and the punishment they receive, in hell for all eternity or in purgatory for eons. All this serves as a caveat to Dante and his readers.

The author adheres to the concept of sins being not only bad behavior (many kinds, such as hypocrisy, in addition to those in the Ten Commandments), but also bad character traits such as envy, whether or not they are played out in negative actions. Of the Seven, Dante dooms the gluttonous and wrathful to everlasting punishment in the Inferno, but not the envious, with the single exception of those who betrayed the one they envied under semblance of kindness, thus practicing hypocrisy. These are covered with ice forever. Dante confesses to the first of the Seven, the defect of pride, as his own besetting sin, but prideful sinners he places only in the Purgatorio, where, after enormous eons, they will be purged of their sins, forgiven, and proceed to Paradiso. Dante believes, however, that a really proud man is not envious.

On the Second Terrace of the Purgatorio, we find redeemable envious persons spending varying lengths of time for this sin.

There Dante and his guide Vergil first encounter "Spirits invisible, who courteously

> Unto love's table bade the welcome guest.
> 'This circuit,' said my teacher, 'knots the scourge,
> For envy; and the cords are therefore drawn
> By charity's correcting hand.' ...
> Then more than erst I oped mine eyes; before me view'd;
>   and saw Shadows with garments dark as was the rock;

Dante hears the spirits or "shades" beg for the prayers of the saints.

> I do not think there walks on earth this day
> Man so remorseless, that he had not yearn'd
> With pity at the sight that next I saw.
> Mine eyes a load of sorrow teem'd, when now
> I stood so near them, that their semblances
> Came clearly to my view. Of sackcloth vile

Their covering seem'd; and, on his shoulder, one
Did stay another, leaning; and all lean'd
Against the cliff. E'en thus the blind and poor,
Near the confessionals, to crave an alms,
And, each his head upon his fellow's sunk;
Most to stir compassion, not by sound
Words alone, but that which moves not less,
The sight of misery. And as never beam
Of noon-day visiteth the eyeless man,
E'en so was heaven a niggard unto these
Of his fair light: for, through the orbs of all,
A thread of wire, impiercing, knits them up,
As for the taming of a haggard hawk.
On the other side me were the spirits, their cheeks
Bathing devout with penitential tears,
That through the dread impalement forced a way.
[These souls had progressed farther on their passage to
Paradiso.]

Dante cites only two souls by name doing penance here, that of
a Sierese woman, who described her own case, which was really
one of schadenfreude:

Though Sapia named,
In sapience I excell'd not; gladder far
Of other's hurt, than of the good befel me. ...
It so bechanced, my fellow-citizens
Near Colic met their enemies in the field;
And I pray'd God to grant what He had will'd.
There were they vanquish'd, and betook themselves
Unto the bitter passages of flight.

Apparently Dante saw fit to punish the envious by taking away
their vision because most things envied were (and are) concrete,

visible objects in reality, not abstract advantages. The cords of the whip that scourge the envious are drawn from charity (love), the quality the envious lack. They lean on one another for mutual aid and eventually learn love.

Another sinner punished for envy was Guido del Duca, who admits: "My blood was so inflamed with envy, that if I had seen a man make him glad, thou wouldst have seen me suffused with lividness."

I surmise that the reason for only these named examples of envy getting a person to Purgatorio, in contrast to the many examples of other types of sinners described by Dante, is the occult nature of this sin and how few people Dante (or any of us) knew or had heard of who would admit to what was actually in both a case of schadenfreude.

In the fourteenth century Petrarch (of sonnet fame) wrote *De remediis utriusque fortunae (Remedies for Fortune Fair and Foul)*, in two volumes, the first about a number of usually happy circumstances, the second about many of life's standard tragedies. In the translation of Twyne, Petrarch's view of life is summed up in "[F]latteryng fortune is more to be feared, and faire more perilous, than threatnyng fortune." This is because when things are going well, fortune is playing with us, and we are being set up for a disappointment and a fall. In adversity, reality has set in and we are prepared for the worst.

Rawski, the world's leading Petrarch scholar and translator of Petrarch's Latin, describes this work as "quasi-Academic disputation". This is what reminds me, a rank amateur, of Socrates' incessant demands for choices between extremes, in questions that seem to me to be better answered by "it depends" or "sometimes". In Petrarch's study, Reason, representing philosophy, proceeds in an all-or-none, black-and-white fashion, not allowing for shades or nuances. Rawski considers Petrarch's the "basic book" of the Renaissance. Nothing else was so much read and paraphrased until after Erasmus.

The work consists of several hundred short segments about various life situations (e.g., relationship between brothers, serious illness, etc.). Each segment consists of a dialogue between the personification of the author's leading passion in that situation (e.g., Hope or Joy if Fortune has been favorable; Fear or Sorrow if unfavorable) and the braking force of the philosopher Reason. The author comments on envy in various connections and also devotes an entire section (a kind of chapter) to envying and another to being envied. Often the author's personification makes his point repeatedly, hoping for a more favorable response from Reason if he just keeps dunning, but I have omitted some of this redundancy.

We begin with some of the references to envy scattered through other chapters.

Joy: I have earned the laurel wreath.

Reason: He who toils to earn, earns envy. This is the price, alike in scholarship and in armed conflict.... [N]othing has escaped the contagion of envy and greed....

Joy: I have loving brothers.

Reason: A rare thing indeed. Parents nearly always are loving, but brothers often envy, often despise each other.

Joy: I have brothers who love me very much.

Reason: It should be so, unless envy stands in the way.

Joy: I have great power.

Reason: Hence much envy....

Reason: The cause of all ingratitude is threefold: Envy, which feels that benefits bestowed upon others are injurious to its own interests and neglects to consider the benefits it received in the past. Pride.... Greed.

Joy: I have collected a great treasure.

Reason: And you have created worries and envy for your-self, incitement for your enemies and longing for thieves. ...

Reason: Four obstacles to peace: envy, avarice, wrath, and pride. ...

Petrarch's chapter on being envious consists of a dialogue between the envious author Sorrow and Reason.

Sorrow: I am envious.

Reason: A fine passion, if it desires what benefits you. But if it desires what is bad for others, it is malice, and worse than avarice. The wise man, whom I just quoted, says it well: The eye of the envious is wicked. ... The eye of the covetous man is insatiable.

Sorrow: I am tormented by my envy.

Reason: "Than envy Sicilian tyrants invented no worse tor-ture"—as Horace says.

And this a pestilent south wind has transferred to the tyrants of your days.

Sorrow: I am wracked by envy.

Reason: Thus you sin, suffering deserved justice at the same time.

Sorrow: The good fortune of my neighbor makes me envious.

Reason: Good Lord, I believe you! But none of you envy the kings of the Parthians or the Persians, nor does any one of them envy you. There were the days when you envied each other, because the great size of your realms made you neighbors. Why is it not enough to be vexed with your own troubles, of which you have many indeed? Do you also have to be racked by someone else's good fortune and become completely wretched and ill?

Sorrow: I envy the neighbors.

Reason: An old story! Envy is bleary-eyed and cannot see far. Proximity and prosperity are the parents of envy.

Sorrow: I am envious of other people's possessions.

Reason: If you are envious, you must needs be also a petty coward. Of all vices, none is more base than envy. It cannot affect high minds and is more agonizing than the other vices. All the others aim at some good, although it may be a fallacious one. But envy thrives only on ills, is tormented by goodness, and suffers from the very affliction it desires for others. Therefore, I like the saying of Alexander of Macedonia:

Envious men are nothing else but their own torment or their own tormentors.

Truly grave words to come from such a young boy!

✻

An entire chapter shows how "Being Envied" is almost as bad.

Sorrow: I am envied by many.

Reason: Better to be envied than to be wretched.

Sorrow: I am troubled by the envy of my enemies.

Reason: And what friend of virtue was ever spared this tribulation: Examine in your mind every country, every age, peruse every history book, and you will scarcely find one great man untouched by this plague. I do not want to enter into a discussion that would lead us too far afield—but if you remember anything at all that you have read, you cannot be ignorant of many whose company should not only comfort you but make you proud.

Sorrow: I am being envied.

Reason: Forgo honors and public office, give up aspiring to have people talk about your stately bearing and your magnificent retinue. Keep out of the eyes of wicked enviers as much as possible, lest by your look, words, or guise you invite them to point to you with their finger. The mob and their viciousness dwell in the streets, as do nearly all ills. There is no better way to vanquish such foes than by flight or going into hiding.

Sorrow: But malice follows me wherever I flee or hide.

Reason: Remove the cause of evil and you shake off evil as such. Use great wealth sparingly, dispose of or hide whatever may inflame greedy minds by its beauty. If you have anything that you cannot or do not want to get rid of, use it moderately. Envy is inflamed by pretentious display but soothed by humility. There are also certain potent remedies which ward off envy. Yet they are worse than the illness itself, namely, misery and a disreputable life. About the first it has been said elsewhere that misery alone is free from envy. And to the second applies a saying of Socrates. When Alcibiades asked him in what way to avoid envy, Socrates replied: "Live like Thersites, about whose life, should you not know it, you can read in Homer's Iliad." An ironic and typically Socratic reply, because it makes no sense to shun virtue in order to escape envy, and it is better to be Achilles, and suffer envy, than Thersites, without it. Nevertheless, it is a known fact that, in order to live safe, some great men, at times, have hidden their virtue and their intellect.

Sorrow: I am burdened by the envy of many.

Reason: Some say there is another way to stamp out envy—through blazing glory. This path is rarely chosen, and many who try to climb it slide back into what they tried to escape.

Petrarch sums up the contradictoriness of Fortune thus: "Fortune, when she is opposite, is more profitable to men than when she is favourable. For in prosperity, by a show of happiness and seeming to caress, she is ever false, but in adversity when showeth herself inconstant by changing, she is ever true. In that she deceiveth, in this she instructeth."

Though composed in Latin in the fourth century, a work translated and popular in the Renaissance is Prudentius' *Psychomachea*.[2] This work features a battlefield with a host of sins/vices/unpleasant-nesses of character arrayed in combat against their good counterparts. The author makes no mention of envy. This comes as no surprise because envy is difficult to personify, residing, when uncontaminated by expressive behavior, within the individual's consciousness.

In the latter third of the fourteenth century, one of the earliest treatments of the Seven (and second in quality only to that in *The Fairie Queene*, in the esteem of Bloomfield) is the allegorical poem about the dream or vision of Piers Plowman, by the parish cleric (frequently out of work) William Langland. His poetic device involves no particular meter but natural speech rhythms, and no rhyming but lines with a break midway, and usually two (rarely three) alliterations in the first half, repeated once in the second half. Four versions appear, under different titles, one published before the peasants' uprising of 1381 protesting social wrongs (*Piers Plowman*, the A-Text), which omits Wrath entirely, possibly because it is sometimes appropriate, as in the "righteous indignation" the peasants were displaying. This A-Text rejects wisdom and learning, but the B- and C-Texts reverse this. The second (*The Vision of Piers Plowman*, the B-Text) appeared after the revolt, includes Wrath, and makes no changes in Envy. The third is *Piers the Plowman* (C-Text), and represents Piers as a man of integrity who appears only later in the poem and in the end becomes a symbol of Christ. There is also a Z-Text, which I have not found. The poet's use of "passus" for segments or cantos suggests "steps" through life. The versions and the translations vary more toward the end.

Unlike Dante's and Milton's cosmic quests for salvation and understanding, Langland's search for Truth and Salvation does not involve peregrinations into diabolical or celestial realms. Langland's protagonist, like Dante, is the poet himself, who travels by foot around England, frequently falling asleep and dreaming further explications of the way to salvation. In one chapter, "The Harrowing of Hell" (an archaic term for Christ's rescue of the unbaptized virtuous from hell), however, he dreams himself at the gates of hell with Mercy, rejoicing in the release of the righteous, unlike Dante, who sees no hope for virtuous pagans like Vergil, even though they obeyed "natural law", meaning the right-minded, logical ways to be a good person. Will (a play on headstrong "will" but also the poet himself) dreams long stretches of the book, in which he is learning from personified Wisdom, Conscience, Mercy, Patience, et al., and finally from the good man Piers himself, who later morphs into a symbol of Christ.

In Passus V, the poet dreams of the king and his knights going to church, where Conscience is preaching. As a result of this sermon, representative parishioners approach the altar to ask forgiveness, including the personified Seven, in the form of a satire on human vices, followed by Robert the Robber, whose sloth makes him eschew working for an honest living. In Langland's treatment, Pride is little other than vanity. Lechery is presented not as we use the term but much like Gluttony, ending with a vow to "dyne but ones on Saterday" and "drynke ... but myd with doke" (drink with the duck, i.e., go on the wagon). Gluttony also is drunk all weekend. If you read the sound, the modern word is usually apparent.

"Envye" is given long coverage. We note that in Langland's listing of the Seven, Covetousness is separate and equal. But on to "Envy":

> Envye with hevy herte asked after shrifte
> And carefully *mea culpa* he comsed to shewe.
> He was as pale as a pelet, in the palsy he semed,
> And clothed in a kaurymaury—I kouthe it nought
>   discryve—
> In kirtel and courtery, and a knyf by his syde;
> Of a freres frokke were the foresleves.
> And as a leek that hadde yleye long in the sonne,
> So loked he with lene chekes, lourynge foule,
> His body was to-bollen for wrathe, that he boot hise
>   lippes,
> And wryngynge he yede with the fust—to wreke hymself
>   he thoughte
> With werkes or with wordes whan he seyghe his tyme.
> Ech a word that he warp was of a neddres tonge:
> Of chidynge and of chalangynge was his chief liflod.
> With bakbitynge and bismere and berynge of fals
>   witnesse:
> This was al his curteisie where that evere he shewed
>   hym.
> "I wolde ben yshryve," quod this sherewe, and I for
>   shame dorste.
> I wolde be gladder, by God! that Gybbe hadde
>   meschaunce

Than though I hadde this wouke ywonne a weye of Essex
    chese.
I have a neghebore neigh me, I have anoyed hym ofte,
And lowen on hym to lordes to doon hym lese his silver,
And maad his frendes be his foon thorugh my false
    tonge.
His grace and his goode happes greven me ful soore.
Bitwene mayne and mayne I make debate ofte,
That bothe lif and lyme is lost thorugh my speche.
And when I mete hym in market that I moost hate,
I hailse hym hendely, as I his frend were;
For he is doughtier than I, I dar do noon oother;
Ac hadde I maistrie and myght—God woot my wille!
And whan I come to the kirk and sholde knele to the
    Roode
And preye for the peple as the preest techeth—
For pilgrymes and for palmeres, for al the peple after—
Thanne I crye on my knees that Crist gyve hem sorwe
That baren awey my bolle and my broke shete.
Awey fro the auter thanne turne I myne eighen
And biholde how [H]eyne hath a newe cote;
I wisshe thanne it were myn, and al the web after,...
And of his lesynge I laughe—that li[ght]eth myn herte;
Ac for his wynnynge I wepe and waille the tyme;
And deme men that thei doonille, there I do wel werse:
Whoso undernymeth me herof, I hate hym dedly after.
I wolde that ech a wight were my knave,
For whoso hath moore than I, that angreth me soore.
And thus I lyve lovelees like a luther dogge
That al my body bolneth for bitter of my galle.
I myghte noght ete many yeres as a man oughte,
For envye and yvel wil is yvel to defie.
May no sugre ne swete thyng aswage my swellyng,
Ne no diapenidion dryve it fro myn herte,

Ne neither shrifte ne shame, but whoso shrape my
  mawe?"
"Yis, redily!" quod Repentaunce, and radde hym to the
  beste,
"Sorwe for synnes is savacion of souls."
"I am evere sory," quod [Envye], "I am but selde oother
And that maketh me thus megre, for I ne may me venge.
Amonges burgeises have I be [bigg]yng at Londoun,
And gart bakbityng be a brocour to blame mennes ware.
When he solde and I nought, thanne was I redy
To lye and to loure on my neghebore and to lakke his
  chaffare.
I wole amende this if I may, thorugh myght of God
  Almighty."

Not a nice person, "Envye", but we wish him well in his "amend-ing".

Near the end of the work, the versions and the translations diverge. Conscience directs all Christians to build a fortress (also called a "castle") besieged by the Devil (or Antichrist), the World, the Flesh, and (who else?) the Seven. The author arms seven sisters to oppose the Seven, e.g., Humylyte versus Pride, Abstynence (with a bow) against Lecherye, Chestyte or Contynense (with a sling) against Sloth, Luyberalyte against Greed, Good Occupacyon or Good Besynes against Covetyse, and, finally, Charyte against Envye. What about Glotonye? Envy sends the Friars to college to learn philosophy and law, in hopes that they will come out with the belief that all should share (Envy means for others to share with him). As the minions of evil storm the castle, mankind and the Virtues combat them all, but are often tricked by persons in the church offering too easy penances for sin, causing sinners to forget their repentance. Langland gives us no easy happy ending. Tolkien also noted that when fighting evil, the best you can hope for is to fight to a draw and have to return, exhausted, to fight again the following day.

✳

Many sermons inveighing against envy have come down to us from the Renaissance. One such is Chaucer's "The Persones Tale" in his well known *The Canterbury Tales.* It is really not a tale at all but a sermon delivered by the parson when cornered into fulfilling his obligation to share a story with the other pilgrims. The parson quotes Augustine's definition of envy as equivalent to our schadenfreude, i.e.,

> sorwe of other mennes wele, and joye of other mennes harm. This foule synne is platly agayns the Holy Gost....Cartes than is envye the worste synne that is; for sothely alle other synnes ben somtyme oonly agains oon special vertu; but cartes envye is agayns alle vertues and agayns al goodnes; for it is sory of alle the bountees of his neighebor; and in this maner it is divers from all the synnes; for wel unnethe is ther any synne that it ne hath som delit in itself, sauf oonly envye, that ever hath in itself anguisch and sorwe. The spices of envye ben these. Ther is first sorwe of other mennes goodnes and of her prosperite; and prosperite is kyndely matier of joye; thanne is envye a synne agayns kynde. The secounde spice of envye is joye of other mennes harm; and that is proprely lik to the devyl, that ever rejoyeth him of mennes harm. Of these tuo spices cometh bacbityng; and this synne of bakbytyng or detraccioun hath certain spices, as thus: som man praiseth his neighebor by a wickid entent, for he makith alway a wickid knotte atte last ende; alway he makith a *but* at the last ende, that is thing of more blame, than worth is al the praysing. The secounde spice is, that if a man be good, and doth or saith a thing to good entent, the bacbiter wol tome al thilke goodnes up-so-doun to his schrewed entent. The thridde is to amenuse the bounte of his neighebor. The ferthe spiece of bakbytyng is this,

that if men speke goodnes of a man, than wil the bakbiter seyn, "Parfay, yit such a man is bet than he;" in dispraysynge of him that men praise. The fifte spice is this, for to consente gladly and herken gladly to the harm that men speke of other folk.

The parson warns also against "grucching or murmuracion.... Agayns god it is, whan a man gruccheth agayn the peynes of helle, or agayns poverte, or los of catel, or agayn reyn or tempest.... And alle thise thinges sholde men suffer paciently, for they comen by the rightful jugement and ordinance of god."

Against envy, the parson advises that we love our enemy, pray for him, and "doon him bountee". "Certes, thane is love the medicine that casteth out the venim of Envye fro mannes herte."

These ideas are in line with Chaucer's concept that in humankind there is a natural aristocracy of virtue that outranks the artificial aristocracy based on the randomness of birth, a belief developed in "The Franklin's Tale". This reversal of the usual stand, that virtue should outrank birth, is one with which moralists over the centuries (and I) agree.

John Gower, a fourteenth-century English poet and contemporary of Langland's and Chaucer's, was a friend of Chaucer and as well known in his time as Chaucer. Although he and Langland were both writing in London at the same time, there is no evidence that they were acquainted.

The first of Gower's three major works, *Mirour de l'Omme*, a poem in twelve-line stanzas, which survives in a single damaged manuscript, is dated to 1376–1379. It is written in Anglo-Norman, which has only recently been translated into English prose by William Burton Wilson, who also prepared a dictionary of Anglo-Norman. He omits many stanzas of the original, but uses prose to preserve the repetitious, verbose, redundant form of the original. (Authors and publishers in those times were not handy with the red pencil.) Indeed, some of Gower's stanzas consist of a single sentence replete with dangling clauses and anacoluthons, which Wilson had to restructure to conform with current usage. I notice also that the tense shifts back and forth from past to present.

Gower's work ambitiously attempts to explicate the cause, condition, and remedy for man's condition on earth. In Gower's view, the Devil, though male, conceived and begot Sin, a very evil, ugly, and vile daughter. He was also enamored of her and incestuously engendered upon her a son, Death. In order to have his will with mankind, the Devil had Sin espouse her own son Death, by whom she had seven daughters, the seven deadly sins. The Devil then called a parliament of all his minions except Death, to whom he bragged how he had brought mankind down from Paradise into a land of misery and now intended to drag them down farther into hell. The World and Death promised help with the Devil's plan. To this end, the Devil sent Temptation to teach mankind about the promises of pleasure and wealth, to which Flesh consented. But the Soul of man suffered and called on Reason and Fear to persuade man to abandon his folly. Reason reasoned with the Flesh, and when the Flesh saw the horrible face of Death, it returned to the Soul.

Taking up the fight, Sin agreed to marry her seven daughters (the deadlies) to the World to entrap mankind further. Each of the seven sisters rode to a spectacular wedding in her own elegant equipage, and each carrying a bird.

> Then came Envy in her turn, mounted on a dog and carrying on her right fist a sparrow-hawk that was moulting; her face was much discolored and pale from the evils she was thinking about, and the mantle she wore was of proper purple, well embroidered with burning hearts, and amidst them, well-placed, were serpent tongues scattered daintily everywhere.

When man, who stood far off listening, saw such revelry and such joy, his Flesh day and night tried various ways to reach such great delight; but the Soul, which guides Reason to the Flesh (which so greatly plays the fool with Conscience) resisted so that the Flesh did not dare to bound off; rather, for the moment it stayed very quiet and followed the Soul like a good servant.

Therefore after the wedding the World engendered five more daughters "ugly and deadly" on each of the seven. These were what we might call modes of expression, and each was said to have servants to help with the evil. For example, Envy's first daughter was Detraction who had a chamberlain Malebouche (Badmouth) and two other servants, Defamation and Reproof. The second daughter was Sorrow-for-Others'-Joy, whose chambermaid was Dissension. The third was Joy-for-Others'-Grief, with three daughters, but Wilson translates only the stanzas about Detraction. The fourth is Supplanting (or crowding someone else out), often by trickery. Supplanting has three servitors in her retinue, Ambition, Circumvention, and Confusion, all working to augment the evil. The fifth daughter is False-semblance, the most perilous and contriving of all, assisted by Two-tongued, who has a kind of partner called False-thought. The third assistant is Dissimulation.

Finally Gower describes the sister Envy, herself, the mother of all these. He equates Envy with the deadly dragon in Revelation with whom the archangel Saint Michael fought. He says that envy is the most unnatural of evils because if you give anything to the envious, he will only reward you with evil. Gower credits King Solomon with describing envy as having an evil eye, a mouth of detraction, and a foot of defamation. Gower compares envy to consumption (tuberculosis), an unnatural fire that dries up the heart, leaving "not a single drop of the liquor of good love with which to water charity". "Envy brings more pain to her bearer than to the person against whom she is directed."

Gower's allegory goes on to have God Himself engender seven daughters, the virtues, to counteract the sins, Envy's counterpart being Charity.

In the nineteenth century an English parson somehow acquired three Renaissance plays by an unknown author, now catalogued by the parson's name as the Macro plays, dated from the early fifteenth century. Only one of those three, *The Castle of Perseverance*, deals with our topic. This play even uses two letters no longer in use in the language, for the combined aspirated and vocalized "th", one called the "thorn" and the other the "crossed d". The playwright gives instructions not only for staging his work but even for advanced publicity. He advises the company to send out the announcement, called the "banns", that the traveling company will arrive in a week and perform on the bank of a stream. The audience sits on the slope, and as the scene changes, they move up- or down-stream. The staging itself uses seven "scaffolds"[3], on which the prominent characters climb to talk across to each other. Avaricia summons: "Pryde, Wrathe, and Envye, Com forth, the Duelys chyldren thre!" Envy (portrayed as an archer) tells us:

> I clymbe from this crofte.
> Wyth Mankynde to syttyn on loft.

As a character trying to lead us astray, Envy's advice is bad, and he warns us:

> It is myn offyce fowle to speke,
> Fals sklaundrys to bere abowte....
> A ful fowle defamacyoun.
> Therefore this bowe I bere.

Envy admits to being one of the three sins of the devil (in contrast to the four sins of the flesh):

> Belsabubbe, now have good day,
> For we wyl wenden in good aray,
> All three in fere, as I thee say,
> Pryde, Wrathe, and Envye.

Envy also makes a point frequent in Renaissance literature that Envy and Wrath go together (often teaming up with Covetousness):

> Whanne Wrathe gynnyth walke in ony wyde wonys,
> Envye flet as a fox and folwyth on faste. ...
> Goo we to Coveytyse, all thre at onys.

Envy's advice is to follow through with harmful behavior:

> Envye with Wrathe must drive
> To haunte Mankynde also.
> Whanne any of thy neyborys wyl thryve
> Loke thou haue Envye therto.
> On the hey name I charge the belyue
> Bakbyte hym, whowso thou do.
> Kyll hym anon wythowtyn knyve
> And speke hym sum schame were thou go,
> Be dale or downys drye.
> Speke thi neybour mekyl schame:
> Pot on hem sum fals fame,
> Loke thou vndo hys nobyl name
> Wyth me, that am Envye.

When Envy (along with the other sins) gets his comeuppance at the end of the play, he admits, "Al myn enmyte is not worth a fart."

✳

In mid-fifteenth century, a work appeared (author unknown, later edited by Arthur Brandeis, whose marginal notes help with the Middle English) called *Jacob's Well, An English Treatise on the Cleansing of Man's Conscience.*[4] It contains chapters on the various "synnes", including one on the "wose" (ooze) of "enuye". The author tells how a "modyr conceyvid two dowthterys". The "fadyr" was the "deuil", for the "feend wolde that alle men werryn evylle, & that no man were good". "[T]hrugh his enuye, deth of dampnacyoun entryd in to mankynde." One of the daughters took "ioye of thir neyghbourys harme", the other "sorwe of thir neyghbourys good". The author indicates that "Enuye is werst of alle synnes" because it is contrary to all virtues and goodness.

The author goes on to describe how envy has three "corners", the first in the "herte", consisting of judging falsely of others, thinking badly of others' goodness, and being sorry for others' welfare. The second, in the "mowth", consists of spreading calumny, "bacbyting", and sowing discord. People who do this are "chylderin of the fende and contrarye to crist". Finally, the third corner consists of "dedes" or "werkys" that aim to bring down the envied one, ruining him, discrediting his good name.

"Enuye" turns all good into bad, "gold to copyr, precyouse stonys in-to wose, corne in-to chaffe, wyne in-to watyr, hony into galle, ioye into sorwe". "All goodness in him that hath envye is turnyd in-to wyckydnes, alle virtues are turnyd in-to synne, all his neybourys dyssesys he enjoyeth." "Enuye is contrarie to the holy gost, and the synne that god most hatyth." The author teaches that envy is only a venial sin when its focus is "natural desires" (possessions), but becomes deadly when its focus is the prosperity of others.

He enjoins us to "caste out…this wose of enuye in thise cornerys; that is, out of thin herte, out of thi mowth, & out of thi werkys, & forsake the sede of dyscord" because "doctourys seyth that enuye…is turnyd in-to wyckydnes."

He goes on to classify envy with five other sins opposed to the Holy Ghost, the other four having to do with failing to repent. Like Chaucer in "The Parson's Tale", this author acknowledges the legitimacy of concern for the harmful effects that the neighbor's prosperity might have on oneself, and being troubled over this is neither envy nor a sin.

He opposes hypocrisy: one who "[s]pekyth faire beforn an-othere, & bakbyteth hym behynde.... [A] bakbytere is werse than a theef; for it is werse to stelyn away a mannys good name than his catell."

He advises us to "delue ... out this wose of enuye tyl thou fynde & fele a syker [solid] grownd, that is, frenschyp, that is, loue." He ends with two stories in which the virtuous come to a happy end.

I must add that we haven't progressed far in half a millennium.

In the second half of the sixteenth century, Renaissance literature reached its pinnacle (according to Bloomfield and other medievalists) in Spenser's *The Faerie Queene.* For this epic poem Spenser invented an elegant stanza form of nine lines, the first eight in iambic pentameter, the final verse with an added foot, making it iambic hexameter. Plurals are often in the Germanic "n". If you pronounce the terminal words, you will hear the ababbcbcc scheme. The poem presents several tales centered around King Arthur, and Spenser's assumption of his readers' knowledge of the Arthur lore presents problems even for Spenser scholars. One such story is an odyssey dealing with the pilgrimage through life of the Red Cross Knight, and, as in other quests, such as *Don Quixote,* there are other interwoven tales. Along the road, Spenser deals with envy frequently, often along with the other six deadly sins, and he specifically notes his good characters to be free of envy. The poet fears the envy of rival poets and in two introductory sonnets asks his patrons' help in circumventing their envy (see chapter on envy in authors).

Our author Spenser cites the belief common to this day, in many cultures, that when things are going well, especially unexpectedly so, the prudent course is to hide one's good fortune, or heaven will look down and destroy one's happiness.

Two lovers realize that no one can have it all:

> For th' heavens, envying our prosperities,
> Have not vouchsaft to graunt us twine
> The gladfull blessing of posteritie,
> Which we might see after our selves remaine
> In th' heritage of our unhappie paine.

Again

> For heaven, first author of my languishment,
> Envying my too great felicity,
> Did closely with a cruell one consent
> To cloud my daies in dolefull misery,
> And make me loath this life, still longing for to die.

Similarly with fortune:

> Unhappy knight! Upon whose hopeless state
> Fortune, envying good, hath felly frowned,
> And cruell heavens have heapt an heavy fate:
> I rew that thus thy better dayes are drowned
> In sad despaire, and all thy senses swowned
> In stupid sorrow, with thy juster merit
> Might else with felicitie bene crowned.

In addition to these references, Envy is thrice personified as one of the characters. First, following that tradition of heroes going to the underworld for advice (Gilgamesh, Odysseus, Aeneas, Dante), the Red Cross Knight and a character named Duessa encounter a procession of the Sins. Each of the Seven rides a different beast (various animals were often considered in Medieval times attached to the Sins), and each partakes of traits illustrating the sinful condition. In Spenser, as in other Renaissance literature, snakes are often associated with envy, often coming out of the mouth as a tongue.

In his description of the procession of the Seven, Spenser writes:

> And next to him malicious Envy rode
> Upon a ravenous wolfe, and still did chaw
> Between his cankred teeth a venemous tode,
> That all the poison ran about his chaw;
> But inwardly he chawed his owne maw
> At neighbours welth, that made him ever sad,
> For death it was, when any good he saw;
> And wept, that cause of weeping none he had;
> But when he heard of harme he wexed wondrous glad.
>
> All in a kirtle of discolourd say.
> He clothed was, ypaynted full of eies;
> And in his bosome secretly there lay
> An hatefull Snake, the which his taile uptyes
> In many folds, and mortall sting implyes.
> Still as he rode he gnasht his teeth to see
> Those heapes of gold with griple Covetyse;
> And grudged at the great felicitee
> Of proud Lucifera, and his owne companee.
>
> He hated all good workes and vertuous deeds,
> And him no lesse, that any like did use;
> And who with gratious bread the hungry feeds,
> His almes for want of faith he doth accuse.
> So every good to bad he doth abuse;
> And eke the verse of famous Poets witt
> He doth backebite, and spightfull poison spues

From Leprous mouth on all that ever writt.
Such one vile Envy was, that fifte in row did sitt.

Later in the poem the protagonist encounters a pair of vile old
women, personification of Envy and Detraction (malicious gossip,
slander, backbiting, etc.). Spenser writes:

When as two old ill favour'd Hags he met,
By the way side being together set;
Two griesly creatures: and, to that their faces
Most foule and filthie were, their garments yet,
Being all rag'd and tatter'd, their disgraces
Did much the more augment, and made most ugly cases.

The one of them, that elder did appeare,
With her dull eyes did seeme to looke askew,
That her mis-shape much helpt; and her foule heare
Hung loose and loathsomely: Thereto her hew
Was wan and leane, that all her teeth arew,
And all her bones might through her cheekes be red:
Her lips were, like raw lether, pale and blew:
And as she spake therewith she slavered;
Yet spake she seldom, but thought more the lesse she
    sed.

Her hands were foule and durtie, never washt
In all her life, with long nayles over-raught,
Like puttocks clawes; with th' one of which she scracht
Her cursed head, although it itched naught:
The other held a snake with venime fraught,
On which she fed and gnawed hungrile,
As if that long she had not eaten ought;
That round about her jawes one might descry
The bloudie gore and poyson dropping lothsomely.

Her name was Envie, knowen well thereby,
Whose nature is to grieve and grudge at all
That ever she sees doen prays-worthily;
Whose sight to her is greatest crosse may fall,
And vexeth so that makes her eat her gall;
For, when she wanteth other thing to eat,
She feedes on her owne maw unnaturall,
And of her owne foule entrayles makes her meat;
Meat fit for such a monsters monsterous dyeat.

And if she hapt of any good to heare,
That had to any happily betid,
Then would she inly fret, and grieve, and tear
Her flesh for felnesse, which she inward hid:
But if she heard of ill that any did,
Or harme that any had, then would she make
Greate cheare, like one unto a banquet bid,
And in anothers losse great pleasure take,
As she had got thereby and gayned a great stake.

Her companion Spenser described thus:

The other nothing better was then shee,
Agreeing in bad will and cancred kynd;
But in bad maner they did disagree,
For what so Envie good or bad did fynd
She did conceale, and murder her owne mynd;
But this, what ever evill she conceived,
Did spred abroad and throw in th' open wynd:
Yet this in all her words might be perceived,
That all she sought was mens good name to have
   bereaved.

For, whatsoever good by any sayd
Or doen she heard, she would streightwayes invent
How to deprave or slaunderously upbrayd,
Or to misconstrue of a mans intent,
And turne to ill the thing that well was ment:
Therefore she used often to resort
To common haunts, and companies frequent,
To hearke what any one did good report,
To blot the same with blame, or wrest in wicked sort.

And if that any ill she heard of any,
She would it eeke, and make much worse by telling,
And take great joy to publish it to many,
That every matter worse was for her melling:
Her name was hight Detraction, and her dwelling
Was neare to Envie even her neighbour next;
A wicked hag, and Envy selfe excelling
In mischiefe; for her selfe she onely vext,
But this same both her selfe and others eke perplext.

Her face was ugly, and her mouth distort,
Foming with poyson round about her gils,
In which her cursed tongue, full sharpe and short,
Appear'd like Aspis sting that closely kils,
Or cruelly does wound whom so she wils:
A distaffe in her other hand she had,
Upon the which she litle spinnes, but spils;
And faynes to weave false tales and leasings bad,
To throw amongst the good which others had disprad.

Immediately thereafter, in a manner unclear to me, Spenser has
Envy and Detraction somehow produce an offspring, a Blatant Beast:

These two now had themselves combynd in one,
And linckt together gainst Sir Artegall:
For whom they wayted as his mortall fone,
How they might make him into mischiefe fall,
For freeing from their snares Irena thrall:
Besides, unto themselves they gotten had
A monster, which the Blatant Beast men call,
A dreadfull feend, of gods and men ydrad,
Whom they by slights allur'd, and to their purpose lad.

Such were these Hags, and so unhandsome drest:
Who when they nigh approching had espyde
Sir Artegall, return'd from his late quest,
They both arose, and at him loudly cryde,
As it had bene two shepheards curres had scryde
A ravenous Wolfe amongst the scattered flockes:
And Envie first, as she that first him eyde,
Towardes him runs, and, with rude flaring lockes
About her eares, does beat her brest and forhead
knockes.

Then from her mouth the gobbet she does take,
The which whyleare she was so greedily
Devouring, even that halfe-gnawen snake,
And at him throwes it most despightfully:
The cursed Serpent, though she hungrily
Earst chawd thereon, yet was not all so dead
But that some life remayned secretly;
And, as he past afore withouten dread,
Bit him behind, that long the marke was to be read.

Thereto the Blatant Beast, by them set on,
At him began aloud to barke and bay
With bitter rage and fell contention,

That all the woods and rockes nigh to that way
Began to quake and tremble with dismay;
And all the aire rebellowed againe,
So dreadfully his hundred tongues did bray:
And evermore those hags themselves did paine
To sharpen him, and their owne cursed tongs did straine.

And still among most bitter wordes they spake,
Most shamefull, most unrighteous, most untrew,
That they the mildest man alive would make
Forget his patience, and yeeld vengeaunce dew
To her, that so false sclaunders at him threw:
And more, to make them pierce and wound more deepe,
She with the sting which in her vile tongue grew
Did sharpen them, and in fresh poyson steepe:
Yet he past on, and seem'd of them to take no keepe.

In another section Spenser has us encounter a "monstrous rablement" in which envy is attached to covetousness, foul speech (slander, lies, etc.) as well as the evil eye, which throughout our and other cultures has been held to be both an expression of envy and its retaliation:

The first troupe was a monstrous rablement
Of fowle misshapen wightes, of which some were
Headed like Owles, with beckes uncomely bent;
Others like Dogs; others like Gryphons dreare;
And some had wings, and some had clawes to teare:
And every one of them had Lynces eyes;
And every one did bow and arrowes beare.
All those were lawlesse lustes, currupt envyes,
And covetous aspects, all cruell enimyes.

Those same against the bulwarke of the Sight
Did lay strong siege and battailous assault,

Ne once did yield it respitt day nor night;
But soone as Titan gan his head exault,
And soone againe as his light withhault,
Their wicked engins they against it bent;
That is, each thing by which the eyes may fault
But two then all more huge and violent,
Beautie and Money, they that Bulwarke sorely rent.

A battle ensues between Sir Callidore and the Blatant Beast.
Spenser has the Beast fight with slander:

And them amongst were mingled here and there
The forks of Serpents, with three forked stings,
That spat out poyson, and gore-bloudy gere,
At all that came within his ravenings;
And spake licentious words and hatefull things
Of good and bad alike, of low and hie,
Ne Kesars spared he a whit, nor Kings;
But either blotted them with infamie,
Or bit them with his banefull teeth of injury.

The battle rages on.

Tho, when the Beast saw he mote nought availe
By force, he gan his hundred tongues apply,
And sharpely at him to revile and raile
With bitter termes of shamefull infamy;
Oft interlacing many a forged lie,
Whose like he never once did speake, nor heare,
Nor ever thought thing so unworthily:
Yet did he nought, for all that, him forbeare,
But strained him so streightly that he chokt him neare.

At last, when as he found his force to shrincke

And rage to quaile, he tooke a muzzel strong
Of surest yron, made with many a lincke:
Therewith he mured up his mouth along,
And therein shut up his blasphemous tong,
For never more defaming gentle Knight,
Or unto lovely Lady doing wrong;
And thereunto a great long chaine he tight,
With which he drew him forth, even in his own despight.

Him through all Faery land he follow'd so,
As if he learned had obedience long.
That all the people, where so he did go,
Out of their townes did round abut him throng,
To see him leade that Beast in bondage strong;
And seeing it much wondred at the sight:
And all such persons as he earst did wrong
Rejoyced much to see his captive plight,
And much admyr'd the Beast, but more admyr'd the
     Knight.

One hopes this is the last we hear of the Beast, but, alas, he is
not finished.

Thus was this Monster, by the maystring might
Of doughty Calidore, supprest and tamed,
That never more he mote endammadge wight
With his vile tongue, which many had defamed,
And many causelesse caused to be blamed.
So did he eeke long after this remaine,
Untill that, (whether wicked fate so framed
Or fault of men) he broke his yron chaine,
And got into the world at liberty againe.

Thenceforth more mischiefe and more scath he wrought
To mortall men then he had done before;
Ne ever could, by any, more be brought
Into like bands, ne maystred any more:
Albe that, long time after Calidore,
And good Sir Pelleas him tooke in hand,
And after him Sir Lamoracke of yore,
And all his brethren borne in Britaine land;
Yet none of them could ever bring him into band.

So now he raungeth through the world againe,
And rageth sore in each degree and state;
Ne any is that may him now restraine,
He growen is so great and strong of late,
Barking and biting all that him doe bate,
Albe they worthy blame, or cleare of crime:
Ne spareth he most learned wits to rate,
Ne spareth he the gentle poets rime;
But rends without regard of person or of time.

Christopher Marlowe's play *The Tragicall History of the Life and Death of Doctor Faustus* (published in 1604, eleven years after Marlowe's death), which was based on a 1587 text by an unknown author, *The History of the Damnable Life and Deserved Death of Doctor John Faustus*, presents several devils (Lucifer, Belzebub, and Mephistophilis) entertaining Faust with a procession of the Seven Deadly Sins. Faustus questions each, and Envy's oft-quoted reply is: "I am Envy, begotten of a chimney-sweeper and an oyster-wife.[5] I cannot read and therefore wish all books burned. I am lean with seeing others eat. O, that there would come a famine over all the world that all might die and I live alone! Then thou shouldst see how fat I'd be. But must thou sit and I stand? Come down, with a vengeance!"

Marlowe does nothing more with Envy or the other Sins after this episode. Nor, in fact, would Faustus have any use for Envy, having consummated his "Faustian bargain".

Othello is often cited as Shakespeare's example par excellence of jealousy and envy. And so he is, with not only the paranoid delusion in Othello's head involving his wife and Cassius, but also the subsidiary theme of Iago's jealousy regarding Othello's presumed earlier seduction of Iago's wife Amelia. These are typical three-person jealous love triangles. At the beginning of the play, however, occurs an example of authentic two-person envy. Iago envies the goodness of Othello's character. Also, because Iago envies Cassius for whom he has been passed over for promotion in favor of the less experienced but more academic military officer, Iago sets in motion vengeance through lies and duplicity about Desdemona's alleged infidelity.

In Shakespeare's best known sonnet (#29), beginning "When in disgrace with fortune", after considering all the advantages others enjoy, the protagonist reverts to one of the recommended treatments for envy, i.e., to compare his own advantage and be content.

In Shakespeare's *Romeo and Juliet*, the hostility between the houses of Montague and Capulet is never explained. But Shakespeare's earlier mid-sixteenth-century source, *Romeus and Juliet* by Arthur Brooke, cites envy as the cause of this ancient enmity:

> There were two auncient stockes, / which Fortune high dyd
> place
> Aboue the rest, indewd with welth, / and nobler of
> their race,
> Loued of the common sort, / loued of the Prince alike:

And like vnhappy were they both, / when Fortune list to
strike.
Whose prayse with equall blast, / fame in her trumpet
blew:
Thc one was cliped Capelet, / and thother Montagew.
A wonted vse it is, / that men of likely sorte
(I wot not by what furye forsd) / enuye eche others porte.
So these, whose egall state / bred enuye pale of hew,[6]
And then of grudging enuyes roote, / blacke hate and ran-
cor grewe.
As of a little sparke, / oft ryseth mighty fyre,
So of a kindled sparke of grudge, / in flames flashe out
theyr yre.
And then theyr deadly foode, / first hatchd of trifling stryfe:
Did bathe in bloud of smarting woundes, / it reued breth
and lyfe.
No legend lye I tell, / scarce yet theyr eyes be drye:
That did behold the grisly sight, / with wet and weping eye.[7]
But when the prudent prince, / who there the scepter helde
So great a new disorder / in common weale behelde:
So ientyl meane he sought, / their choler to asswage:
And by perswasion to appease, / their blameful furious
rage.
But both his words and tyme, / the prince hath spent in
vayne:
So rooted was the inward hate, / he lost his buysy payne.
When friendly sage aduise, / ne ientyll words auayle:
By thondring threats, and princely power / their courage
gan he quayle.
In hope that when he had / the wasting flame supprest,
In time he should quyte quench the sparks / that boornd
within their brest.

And the story continues, as in Shakespeare.

❋

Just beyond the Renaissance, like a bookend closing off the other end from Dante's epic poem, is Milton's[8] seventeenth-century monumental epic poem *Paradise Lost*. Milton attributes to envy the two critical prodromata of the Fall of mankind (i.e., Satan's unsuccessful rebellion against God resulting in his expulsion from paradise, and his temptation of Eve), plus another, albeit unsuccessful, attempt, i.e., the Temptation of Christ in the Wilderness.

Satan is seen by some scholars as the hero of the poem; he is certainly the most interesting character. In his arrogance he envied and resented God for the fact that he was in second position, and tried to arrange, since he could not have paradise, that no one else dwell there either.

> Th' infernal Serpent; he it was, whose guile
> Stird up with Envy and Revenge, deceiv'd
> The Mother of Mankind, what time his Pride
> Had cast him out from Heav'n, with all his Host
> Of Rebel Angels, by whose aid aspiring
> To set himself in Glory above his Peers,
> He trusted to have equal'd the most High,
> If he oppos'd; and with ambitious aim
> Against the Throne and Monarchy of God
> Rais'd impious War in Heav'n and Battel proud
> With vain attempt. Him the Almighty Power
> Hurld headlong flaming from th' Ethereal Skie
> With hideous ruine and combustion down
> To bottomless perdition, there to dwell
> In adamantine Chains and penal Fire,
> Who durst defie th' Omnipotent to Arms.

Next, Satan suffered envy of "this new favorite of Heav'n" (our human race, "a little lower than angels") and the beautiful world

God had given mankind, in contrast to the Hell to which Satan had been consigned by God. Begrudging Adam and Eve's felicity (the joys of carnal love and of the table), Satan, the "marplot of Eden" set about ruining mankind's position of innocence in the Garden by deceiving Eve.

> The Spirit maligne, but much more envy seis'd
> At sight of all this World beheld so faire.

Eve, apparently, wants to be educated, since when Satan tempts her with the fruit of the Tree of the Knowledge of Good and Evil, she complains to Adam of:

> "Envious commands
> Designed to keep [us] low
> When knowledge might exalt." [9]

But Adam reminds her:

>   "for thou know'st
> What hath been warned us, what malicious foe,
> Envying our happiness, and of his own
> Despairing, seeks to work our woe and shame
> By sly assault; ...
> Conjugal love, than which perhaps no bliss
> Enjoyed by us excites his envy more."

These reactions by Satan illustrate one of the cardinal features of envy: wishing to spoil for the other what he cannot have for himself. His revenge for God's favoritism completed, Satan has no future.

> All hope excluded thus, behold in stead
> Of us out-cast, exil'd, his new delight,
> Mankind created, and for him this World,
> So farwel Hope, and with Hope farwel Fear,

Farwel Remorse: all Good to me is lost;
Evil be thou my Good; by thee at least
Divided Empire with Heav'ns King I hold
By thee, and more than half perhaps will reigne;
As Man ere long, and this new World shall know.
Thus while he spake, each passion dimm'd his face
Thrice chang'd with pale ire, envie and despair,
Which marrd his borrow'd visage, and betraid
Him counterfeit, if any eye beheld.

Milton's description of Satan's face "with pale ire, envie and despair" is sometimes quoted as the ultimate conjunction. It is used by Melville, out of quotes, as characterizing Claggart, who envies Billy Budd.

Finally, in similar Renaissance style, John Bunyan's seventeenth century allegory of life as a journey through temptations and decisions, *The Pilgrim's Progress,* has his protagonist Faithful meeting many characters representing virtues and vices. In the town of Vanity Fair, where Faithful is taken to court for "slandering the citizens", a witness named Envy is called. However that character does not demonstrate (to me) any speech recognizably implied by his name. (In fact I might have expected "Pride" to represent this town.) After being sworn in, he testifies, "My lord, This man, notwithstanding his plausible name, is one of the vilest men in our country; he neither regardeth prince nor people, law nor custom: but doth all that he can to possess all men with certain of his disloyal notions, which he in the general calls principles of faith and holiness. And in particular, I heard him once myself affirm that Christianity and the customs of our town of Vanity were diametrically opposite, and could not be reconciled. By which saying, my lord, he doth at once not only condemn all our laudable doings, but us in the doing of them."

Questioned further, he indicated that he "would not be tedious to the court" and that if anything be lacking to "despatch him, I will enlarge my testimony". Detraction and defamation (in this case perjury) are aspects of envy, which Bunyan may have had in mind.

The only other (stretched) connection to envy that I can think of is that this is meant to imply envy of another's virtue, a cause for envy cited by Bacon and others. But many other characters in *Pilgrim's Progress* could be interpreted as envious for the same reason.

All these early works picture envy in a terrible light, to be fought, but I have found in them no help in coming to grips with this soul-searing universal problem, appropriately called by Elliott, "the last dirty little secret"—except to love. Easy to say; hard to do.

Notes

1. I was interested to learn recently that apocryphal writings from the late pre-Christian and the early Christian eras also contain accounts of visits to heaven and to hell. The Book of Enoch, an account of Enoch, a virtuous man mentioned in Genesis, records that he was taken through the heavenly realms by Uriel, an angel, a visit similar to Dante's to Paradiso. The Gospel of Nicodemus relates that after Jesus ascended to heaven following his crucifixion, He journeyed to hell to rescue the virtuous pagans and also innocent children, who died too young to have sinned. His benevolence in hell is called "the Harrowing of Hell" and is referred to in *Piers Plowman*. These two books are not included in either the Catholic or the Protestant scriptures.

2. "Psychomachea" is an entire genre of literature dealing with the struggle between good and evil, and Prudentius' work is usually referred to as *Prudentius' Psychomachea*. The translation I used calls Prudentius' version *Battle for Mansoul*, i.e., the soul of man.

3. This term was used for portable theatrical platforms that could move with the troop.

4. I have not found an explanation of "Jacob" in the main title, but I assume the "Well" is for cleansing. This work also uses those two symbols for letters representing the hard and soft sounds of "th".

5. I.e., dirty and smelly.

6. Envy seems to be traditionally pale, as in *Paradise Lost* and *Billy Budd*.

7. Similar constant feuding and strife between families and clans, usually attributed to competition and envy, are seen in the Icelandic sagas.

8. Milton expressed the hope that he would leave something worthy to be read by posterity in subsequent centuries.

9. Cf. the Greek belief that Zeus feared competition from mankind when Prometheus took to earth the arts of civilization.

Chapter 10

Envy in Modern Fiction
(Literary and Cinematographic)

M odern (nineteenth- and twentieth-century) fiction rarely uses envy as a major theme. As our society has become increasingly secular, fiction has moved toward entertainment (sometimes with psychologic and social insights) rather than a device for moral instruction. This trend has accelerated as fiction has become increasingly pictorial in cinema, with less discretionary time spent with the printed word.

We shall begin with a novel in which the title character is the object of envy and, despite his innocence, is brought down by the manipulations of the envier.

I refer to our own Herman Melville's *Billy Budd, Sailor,* the classical work that virtually everyone with an insight into envy cites as prototypic of malignant vengeance aimed at destroying the innocent envied person. Just as happens in real life, the machinations of envy are displayed in behavior, but the word "envy" itself does not occur until well into the novel, and then only a handful of times, once out of quotes, "pale ire, envy, and despair", taken directly from Milton's description of Satan's envy in *Paradise Lost.*

In Melville's novel, the title character is a young, handsome, sunny, charismatic deck hand (or "foretopman") who has been impressed into His Majesty's service on a battle frigate soon after an insurrection on a sister ship.

Melville's paragraphs laying out the master-at-arms' subjection to envy:

> Now envy and antipathy, passions irreconcilable in reason, nevertheless in fact may spring conjoined like Chang and Eng[1] in one birth. Is Envy then such a monster?
>
> Well, though many an arraigned mortal has in hopes of mitigated penalty pleaded guilty to horrible actions, did ever anybody seriously confess to envy? Something there is in it universally felt to be more shameful than even felonious crime. And not only does everybody disown it, but the better sort are inclined to incredulity when it is in earnest imputed to an intelligent man. But since its lodgment is in the heart not the brain, no degree of intellect supplies a guarantee against it. But Claggart's was no vulgar form of the passion. Nor, as directed against Billy Budd, did it partake of that streak of apprehensive jealousy that marred Saul's visage perturbedly brooding on the comely young David. Claggart's envy struck deeper. If askance he eyed the good looks, cheery health, and frank enjoyment of young life in Billy Budd, it was because these went along with a nature that, as Claggart magnetically felt, had in its simplicity never willed malice or experienced the reactionary bite of that serpent. To him, the spirit lodged within Billy, and looking out from his welkin eyes as from windows, that ineffability it was which made the dimple in his dyed cheek, suppled his joints, and dancing in his yellow curls made him pre-eminently the Handsome Sailor. One person excepted [the scholarly Captain Vere], the master-at-arms was perhaps the only man in the ship intellectually capable of adequately appreciating the moral phenomenon presented in Billy Budd. And the insight but intensified his passion, which assuming various secret forms within him, at times assumed that of cynic disdain, disdain of innocence—to be nothing more than innocent! Yet in an aesthetic way he saw the charm of it, the

courageous free-and-easy temper of it, and fain would have shared it, but he despaired of it.

With no power to annul the elemental evil in him, though readily enough he could hide it; apprehending the good, but powerless to be it; a nature like Claggart's, surcharged with energy as such natures almost invariably are, what recourse is left to it but to recoil upon itself and, like the scorpion for which the Creator alone is responsible, act out to the end the part allotted it.

Envying the insouciant swabbie, Claggart spreads lies about Billy, putting Captain Vere, under threat of insurrection in wartime, into the position of having to hold a summary hearing, a so-called "drum court", where he has to believe the statements of his own master-at-arms or face presumed sedition himself. Billy, inarticulate and tongue-tied, trying to defend himself, inadvertently strikes and kills the lying master-at-arms.

The captain has Billy hanged from the yardarm, as Billy cries, "God bless Captain Vere."

Billy Budd is always mentioned in any serious discussion of envy. The novel portrays one common device used by envious persons: malicious lies and character assassination. Schoeck commented on the fact that several otherwise competent literary critics completely missed the envy motive in this novel, in one case calling Billy a Christ figure, in another the whole novel a gingerly portrayal of homosexuality at sea in the nineteenth century. Even John Updike, in a recent essay on final works of authors who realize that their own death is near, included *Billy Budd* without mention of envy. This failure to recognize envy when it is skirted artistically accords with Schoeck's (and others') observation of our repression and reluctance to recognize and confront envy in our time.

Melville's work was published posthumously from not quite "fair copy" (as they had to do in pre-typewriter days) with the help of Melville's widow, but no further interpretation from Melville. The author even left it uncertain whether he wished the novel to be called *Billy Budd, Foretopman,* or *Billy Budd, Sailor.* It has been published both ways and also as just *Billy Budd.*

We turn to the French *Frederick Bastien*: *Envy* by Eugène Sue.

A French novel of the nineteenth century, translated into English but never popular in our country,[2] this novel treats of the destructive effects of envy on a nineteen-year-old, and his later redemption. Son of an intelligent and sensitive young mother and a boorish father, Frederick has occasion to visit a servant in the castle of the marquis in their valley. From time to time he catches fleeting glances of the nobleman mounted on horseback, contemporary of Frederick's. Formerly an apt pupil, he goes into an academic tailspin and a depression, which makes his mother frantic with worry. As the novel advances, Frederick plans to kill the marquis, but the attempt is aborted by chance. He ponders suicide, but this also fails, due to the intervention of M. David, a visiting family friend. This man sizes up the situation correctly and enables Frederick to acknowledge his envy and deal with it constructively.

M. David confronts Frederick:

> "I am certain that envy was the germ of your hatred toward Raoul de Pont Brillant. ...
>
> "Now let us see, my child; what did you envy the most in the young Marquis of Pont Brillant? His riches? So much the better. Envy them ardently, envy them sincerely, and in this incessant, energetic envy, you will find a lever of incalculable power. You will overcome all obstacles. By means of labour, intelligence, and probity, you will become rich. Why not? Jacques Lafitte was poorer than you are. He wished to be rich, and he became a millionaire twenty times over. His reputation is without a stain, and he always extended a hand to

poverty, always favoured and endowed honest, courageous work. How many similar examples I could cite you!

Blessed are these sentiments that the sight of wealth inspires in you, if it throws you among the people of courage who fight for the imperishable cause of equality and human brotherhood.

Frederick starts to get the idea.

"And you felt envy, keenly and deeply, did you not, when you compared the obscurity of your name and your poor, humble life with the splendid life and illustrious name of the young Marquis of Pont Brillant?"

"It is only too true."

"Up to that point, these sentiments were excellent."

"Excellent?"

"Excellent! You brought with you from the castle living and powerful forces; they ought, wisely directed, to have given the widest range to the development of your faculties. Unhappily, these forces have burst in your inexperienced hands, and have wounded you, poor dear child! Thus, to return to yourself, all your pure and simple enjoyments were destroyed by the constant remembrance of the splendours of the castle; then in your grievous, unoccupied covetousness, you were forced to hate the one who possessed all that you desired; then vengeance."

...

"[I]t was remorse for that base and horrible act that led me to think of suicide."

...

"Let us see,"' pursued David, with increasing animation; "for what else did you envy this young marquis? The antiquity of his name? Envy it, envy it, by all means. You will have what is better than an ancient name: you will make your own name illustrious, and more widely celebrated than that of Pont Brillant. Art, letters, war! how many careers are open to your ambition! And you will win reputation. I have studied your works; I know the extent of your ability, when it is increased tenfold by the might of a determined and noble emulation."

...

"Let us go farther. Did the wealth of the marquis fill your heart only with covetous desire, instead of a sentiment of hatred and revolt against a society where some abound with superfluous possession, while others die for want of the necessaries of life? Very well, my child, that is an excellent sentiment; it is sacred and religious, because it inspired the Fathers of the Church with holy and avenging words. So, at the voice of great revolutions, the divine principle of fraternity, of human equality, has been proclaimed.

"Yes," added David, with a bitter sadness, "but proclaimed in vain. Priests, denying their humble origin, have become accomplices of wealth and power in the hands of kings, and have said to the people, 'Fate has devoted you to servitude, to misery, and to tears, on this earth.' Was not this a blasphemy against the fatherly goodness of the Creator,—a base desertion of the cause of the disinherited? But in our day this cause has valiant defenders." etc., etc., etc.

...

"Let us go on," continued David, unwilling to leave the least doubt in Frederick's mind; "does the envy you feel when you hear the ancient name of Pont Brillant manifest itself by a violent hatred of aristocratic tradition, always springing up, sometimes feudal, and sometimes among the citizenship? Exalt this envy, my child. Jean Jacques [Rousseau], in protesting against the inequality of material conditions, was sublimely envious, and our fathers, in destroying the privileges of the monarchy, were heroically, immortally envious."

"Oh!" exclaimed Frederick, 'how my heart beats at your noble words, M. David! What a revelation! What was killing me, I realize now, was a cowardly, barren envy. Envy for me was indolence, despair, death. Envy ought to be action, hope, and life. In my impotent rage I only knew how to curse myself, others, and my own nonentity. Envy ought to give me the desire and strength to come out of my obscurity, and I will come out of it."

Later reassuring his mother, Frederick explains, "Envy, like hatred, can become fruitful, heroic,—sublime."

Frederick's love for his mother displays a hint of envy by proxy—he believes his mother deserves better, and she does, eventually, after her boorish husband's death, marry the loving and sensitive David.

During a flood in the valley Frederick saves the marquis and others from drowning and is recognized by the populace, who erect a plaque to commemorate his heroism. Plans are set in motion for him to go on to Polytechnic School, since he has made great strides in geometry in three weeks.

In this way, Sue, the author, stresses the positive use of envy as a goad to self-realization. Schoeck comments on the accuracy of the psychologic workings of envy in this novel. And if the novel's ending is a little pat, it makes the point of striving to achieve what one envies.

Another nineteenth-century French novelist, Honoré de Balzac, wrote, at breakneck speed, more than a hundred novels, known collectively as *La Comedie Humaine.*[3] In this compendium of human foibles, *Cousin Bette* is the novel which, though multi-themed, has a title character characterized by envy. Falling onto the charity of relatives who barely tolerate her, with only one older male cousin helping her and showing her kindness, this prototypic "poor relation", though repeatedly downplaying herself as "only an old maid", analyzes her situation intelligently, makes wise choices, and creates for herself a good life while the well-to-do relatives are victims of their own flaws and folly. Hear Balzac's description of Bette:

> A peasant woman of the department of the Vosges in the fullest meaning of that term, thin, dark-hued, with gleaming black hair, thick eyebrows meeting in a tuft, arms of great power and length, thick feet, and a few warts on the long, simian face,—such is a concise portrait of this spinster cousin.
>
> The family of the two brothers, who lived together, sacrificed the plain daughter to the pretty daughter, the bitter fruit to the dazzling flower. Lisbeth worked while Adeline was petted and indulged; and there came a day when the former, alone with Adeline, tried to disfigure the latter's nose,—a true Grecian nose, the admiration of old women.
>
> Though whipped for this particular misdeed, she never could be prevented from tearing the dresses and spoiling the collars of the petted darling.

The "almost too kind and sweet-natured" Adeline brought Bette to Paris intending to rescue her from poverty and arrange a marriage. But first her older male cousin began by helping her learn a trade, apprenticing her to the embroiderers to the imperial court.

> Cousin Lisbeth, called "Bette" for short, became henceforth a worker of gold and silver lace. Energetic, like all mountaineers, she had the courage to be taught to read, write,

and cipher, for the baron proved to her the need of those accomplishments if she was ever to have an establishment of her own in the trade. She resolved to make her fortune; and in two years she actually metamorphosed herself. In 1811 the peasant woman of Lorraine was a rather pleasing, capable, and intelligent forewoman in a prosperous house.

The rest of the family fell on hard times, but Bette kept her financial situation separate and eventually set up her own embroidery business.

[Bette] gave up all idea of competition with her beautiful cousin, whose many superiorities she inwardly acknowledged; but envy lurked in her breast, as a germ of the plague lurks in a bale of woollen stuffs only to burst forth and ravage a city when the bale is opened. [reference to tularemia]
Whenever Bette saw her cousin cheerful and hopeful, she would say, ... "We may expect some day to see *my* poor cousin's name in the police reports."

Adeline "ate from silver and gold dishes and never appeared at receptions without wearing in her hair and round her neck diamonds as large as hazelnuts."

From time to time, however, she [Bette] would say to herself, "Adeline and I are of the same blood; our fathers were brothers; yet she lives in a mansion, I in a garret."
Many times the Baron had solved the problem of finding her a husband, but although attracted at first, she would soon refuse, afraid of being reproached for her lack of education, her ignorance, or her poverty.
The restive, independent, wilful spirit, and the inexplicable untamability of this woman, for whom the baron had four times found a husband (a clerk in his ministry, a major, a

purveyor, and a retired captain), and who had refused a dealer in the gold-lace trade, who afterwards became wealthy, fully accounted for the nickname of "Nanny-goat" which the baron bestowed upon her. And yet the name only answered to the external oddities of her behavior, to those surface exhibitions which we make to each other in our social state. This woman, if carefully observed, would have betrayed the ferocious side of the peasant class; she was still the child who longed to tear the nose from her cousin's face, and, if she had not acquired a stock of common-sense, might even now kill her in a paroxysm of jealousy.

It was only through her acquired knowledge of life and of the laws that she was able to control those rapid impulses by which the people of isolated regions and savages pass from feeling to action. Possibly the whole difference between the natural man and the civilized man lies here. The savage has feelings only; the civilized being has feelings and ideas. Therefore among savages the brain receives, as it were, few imprints; it is wholly in the grasp of the feeling that invades it. But in civilized man ideas descend upon the heart and transform it; he is possessed by many interests, many feelings, whereas the savage has but one idea, one feeling, at a time. That is the cause of the momentary power of the child over its parents,—a power which ceases as soon as the child's desire is satisfied; but in the man who lives close to nature that cause is continuous. Cousin Bette, the Lorraine savage, more or less treacherous, belonged to the category of such natures, who are not so uncommon among the masses as people think for,—a fact which goes far to explain their conduct in revolutions.

Eventually Bette finds herself a husband who will help her and continues with her business, but never conquers her envy, while the family struggles with financial problems that they eventually more or less surmount.

But Bette's tuberculosis claims her life, while she takes the secret of her envy to the grave.

> Lisbeth, unhappy enough already at the good fortune of the family, could not endure this additional happiness [payment of a threatening debt by a relative]. She grew so rapidly worse that Bianchon announced she must die in a week, — conquered at last in the long struggle where she had scored so many victories. She kept the secret of her hatred through the weary dying anguish of pulmonary consumption; and found supreme satisfaction in seeing Adeline, Hortense, Hulot, Victorin, Steinbock, Celestine, and the children, in tears around her bed, considering her the angel of the family.

Another French author, the eighteenth-century Encyclopedist Diderot, left a portrait of a sycophant, hence very unattractive, a man of high intelligence and musical ability (nephew of the composer Rameau), who envied those gifted in intellectual and artistic creativity, but was unwilling to pursue the kind of life that leaves traces for upcoming generations:

> *Now* you are going beyond me. What you say seems like philosophy, and I warn you that I never meddle with that. All that I know is that I should be very well pleased to be somebody else, on the chance of being a genius and a great man; yes, I must agree, I have something here that tells me so. I never in my life heard a man praised, that his eulogy did not fill me with secret fury. I am full of envy. If I hear something about their private life that is a discredit to them, I listen with pleasure: it brings us nearer to a level; I bear my mediocrity more comfortably. I say to myself: Ah,

thou couldst never have done *Mehemet,* nor the eulogy on Maupeou. So I have always been, and I always shall be, mortified at my own mediocrity. Yes, I tell you I am mediocre, and it provokes me. I never heard the overture to the *Indes galantes* [composition of his uncle Rameau] performed, nor the *Profonds abimes de Tenare, Nuit, eternelle nuit,* [also by Rameau] sung without saying to myself: That is what thou wilt never do. So I was jealous of my uncle....The something which is here and speaks to me says: Rameau, thou wouldst fain have written those two pieces: if thou hadst done those two pieces, thou wouldst soon do two others; and after thou hadst done a certain number, they would play thee and sing thee everywhere. In walking, thou wouldst hold thy head erect, thy conscience would testify within thy bosom to thy own merit; the others would point thee out, There goes the man who wrote the pretty gavottes [and he hummed the gavottes. Then with the air of a man bathed in delight and his eyes shining with it, he went on, rubbing his hands:] Thou shalt have a fine house [he marked out its size with his arms], a famous bed [he stretched himself luxuriously upon it], capital wines [he sipped them in imagination, smacking his lips], a handsome equipage [he raised his foot as if to mount], a hundred varlets who will come to offer thee fresh incense every day [and he fancied he saw them all around him, Palissot, Poinsinet, the two Frdrons, Laporte, he heard them, approved of them, smiled at them, contemptuously repulsed them, drove them away, called them back; then he continued:] And it is thus they would tell thee on getting up in a morning that thou art a great man; thou wouldst read in the *Histoire des Trois Siecles* that thou art a great man, thou wouldst be convinced of an evening that thou art a great man, and the great man Rameau would fall asleep to the soft murmur of the eulogy that would ring in his ears; even as he slept, he would have a complacent air; his chest would expand, and rise, and fall with comfort; he would move like a great man. ... [and as he talked he let himself sink softly on a bench, he closed his eyes, and imitated the blissful sleep that his mind was picturing. After relishing the sweetness of this repose for a few instants, he awoke, stretched his arms, yawned, rubbed his eyes, and looked about him for his pack of vapid flatterers].

Rarely do the envious admit not having been willing to work for the distinction they envy in another and being happy when those they envy display their flaws.

We turn to depictions of envy in Russia, which is commonly believed to be a sinkhole for envy.

The engine that drives Russia is envy.
—Russian maxim

In Yuri Olesha's 1927 novel *Envy* coming out of communist USSR, the protagonist Nikolai is identified by another character as "Nikolai Kavalerov, the Envious". Nikolai grew up in a bourgeois family before the Revolution. He finds himself on the cusp between the old comfortable landowning class and the new cold, competitive Soviet efficiency-oriented managerial class, represented by Volodia, a hard young man whose dedication to the Party exceeds his love for his fiancée. An older manager, Andrei Petrovich Babichev, retains some of the warmth and compassion associated with pre-Revolutionary days, runs a food plant, and is referred to, contemptuously, by Nikolai as "the sausage maker". Not completely integrated into the modern mechanical, emotionless world, he actually shows pity for Nikolai; when Andrei finds Nikolai drunk in a gutter outside a tavern on a rainy night, he carries Nikolai home and installs him on a couch with clean bedding. After staying there for a month, Nikolai plans to give up Andrei's comfortable apartment. In a six-page letter he explains why, in as explicit, brutal, vitriolic, envy-dripping language as I have found anywhere except in Joan Frank's piece (cf. my chapter 11):

Andrei Petrovich:
You took me in out of the cold. You took me in under your wing. I slept on your delightful sofa. You know how lousily I had lived before that. Came the blessed night. You took pity on me, gathered up a drunk.

You put me between linen sheets. The material was so smooth and cool; it was calculated to soothe my anger and ease my anxiety. It did.

Even mother-of-pearl pillowcase buttons came back into my life—with iridescent rainbow rings swimming in them. I recognized them at once. They emerged from a long-forgotten corner of childhood.

I had a bed.

The word itself had a poetic remoteness for me, like the word 'hoop.'[4]

You gave me a bed.

From the height of your well-being, you lowered a cloud-bed, a halo that surrounded me with magic warmth, wrapped me in memories, nostalgia without bitterness, and hopes. It seemed I could still have much of what had been intended for me in my youth.

You are my benefactor, Andrei Petrovich!

Just think: a famous man made me his close companion! A remarkable public figure settled me in his home. I want to convey my feelings to you.

Strictly speaking, it's all one feeling: hatred.

I hate you, Comrade Babichev.

I'm writing this letter to bring you down a peg.

From my first day with you, I felt afraid. You stifled me. You crushed me under your weight.

You stand in your underpants giving off the beery smell of sweat. I look at you and your face becomes strangely enlarged, your torso becomes bloated—the lines of a clay idol curve out, swell. I want to shout out:

Who gave him the right to crush me?

How am I worse than he?

Is he more intelligent?

Is he richer spiritually?

Is he on a higher level of organization?

Stronger? More important?

Superior not only in position, but in essence?

Why must I acknowledge his superiority?"

...

A month went by. I know the answer. And now I'm not afraid of you. You're just an obtuse dignitary. And nothing more. It was not the importance of your personality that crushed me. Oh no! Now I see through you, look you over: I've got you in the palm of my hand. My fear of you has passed, like something childish. I have thrown you off my back. You're not much really.

At one time I was tortured by doubts. Can it be that I am a nonentity compared to him? I wondered. Can it be that for an ambitious man like me he is plainly an example of greatness?

But it turned out that you are nothing but an empty shell, ignorant and stupid like all figureheads, those who have gone before and those who will come after. And, as it does with all figureheads, your position has gone to your head. Only conceited stupidity could account for the hurricane you raised over a bit of ordinary salami or, for that matter, the fact that you took in off the street an unknown young man.

[He goes on about Andrei's hard young Soviet friend, Volodia.]

At first when you told me that the sofa belonged to him, that when he came back I would have to get the hell out of there, I was offended. But the next minute I understood that you are cold and indifferent to both of us. You are a baron and we are your hangers-on.

But I dare assure you that neither of us will come back to you again. You don't respect people. He will return only if he is more stupid than I am.

It so happens that I do not have to my credit either deportation under the old regime or a revolutionary record. So they won't entrust me with responsible work, like the manufacture of soda pop or the running of a bee farm.

But does that make me an unworthy son of our century, and you a good one? Does that make me nothing and you a big something?

Sure, you found me on the street. ... But how stupidly you behaved!

On the street you decided, well okay, the guy's not much, still let's see if I can fit him in somewhere. A copyreader perhaps, a proofreader, a copyholder. You didn't try to descend from the heights, to approach the young man in the gutter, to understand. You were too full of yourself. You're a bureaucrat, Comrade Babichev.

Who do you think I was? A drowning remnant of the lumpenproletariat? You decided to hold me up? Thanks. I am strong enough, do you hear me, strong enough to drown and to come up again, and to drown once more.

I wonder how you'll react when you read this. Perhaps you will try to have me deported, or put me into an institution. You can do anything: you're a big man, a member of our administration. You even said that your own brother should be shot. You said yourself: we'll clap him into a madhouse.

[He continues about Andrei's brother, Ivan, and the brother's daughter, Volia.]

I am going to protect your brother and his daughter. Listen to me, you obtuse lump who laughed at the branch laden with flowers and leaves, because that exclamation was the only way I could express my ecstasy when I saw her. And you, what words do you use for her? You called me an alcoholic because I addressed a girl in metaphoric language which you couldn't understand... my exalted sausage maker!"

...

How could I have stood a whole month in this humiliating position?

I am not going to take any more of it. Just keep waiting, perhaps fool number one will come back to you. Convey my sympathies to him.

...

But at the very same time as these lickspittles were paying their tribute, when conceit was bloating you, a man lived by your side. Nobody showed him any consideration, nobody asked for his opinion. The man lived alongside you and observed your every movement. He studied you, watched you; not like a slave, from below, but like a human being, calmly. And this man concluded that you are nothing but an exalted clerk, only a very ordinary person brought to an enviable height by purely external circumstances.

...

You tried to make me your fool and I became your enemy. "With whom are you at war, you scum?" you shouted at your brother. I don't know what you had in mind: yourself, your Party, your factories, your stores, your sausages, I cannot tell. But I know whom I am against: a very ordinary middle-class gentleman, an egotist, a voluptuary, a fool: a man who is convinced that he can get away with anything. I am fighting for your brother, for the girl to whom you lied. I am fighting for tenderness, for pathos, for individuality; for names that touch me, like "Ophelia," for everything that you are determined to oppress and erase.

And he finally signs off.[5]

As the story proceeds, Nikolai meets Andrei's older brother Ivan, and they realize that Andrei is the thorn in both their sides.

"Let's drink, Kavalerov," Ivan said. "Let's drink to youth that is past, to the conspiracy of feelings that has failed, to the machine that does not exist and never will." [He refers to a fantasized invention that he clung to as a focus of self-esteem.]

...

"You are a son of a bitch, Ivan Babichev!"
Kavalerov caught Ivan by his collar.
"No," he said, "youth is not past! You hear me, it's not! You're lying. I'll prove it to you...tomorrow, do you hear? I'll kill your brother during the soccer match."

As they drink, Ivan sums it up:

Oh, my dear fellow, I see! You, as I understand it, have sent a powerful man to hell. Don't interrupt. You have conceived a hatred for a man who has gained universal recognition. It seems to you, certainly, that it is he who has insulted you. Don't interrupt me. Drink up. You are sure it is he who is preventing you from proving yourself, that he has stolen your rightful place, that where you think you should excel, he does. And you are seething. ... My friend, envy is eating us away. We envy the future, it is the envy of senility, if you wish. Mankind has grown old. It is the envy of a generation of mankind grown old. Let's talk about envy. ... You, we may say, are a clot of envy. A clot in the bloodstream of the dying era, which envies the New that will take its place.

Kavalerov then tells a story of a party he attended as a child where he envied the little hostess dressed in pink ruffles and bows, so he

> ... tore her ribbons, mussed her curls, scratched her charming features. I grabbed her by the nape of the neck and banged her forehead several times against a column. At that moment I loved that girl more than life itself, worshipped her, and hated her with all my strength. ... I thought I would dishonor her. ... But ... I was the one disgraced. They kicked me out. ... I spoiled their party for them. ... That is how I came to know envy. ... Envy catches you by the throat, squeezes your eyes from their sockets. ... You understand me, don't you? I am speaking of envy.

Ivan's final advice is:

> Avenge yourself. Trust me. Let's go out with a bang. ... You are lucky. While avenging yourself, you can avenge the era which gave you birth. ... Kill him. Leave an honorable memory of yourself, as the hired assassin of the era. Squash your enemy in the door, on the threshold between the two eras. He is swaggering: he thinks he is already across the threshold.

Olesha's children's party story illustrates the futility of the envied one trying to share; it does not alleviate envy but inflames it.

Not the least remarkable feature of this remarkable story is that it did not send the author to Siberia or the firing squad. The Soviet authorities somehow saw it as an indictment against capitalism! *Pravda*'s reviewer wrote: "The novel exposes the envy of small despicable people, the petty bourgeois flushed from their lives by the Revolution: those who are trying to initiate a 'conspiracy of feelings' against the majestic reorganization of our national economy and our daily life."

We shall return to Yuri Olesha in the chapter on authors' envy.

We have seen envy as a theme in Renaissance theater and also in classical theater (*Prometheus Bound*). Another play from Greek classical times, Aristophanes' *Plutus (Wealth)*, is cited by Berke as a treatment of envy. The translations I read did not convey envy to me but the need for most of us to be in moderate need to be motivated to work to support ourselves and in this way to supply each other's needs.

We turn to envy as a theme in Russian theater. Pushkin, born in 1799, the same year as Balzac, produced such an enormous literary output in several genres, until his death at thirty-eight, that he is considered by many scholars the father of modern Russian literature. He hoped to establish a tradition that would elevate Russian theater to a par with Shakespeare's. In his final works, his four so-called "Little Tragedies" (probably intended as the playwright's segue into full-length drama), he moved to blank verse with much enjambment. Aware of the gossip, apocryphal and otherwise, about the Mozart/Salieri relationship, he wrote a one-act, two-scene, nine-page play, *Mozart and Salieri*. Elaine Feinstein calls this play

> ...a study in motivation. The lighthearted, quicksilver, unpredictability of genius is set against the plodding doggedness of mere talent. We are shown envy at work, but

Salieri's conscious mind works up "rational" arguments in defense of the idea that to poison his friend will be an act of justice furthering the cause of art—by protecting the general community of artists from being reduced to worthlessness by Mozart's genius. The working out of Salieri's motivation, at conscious and unconscious levels, is cogent, all the more so because Salieri's destructive envy consorts with real fondness for Mozart, and reverence for his art.

The first scene begins and ends with a soliloquy by Salieri, and Feinstein writes:

> Salieri's two soliloquies... are mighty peaks in Russian blank verse.... John Bayley has written of... Salieri's first soliloquy based on the inexorable, step-by-step unfolding of logical argument.... Acting at once as apologia and exposition, they both reveal the speaker and embody him, making audible in his words a whole background of history and culture.... Salieri's speech is like a feat of classical architecture, a structure massive and elegant, whose symmetry is both severe and self-absorbed.

To cut from this soliloquy would not do it justice:

> Justice, they say, does not exist on earth.
> But justice won't be found in heaven either:
> That's plain as any simple scale to me.
> Born with a love of art, when as a child
> I heard the lofty organ sound, I listened,
> I listened and the sweet tears freely flowed.
> Early in life I turned from vain amusements;
> All studies that did not accord with music
> I loathed, despised, rejected out of hand;
> I gave myself to music. Hard as were

The earliest steps, and dull the earliest path,
I rose above reverses. Craftsmanship
I took to be the pedestal of art:
I made myself a craftsman, gave my fingers
Obedient, arid virtuosity,
My ear precision; killing sound, dissecting
Music as if it were a corpse, I checked
All harmony by algebra. At last,
Having achieved a mastery of theory,
I ventured on the rapture of creation.
I started to compose; in secrecy,
Not dreaming yet of fame. All many a time,
When I had sat in silence in my cell
Two days and more, forsaking sleep and food,
Tasting the bliss and pain of inspiration,
I burned my work and watched indifferently
As my ideas, the sounds I had created
Flared up and disappeared in wisps of smoke.
But what of that? For when the mighty Gluck
Revealed to us his new, enchanting secrets,
Did I not put behind me all I knew,
All that I loved, believed so fervently?
Did I not follow promptly in his path,
As trustful as a traveler redirected
By someone he encounters on his way?
Through zealous, unremitting application
I gained a not inconsequential place
In art's infinity. Fame smiled on me;
I found the hearts of men in harmony
With my creations. Happiness was mine:
My toils, success and fame I enjoyed in peace,
As too the work and the success of friends,
My fellows in the majesty of music.
I knew no envy—never!—not when first

I heard the opening of *Iphigenia*,
Not when Piccini tamed Parisian ears.
Who could have called the proud and free Salieri
A wretched envier, a trampled serpent
Alive yet helpless, biting sand and dust?
No-one!... But now—and *I* who say it—now
I envy—I profoundly envy. Heaven!
O where is justice when the sacred gift,
Immortal genius, comes not in reward
For toil, devotion, prayer, self-sacrifice—
But shines instead inside a madcap's skull,
An idle reveller's? "Oh, Mozart, Mozart!"

In Pushkin's version Salieri drops poison into Mozart's wine in a tavern where they are socializing.

In the deserving/undeserving analysis of Mozart's advantage, we note that Salieri finds Mozart personally undeserving ("idle reveller") but his advantage of creativity overwhelmingly deserving of accolades.

After working in other genres, what might Pushkin have achieved in this, had he lived?

By comparison, we look now at Shaffer's more extensive handling of the Mozart/Salieri envy problem in his stage play and later film titled *Peter Shaffer's Amadeus* to allow scope for artistic license.

Shaffer's treatment of what is known, surmised, and imagined about Salieri's consuming envy of Mozart's genius and bitterness over his own lack of stellar talent includes the fact that on his deathbed Mozart accused Salieri of poisoning him. Many years later on *his* deathbed Salieri admitted having done so, although no one believed him because of the paranoid delusional nature of his psychosis. Shaffer delves into the idea that Salieri had tried to make a deal with God, promising Him to exchange his virtue for the musical genius on which he had set his heart. When Salieri was eclipsed because God had apparently lavished this gift instead on the vulgar, obscene adolescent upstart, Salieri felt betrayed by God. This Salieri-God-Mozart triangular relationship in Shaffer's treatment comes close to the three-person constellation characteristic of jealousy. In an excellent analysis of Salieri's envy, Sheila Rouslin Welt (cited in my chapter 13) makes the point that in an envy configuration, there is usually an authority figure hanging around in the background, and this is often God. Even Shaffer's use of Mozart's middle name as title, *Amadeus*, underscores the idea that Mozart is truly "beloved of God".

In the deserving/undeserving assessment of envy, Shaffer also stresses Salieri's belief in the personal undeservingness of Mozart, in contrast to his artistic deservingness.

Similar envy of talent is portrayed in the screenplay *Andrei Rublev*, an Andrei Tarkovsky film that is on most lists of the world's hundred best. It is the story of a fifteenth-century Russian monk and icon painter, who flees the monastery and wanders through war-ravaged feudal Russia, encountering such barbaric horrors that he loses his faith and becomes mute. Eventually he regains both speech and faith, returns, and begs to be reinstated in the monastery. He attributes his defection to envy of another monk's greater artistic talent: "It ate at my insides like poison, and I had to get away."

Several twentieth-century stage plays use envy to drive the story. William Inge's *Picnic* displays the mutual envy of two sisters, the smart but plain one for the pretty one, the pretty but stupid one for the smart one. Millie, the would-be writer, says, "Madge is the pretty one—but she's so dumb they almost had to burn the schoolhouse down to get *her* out of it!" The ending bodes ill for the pretty one who cannot get her life together but follows a transient ne'er-do-well smooth-talking penniless alcoholic drifter to the big city, removing herself from the envied one, as the envious (like Rublov) often do, but at the same time jeopardizing her own future with the local boy who loves her.

Inge himself, no stranger to envy, committed suicide, disappointed by the critics' and playgoers' greater acclaim for Tennessee Williams and Arthur Miller. The latter's *Death of a Salesman* is said by some to display envy between the two brothers, but I don't read it that way. In Miller's play, the envy obvious to me is that of Willy Loman for his deceased brother who, Willy points out several times, went into the jungle at seventeen and came out at twenty-one, a rich man.

Envy between two brothers is the theme of one of Eugene O'Neill's lesser-known plays, *Beyond the Horizon*. Two brothers with very different personalities and interests nevertheless grow up with a close fraternal bond. The younger, a sensitive dreamer and intellectual, wannabe writer and poet, hates the family farm, longs for travel and adventure, and has arranged to ship on as deck hand with his sea captain uncle, to see the world. However, persuaded by his brother's intended that she really loved him all along, he impulsively abandons his dream of romantic travel to marry the girl next door. The brother, a man of the soil and natural farmer, with no romantic ideas of travel, dumped by his fiancée, in an improbable switch of plans takes his brother's berth on his uncle's ship to get away from the girl who jilted him. This leaves the "poet" to run the farm when the father dies, and the farm quickly runs down under the inept handling of the man who never wanted to be a farmer in the first place. Soon the young couple realizes that their marriage was a mistake, and it is completely destroyed when their small daughter dies. The hope that the wandering brother will return to save the farm is dashed when he writes that he has an opportunity in Argentina. Another five-year interval finds the brother home from South America, having made and lost a fortune in, of all things, wheat futures. The brother with frustrated

wanderlust questions his brother about riding out a typhoon, but
the non-adventurer only replies:

> You ought to have been there. I remember thinking about
> you at the worst of it, and saying to myself: "This'd cure
> Rob of them ideas of his about the beautiful sea, if he could
> see it." ... And as for the East you used to rave about—well,
> you ought to see it, and *smell* it! One walk down one of
> their filthy narrow streets with the tropic sun beating on it
> would sicken you for life with the "wonder and mystery"
> you used to dream of.

"So all you found in the East was a stench?" says the disgusted
brother about his brother's squandered opportunity. [Envy is at
its worst when the advantage is wasted on the advantaged one,
who does not even appreciate or use it. Educational opportunities
often elicit envy like this.]

By then the natural farmer has lost interest in the land and
returns to another business opportunity in Argentina. Again they
hope for help from him with the farm, although pride prevents asking for money. The failed farmer says to his wife, "Andy's made a
big success of himself—the kind he wanted. And now he's coming
home to let us admire his greatness. ... What am I talking about?
My brain must be sick, too." [He displays the guilt and shame we
feel when we envy those we love.]

> But the speculator has again lost most of his gains.
> The switch in life goals has wreaked havoc on both.

O'Neill's magnum opus, *Long Day's Journey into Night,* presents an older brother who admits that envy caused him to drag
his younger brother with him into a life of alcoholic indolence. In
a drunken confession extending over several speeches, the older
brother takes both credit and blame for his younger brother's life:

No one is prouder you've started to make good. Why shouldn't I be proud? Hell, it's purely selfish. You reflect credit on me. I've had more to do with bringing you up than anyone. I wised you up about women, so you'd never be a fall guy, or make any mistakes you didn't want to make! And who steered you on to reading poetry first? ...I did! And because I once wanted to write, I planted it in your mind that someday you'd write! Hell, you're more than my brother. I made you! You're my Frankenstein! [he meant "Frankenstein's monster"] ...Listen, Kid, you'll be going away [to a tuberculosis sanitarium]. May not get another chance to talk. Or might not be drunk enough to tell you truth. So got to tell you now. Something I ought to have told you long ago—for your own good. Not drunken bull, but 'in vino veritas' stuff. You better take it seriously.

Want to warn you—against me. Mama and Papa are right. I've been rotten bad influence. And worst of it is, I did it on purpose....You listen! Did it on purpose to make a bum of you. Or part of me did. A big part. That part that's been dead so long. That hates life. My putting you wise so you'd learn from my mistakes. Believed that myself at times, but it's a fake. Made my mistakes look good. Made getting drunk romantic. Made whores fascinating vampires instead of poor, stupid, diseased slobs they really are. Made fun of work as sucker's game. Never wanted you succeed and make me look even worse by comparison. Wanted you to fail. Always jealous of you. Mama's baby, Papa's pet! ...And it was your being born that started Mama on dope. I know that's not your fault, but all the same, God damn you, I can't help hating your guts—! ...But don't get wrong idea, Kid. I love you more than I hate you. My saying what I'm telling you now proves it. I run the risk you'll hate me—and you're all I've got left. But I didn't mean to tell you that last stuff—go that far back. The dead part of me hopes you won't get well. Maybe he's even glad the game [addiction] has got Mama again! He wants company, he doesn't want to be the only corpse around the house! ... Make your mind you've got to ... think of me as dead—tell people "I had a brother, but he's dead." And when you come back, look out for me. I'll be waiting to welcome you with that "my old pal" stuff, and give you the glad hand, and at the first good chance I get stab you in the back. ... Only don't forget me. Remember I warned you—for your sake. Give me credit. Greater love hath no man than this, that he saveth his brother from himself.

This play illustrates the way envy is entangled with other emotions, in this case love.

Recently two screenplays and one stage play have explored envy in the context of the Seven Deadly Sins. Wendy MacLeod titled her play simply *Sin*. Adhering to the Greek unity of time, this author's device consists of a woman traffic reporter encountering, in one twenty-four-hour period, seven people representing each of the Seven. Her envious friend is her helicopter coworker, who has recently been passed over for promotion and envies the new news director. He complains above the roar of the motor, "He doesn't even have a liberal arts degree, he has some lame-o degree in communications while *I* have a BA from a very good school, top of my class, *summa* or *magna* or *cum laude* anyway, and I'm flying a helicopter and he's promoted to News Director." She tries to console him, but he continues, "I want to boss, I want to manage, I want to administrate ... he couldn't administrate himself out of a paper bag! He's a hothead, he's a maniac, he's like a serial killer without the van! He's good-looking all right, he's good looking, but this is radio! I ask you. Do you think someone can sound good looking?"

He insists that they detour over the director's home, where a strange expensive car is parked in the driveway. Referring to the car, she reminds him, recalling to us Shakespeare's 29th sonnet, "Face it, Fred, you've got what he wants, you have a wife who loves you ... who buys you shirts [the director had made fun of his clothing] and ... cooks you chicken [Fred complained about his salary] ... you have children, you have a family!"

"I have what he wants?" Fred asks in astonishment.

Sometimes envy works reciprocally, e.g:
"I wish I could just stand up and talk effortlessly and eloquently the way you do."
"I wish I had a sister like yours."

A 1962 French film entitled *Les sept péchés capitaux* (*The Seven Deadly Sins*), combines seven short stories, by different authors, each with different directors. The film is framed by a street carnival at which players throw balls to knock over effigies of the Seven. The Envy segment is based on a short story, *The Cat,* by Simone de Beauvoir. In it a recent bride tries to kill the cat on which her husband lavishes his affection. I interpreted that not as an example of envy but of jealousy in a triangular love affair with one party being an animal. We add that the young wife does envy the cat its preference with the husband. Jealousy gets entangled with envy.

An American film, titled simply *Se7en,* directed by David Fincher, presents a baffling series of murders to a pair of detectives, one newly retired but called back to help his young, inexperienced replacement. The unifying theme, it turns out, is that the highly literate murderer has chosen for victims one far-gone example of each of the Seven Sins. Envy is saved for last. The elderly detective is manipulated, goaded, and inveigled into killing the killer. Knowing the respected detective will be put on the case, the murderer selects himself as the final victim for envying the detective his socially worthwhile and valuable life, in contrast to his own wasted intelligence and opportunities.

Other films use envy alone, without the context of the Seven. One French film, based on a *cause célèbre* in the early years of the twentieth century, is entitled *Murderous Maids*. Two sisters, brought up by nuns in an orphanage, are, at seventeen, placed as domestic servants, as was customary in that time and place. The elder sister persuades the younger to help murder their relatively kind mistress and her daughter, out of envy for the bad luck that landed them in that servile position, instead of having been born to money.

A 2004 American film directed by Barry Levinson is entitled *Envy*. Although simplistic and juvenile (the plot relies on eight-year-old bathroom humor), it nevertheless uses "envy" correctly by our definition, for a pair of lifelong friends, one of whose harebrained schemes is actually successful, making him rich. His sudden riches have no effect on his feelings for the friend he grew up with. Yet all his gifts, efforts to share, kindnesses, and ongoing friendship only make his friend more painfully envious, as is often seen when those we envy try to be kind. The sufferer finally is able to admit the problem to his rich friend.

Another French film, *How I Killed My Father* (in which the killing is psychologic, not actual, but deals with old Oedipal wounds), uses a subplot that illustrates the point made by Schoeck about the role of envy in revolutions, particularly in Africa. Schoeck cites revolutions in which the victors kill all educated citizens, in one case leaving no one with more than a sixth-grade education. In the film the father is a physician who had run a clinic in Algeria, but in the uprisings the militants destroyed his facility, and with it the very thing they needed most at the end of hostilities.

The acclaimed Japanese filmmaker Kurosawa's own favorite film, *Ikura*, shows a bureaucrat who has spent his life stamping and shuffling papers. At the discovery of his cancer, he confronts his wasted existence and tries to remedy it by doing something of value to survive him. He pushes through a petition for a playground that the neighborhood mothers have been requesting for their children. He envies the young, healthy secretary and tells her, "I envy you living. I'd like to live the way you do just one day." The moving final scene shows him on the playground swing, dying as the snow falls.

"The Eye of the Beholder" (taken from the expression "Beauty is in the eye of the beholder" from Margaret Wolfe Hungerford's novel *Molly Bawn,* 1878, which has become almost a cliché in our time) is used as the title of at least two works of fiction revolving around envy.

Fifty years ago, in the flagship segment of Rod Serling's series *The Twilight Zone,* a woman is being given her eleventh (and final) desperate chance at plastic surgery to correct her unsightliness and make her appearance at least acceptable. The film is cleverly shot so that we never see faces of operating-room personnel, but only the gowned and gloved team shuffling back and forth, crossing each other's paths in their work. But when the bandages are removed from her face, the doctors and nurses gasp in despair as they realize that their attempt has failed because she is still what we, the viewers, perceive as stunningly beautiful. At the same time we observe to our horror the grossly misshapen, asymmetric, repugnant faces of those who have been trying to make her "like everyone else".

Gorman's short story by the same title confronts the problem of being envied for being beautiful. A very attractive mother and older sister find that time after time the men in their lives become sidetracked and switch their attention as soon as they meet the gorgeous sister. This teenager is suddenly attacked and her face scarified, with the result that she will never again be outstandingly beautiful, despite the best surgical efforts. Yet the authorities are at a loss to find the perpetrator from the girl's vague clues. Finally the mother's policeman friend tracks down the culprit and motive, and gets the girl to confess to having persuaded her boyfriend to mutilate her so that she can know whether he or any other male really loves her for herself, not her beauty.

Turning to social satire, I have found three twentieth-century works in which the explored premise is that since certain advantages (beauty, strength, talent, intelligence) cannot be given to the have-nots, they should be taken from the haves, that is, society should bring the envied down to the level of the enviers.

In the sixties in England, when parliamentary and other changes were aimed at undoing several kinds of privilege, L. P. Hartley wrote a futuristic novel, *Facial Justice*, illustrating the problems of the envious, the envied, and the society in which leveling happens. Set in a bleak, synthetic post-World War III world, Hartley's society, in which most persons are infertile from radiation, and only a few plants have survived, is run by a dictator who, speaking through a disembodied voice, imposes rules for childish counter-phobic rituals—e.g., spitting in the presence of "bad E" (envy) while performing a little dance for "good E" (equality). All subjects are graded for appearance, Beta being average, Alpha (and Failed Alpha) being attractive, and Gamma in need of repair. Although not required, women at both extremes are pressured to undergo corrective surgery to rectify their advantage or disadvantage and reach the Beta norm, which is a mask-like facies with synthetic skin that does not absorb tears (hence Hartley's title).

Our heroine, Jael 97, a Failed Alpha, procrastinates, delaying the recommended surgery. But when she suffers a bus accident and is taken to the hospital, repair of her injuries leaves her with the Beta physiognomy.

Jael opposes the pressure toward uniformity and tries to muster opposition to the efforts at global standardization, but she can persuade only seven to follow her for a time. Then she attends a concert at which two performers both play Beethoven's *Moonlight Sonata,* one with sensitivity and artistry, the other with wrong notes, chaotic tempi, and no feeling for the music. And so Jael writes a satiric review, indicating that the applause should have been the same for the two performers in a society where appreciation of classical music stigmatizes the unequal.

The novel ends with Jael unmasking the dictator when she takes in out of the rain a frail, dowdy old woman.

Satirizing the post-World War II efforts in Britain to undo privilege—in education, in opportunity, in class—Hartley worked in the enormous gray area between social injustice and ordinary envy. Insufficiently knowledgeable about the British social conditions of Hartley's England, I certainly missed many of his references, but no reader can fail to recognize the colorless, childish, and pointless lives the standardized society was promoting.

At the same time as Hartley, Kurt Vonnegut in our country wrote a science fiction/social fiction satiric novel and a short story, both displaying what happens when the intent is to equalize by bringing the advantaged down to level the playing field. In the novel, *The Sirens of Titan,* we see this treatment only briefly in one society encountered in the hero's intergalactic peregrinations. The central theme of Vonnegut's short story, *Harrison Bergeron,* is the same: since some of the relative disadvantages that drive envy cannot be rectified, the advantages must be taken away from those unequal enough to have them, so as to bring everyone down to the lowest common denominator. Strong, powerful, athletic persons are made to carry weights. Those beautiful of countenance are scarified. The intelligent, represented by Harrison, must wear devices dinning cacophony into their ears so that they cannot think.[6]

✳

Even comic strips and children's literature offer lessons about envy, greed, and contentment with one's lot.

In *Maxine,* a comic about young working women, one segment shows three friends on coffee break discussing an absent fourth, her recent promotions, her child's musical and academic successes, her family's skiing vacation in Europe. The final panel shows the three slumped over their cups, agreeing, "Let's talk about something more cheerful, less depressing."

Dr. Seuss's *Gertrude McFuzz,* a bird character with only one feather in her tail, longs for another feather, like the two in her girlfriend's tail. So she consults her uncle, a doctor, who explains that one tail feather is just right for her, and he urges her to be content. Under Gertrude's nagging, he finally sends her to eat a certain berry. And voila! A second feather sprouts. But Gertrude is greedy, eats more and more berries, and grows a tree of feathers. Then, of course, she is unable to become airborne. As she painfully plucks out one feather after another, she learns her lesson.

A friend and medical school classmate has been doing, in his way, what I have been doing in mine, i.e., writing about human nature so as to help us think about it. In his book of verse, *Wisdom's Way,* Andrew Jannett shares his observations that concur with those of everyone else thinking about our topic:

Envy

Envy is one of the seven capital sins;
Anyone so affected never wins;
Each race, creed, or gender may be afflicted
In greater or lesser degree addicted.

The envious person, you may rely
Watches the car you drive,
The spot on your tie;
He measures your every success,
The wealth you acquire, the way you dress.

Whatever you gain, causes him or her pain;
If you get an award, they'll go insane;
An envier only gets relief when he dies;
That's because, he's closed his eyes.

Envy is difficult to portray in non-literary arts. Medieval art (Bruegel and Hieronymus Bosch come to mind) sometimes represented sinners suffering in hell; sometimes the exact nature of the sin (including envy) was even labeled. Giotto's fresco titled Socle (Envy) has personified envy, represented by a mean woman with a snake curling out of her mouth. This fresco is in the Capella degli Scrovegni nell'Arena (Padua, Italy). Caillot, an early seventeenth-century printer, produced etchings of the Seven Deadly. He portrayed Envy as an old woman with a demon flying around her head, snakes in her hair and one wrapped around her arm. She is biting into what could be a newborn's buttocks. She is followed by a dog with nipples hanging down. One print is held in the Fine Arts Museum in San Francisco, another in Los Angeles. Gericault, a late-eighteenth-century French artist, painted the portrait of a peasant woman whose expression was intended to show envy, hanging now in the Musée des Beaux Arts in Lyon. To me it conveyed only suspicion.

Envy has even been portrayed in at least one other sense modality. A traveling artistic representation of the Seven by Nobi Shioya, entitled "7S: An Olfactory Instillation of the Seven Deadly Sins" came to town recently. It consisted of seven gray cylindrical ceramic vessels suspended at eye level, each with a scent compounded and created by one of the world's seven most highly esteemed perfumieres. Envy smelled slightly musty but not repellent and putrid, as I would have blended it had I been assigned.

Notes

1. The widely displayed conjoined brothers, for whom "Siamese twins" were named.

2. It is quoted extensively because access is difficult. There are only eight copies in American public libraries, and the one I borrowed had uncut pages.

3. The other best known of Balzac's novels is *Père Goriot,* sometimes called "the French Lear".

4. He is referring to the hoops little boys used to roll with a stick.

5. Kavalerov's ravings about the meaning of class in Soviet society and the fact that elevation to managerial class does not bestow innate human superiority—these parts resonate with a work on sociology published in 1972, to which one of my envy sources sent me, *The Hidden Injuries of Class* by Sennett and Cobb. These sociologists make the point that when children of blue-collar workers advance to become "paper pushers", this has the counterproductive effect of eroding both their life satisfaction and their dignity.

6. Though with different intent, the effect is the same in stores that play loud unpleasant music, causing the unwilling hearer to complete her business and exit quickly.

Chapter 11

Authors' Envy of Each Other in Literature and Life

Early and late in their careers, whether acclaimed or obscure, authors are prey to envy. Indeed, some authors claim that envy is worse in their craft than in all others because literary products are so tightly ego-bound. (Of course authors are, by profession, especially articulate about envy along with everything else. Persons having trouble putting a sentence together may feel envy just as keenly.) Authors are particularly sensitive to that important barometer, the *New York Times* bestseller list, their place and their colleagues' on it (or not), and the income it generates.

There are two main types of writing for publication: fiction and nonfiction. Persons in various occupations and professions with special experience, results of experimental trials or other types of study, knowledge, and expertise must write to impart their discoveries to their peers and colleagues, and sometimes to certain segments of the general population. They write for content, and their purpose is to convey information to an audience that needs or would benefit from their findings. Everyone who has gained any kind of original insight must arrange to see it in print, or it will be lost after his lifetime, except for the unreliable recollections of students and others of what they learned from him. (Family history is a particularly apt example of what is lost if it is stored only in human brains.) Except for organization, style is strictly second-ary; accuracy and precision are primary. Authors of this type of literature may envy each other's success in advancing something worth learning, to the point of committing it to print, and the fact that they were able to run the hurdles of getting it published over their signature.

Other authors write straight from their imaginations, and they may jump from what they do—or did originally—professionally. Hence an "author" can be a novelist or a journalist, a philosopher or a historian, an essayist or a psychologist (B. F. Skinner), a phy-sician (Somerset Maugham, Arthur Conan Doyle, and William Carlos Williams) or a scientist (Isaac Asimov is one, and I have a poetry- and science-fiction-writing physicist acquaintance, Geof-frey Landis, whose experiment was sent to Mars and who has had a Nebula Award or two), and there are many others. In general, fiction writers' forte is artistry, even elegance with words, skill with character delineation, and creation of the story. They may envy each other's talent in these dimensions and their colleagues' suc-cess in running the obstacle course of publication.

For inclusion in this chapter, I have identified authors of fiction and nonfiction, whose envy concerns their writing, or "authorship". In fact I shall begin with Schopenhauer because, although a philos-opher, his envy concerning his literary product is most trenchant.

First, however, we look at his comments on envy in general.

I am afraid that no one will be found to be entirely free from it. For that a man should feel his own lack of things more bitterly at the sight of another's delight in the enjoy-ment of them, is natural; nay, it is inevitable; but this should not rouse his hatred of the man who is happier than him-self. It is just this hatred, however, in which true envy con-sists. Least of all should a man be envious, when it is a question, not of the gifts of fortune, or chance, or another's favour, but of the gifts of nature; because everything that is innate in a man rests on a metaphysical basis, and possesses justification of a higher kind; it is, so to speak, given him by Divine grace. But, unhappily, it is just in the case of personal advantages that envy is most irreconcilable. Thus it is that intelligence, or even genius, cannot get on in the world without begging pardon for its existence, wherever it is not in a position to be able, proudly and boldly, to despise the world. ... On the other hand, in the envy that is directed to natural gifts and personal advantages, like beauty in women, or intelligence in men, there is no consolation or hope of one kind or the other; so that nothing remains but to indulge a bitter and irreconcilable hatred of the person who possesses these privileges; and hence the only remaining desire is to take vengeance on him.

But here the envious man finds himself in an unfortunate position; for all his blows fall powerless as soon as it is known that they come from him. Accordingly he hides his feelings as carefully as if they were secret sins, and so becomes an inexhaustible inventor of tricks and artifices and devices for concealing and masking his procedure, in order that, unperceived, he may wound the object of his envy.

For instance, with an air of the utmost unconcern he will ignore the advantages which are eating his heart out; he will neither see them, nor know them, nor have observed or even heard of them, and thus make himself a master in the art of dissimulation. With great cunning he will completely overlook the man whose brilliant qualities are gnawing at his heart, and act as though he were quite an unimportant person; he will take no notice of him, and, on occasion, will have even quite forgotten his existence. But at the same time he will before all things endeavour by secret machination carefully to deprive those advantages of any opportunity of showing themselves and becoming known. Then out of his dark corner he will attack these qualities with censure, mockery, ridicule and calumny, like the toad which spurts its poison from a hole.

Elsewhere he notes, "When someone else's glory increases, yours decreases by comparison. Therefore it is most customary to run down others." Again, "Envy and hatred are very often traceable to a single source." Furthermore, he observes, the "average envier" is spiteful and destructive.

Bad as he finds envy, there is another even worse. "[I]t is *Schadenfreude*, a mischievous delight in the misfortunes of others, which remains the worst trait in human nature. It is a feeling which is closely akin to cruelty, and differs from it, to say the truth, only as theory from practice."

Schopenhauer's thoughts on envy concerning his literary work appear in an essay "On Reputation" and relate to the recognition from peers that he craved for his philosophic writing. He was outraged by the Roman candle-like instant acclaim showered on popular authors. His claims for recognition illustrate envy crowding up to the edge of demand for justice, or Raiga's "*l'envie d'indignation*". He writes: "The general history of art and literature shows that the highest achievements of the human mind are, as a rule, not favourably received at first: but remain in obscurity until they win notice from intelligence of a higher order, by whose influence they are brought into a position which they then maintain, in virtue of the authority thus given them."

In another section:

> It is often only after the lapse of time that the persons really competent to judge them appear—exceptional critics sitting in judgment on exceptional works, and giving their weighty verdicts in succession. These collectively form a perfectly just appreciation; and though there are cases where it has taken some hundreds of years to form it,[1] no further lapse of time is able to reverse the verdict—so secure and inevitable is the fame of a great work.[2]

In contrast:

It is not that a man is thought to be great by masses of incompetent and often infatuated people, but that he really is great which should move us to envy his position; and his happiness lies, not in the fact that posterity will hear of him, but that he is the creator of thoughts worthy to be treasured up and studied for hundreds of years.

"The value of posthumous fame lies in deserving it." A man who basks in unmerited fame "will feel giddy on the heights which he was never meant to climb, ... [and] look upon himself as spurious coin;[3] and in the anguish of threatened discovery and well-merited degradation, he will read the sentence of posterity on the foreheads of the wise—like a man who owes his property to a forged will."

Again:

[T]hat was an incomparably fine saying of Seneca's, that fame follows merit as surely as the body casts a shadow; sometimes falling in front, and sometimes behind. And he goes on to remark that though the envy of contemporaries be shown by universal silence, there will come those who will judge without enmity or favour. From this remark it is manifest that even in Seneca's age there were rascals who understood the art of suppressing merit by maliciously ignoring its existence, and of concealing good work from the public in order to favour the bad. It is an art well understood in our day, too, manifesting itself, both then and now, in an envious conspiracy of silence.

Whether authors ever live to see the dawn of their fame depends upon the chance of circumstances; and the higher and more important their works are, the less likelihood there is of their doing so.[4]

Finally Schopenhauer opines, "an unreasonable value is set upon other people's opinion, and one quite disproportionate to its real worth. Hobbes has some strong remarks on this subject; and no doubt he is quite right. Mental pleasure, he writes, and ecstasy of any kind, arise when, on comparing ourselves with others, we come to the conclusion that we may think well of ourselves." This is the converse of the envier's situation, in which on comparison he finds himself inferior, belittled, and even humiliated.

Schopenhauer and others find it astonishing that even intelligence does not protect against envy. He quotes Cicero: "There is something so penetrating in the shaft of envy that even men of wisdom and worth find its wound a painful one."

Like others, Schopenhauer considers literary envy the worst, both coming and going. A protection against envy is modesty, but this enrages our author all the more.

> If I had to write about *modesty* I should say: I know the esteemed public for which I have the honour to write far too well to dare to give utterance to my opinion about this virtue. Personally I am quite content to be modest and to apply myself to this virtue with the utmost possible circumspection. But one thing I shall never admit—that I have ever required modesty of any man, and any statement to that effect I repel as a slander.
>
> The paltry character of most men compels the few who have any merit or genius to behave as though they did not know their own value, and consequently did not know other people's want of value; for it is only on this condition that the mob acquiesces in tolerating merit. A virtue has been made out of this necessity, and it is called modesty. It is a piece of hypocrisy, to be excused only because other people are so paltry that they must be treated with indulgence.

He implies disdain for the burst of acclaim from the masses for inferior work. He hopes for the slower groundswell of recognition by those whose taste and critical judgment are superior, whose appreciation is hard to acquire but, once gotten, lasting.

Schopenhauer has a word of advice on finding oneself envied.

> For our self-consciousness and our pride there can be nothing more flattering than the sight of envy lurking in its retreat and plotting its schemes; but never let a man forget that where there is envy there is hatred, and let him be careful not to make a false friend out of any envious person. Therefore it is important to our safety to lay envy bare; and a man should study to discover its tricks, as it is everywhere to be found and always goes about *incognito*; for as I have said, like a venomous toad it lurks in dark corners. It deserves neither quarter nor sympathy; but as we can never reconcile it let our rule of conduct be to scorn it with a good heart, and as our happiness and glory is torture to it we may rejoice in its sufferings.

These observations of Schopenhauer's on envy parallel those of other authors, who find literary envy the hardest to bear.

Like Feuerbach and others, Schopenhauer attributed the overwhelming success of Christianity to offering true equality and bliss in the afterlife, beside which all current tribulations are trivial, thus helping the oppressed underclass tolerate envy in the here-and-now.

I was reminded of Schopenhauer's comments by the experience of an acquaintance of mine, a journalist working for a respected newspaper. She related how she and her friends had, over the years, found the writing of one of their colleagues generally poor. To their surprise, this journalist received a book offer. A year later, to their astonishment, he received a second contract. Finally he received a third, with a $125,000 advance. My acquaintance seethed but decided that she could ill afford to let herself be consumed by envious outrage. She handled the problem by sending him a congratulatory telegram. The advantage of this route is that you have absolute control over what you write, and you can edit it, a luxury you don't have once a word is out of your mouth, and you needn't be concerned with your facial expression. An added advantage with the telegram is not having to react to the other's acknowledgment while trying to look sincere. Insofar as possible, my friend forgot the event and moved on with her own work, although, seeing me several months after this happened, she obviously remembered all the details well enough to tell me. I praised her strategy, but sympathized with the pain of envy, complicated by her need for dollars. Probably other factors than writing ability, such as timeliness of the man's material, sold his books.

Similar authorial envy is addressed in Sam Shepard's play, *True West.* One brother, an author, has enjoyed only modest success, but now finds himself so close to signing a contract for a film script that he can taste it. His ne'er-do-well, larcenous, drifter brother shows up, produces an idea for a film, and somehow manages to preempt an advance from his brother's contact. The established author feels cheated and suffers "l'envie d'indignation" especially so because of the lacklustre nature of his brother's idea. He lets himself be talked into writing the outline for his brother, until as they argue, they more or less agree that the idea is worthless. Drinking, they eventually square off in fratricidal rage.

Performed recently in New York, a play about growing up Jewish in Brooklyn after what the author called the Jewish "glory days" of World War II, *Brooklyn Boy* by Donald Margulies displays a successful author on the receiving end of envy by his dying shoe-salesman father, his unsuccessful author wife who has also been unable to carry a pregnancy, and his childhood friend who runs a family deli. The friend and the wife are more overt in acknowl-edging their envy than most, while the father continues a lifelong pattern of downgrading and belittling the son.

Proudly proffering his dying father a copy of his book that is eleventh on the Best Seller list, dedicated "for my mother and my father", the son Eric is appalled by his father's response that he thought there were only ten on the list and his question:

"Don't we get our names? Couldn't you say 'For Phyllis and Manny Weiss'? Then there wouldn't be any confusion. ...It would've given your mother may she rest in peace such *nakhess* to see her name in print. When do people like us ever get to do that? Huh? When we *die*; that's about it. ... Stick it [the book] over there."

The son goes on to ask his father to read the book and to "pre-tend it means something to you".

And the father replies, "You *know* reading's not my thing ... 380-odd pages, that's a hell of a lot to ask from somebody like me."[5]

After leaving his father's hospital room, Eric happens to meet Ira, a friend from childhood. He wishes to get away, but Ira tries to reestablish the friendship. Ira reminds Eric that he went to Brook-lyn College while Eric went to Columbia, and Eric says Ira could have tried for Columbia too.

But Ira protests, "There was *no way* my parents could afford it!"

"What, you think *my* parents were rich? ... They never had any money—I worked my ass off to get a scholarship! Otherwise I never would've gotten the hell out of here!"

"See, it never even *occurred* to me that I could do that! I thought that was for other people. I was smart! I had potential! Nobody ever pulled me aside and told me it was okay to go for it! Nobody!"

"Nobody ever told *me*, either! I figured it out for myself."

"How'd you do it? What is it, a gene? A chemical? What is it you were born with that I wasn't? We were born three days apart! ... [R]ight in this very hospital! Lived three blocks away. Saw each other every day, practically. Now look where *you* are and look where I am."

As they talk, Ira says, "*You're* the published writer. Who am *I*? Just some schmuck who runs a deli."

Then Eric goes to Nina's apartment that they used to share before she insisted on a divorce. He asks her to go on his book tour.

"Shlepping along on your book tour is not my idea of fun. ... You know how it is: I become totally irrelevant. ... You have no idea what it's like having to stand there, smiling like an idiot, hoping *someone* makes eye contact with you. It's demoralizing."

Eric reminds her he always introduced her and told everyone what a wonderful writer she is.

"... and I *hate* it when you do that. It makes me feel like a fucking charity case. ... Everyone knows I haven't had a story published in six years. ... Come on, *six* years? And it hasn't occurred to you I might not be any good? ... I don't know how you put up with me as long as you did. The contagion of failure should've been overwhelming. Between the miscarriages and the rejection letters."

As they sort out his things to go, he pulls out an old cable-knit sweater.

Eric: This is yours.

Nina: It *was* yours. You got it in Maine.

Eric: Yeah, I remember, but I gave it to *you*.

Nina: I know, but I thought you might like to have it back.

Eric: Come on, you loved this sweater.

Nina: I know I did. But I can't see myself wearing it anymore, and I know you were always fond of it, so...

Eric: Do you *hate* me?

Nina: No, it's just ... Whenever I see you or smell your scent on an old sweater, I'm reminded of all the things I failed at.

Sometimes it's better when marriage partners follow different vocations or specialties, so that domains of success are more disparate.

An excellent review of the New York production of Margulies' play, entitled "Prisoners of Envy" by John Lahr, appeared in *The New Yorker* magazine.

Molly Giles also approaches the problem of envy in the lives of authors who are also friends. In her short story "The Blessed Among Us", a party is given to congratulate and honor one member of a writers' workshop whose novel has been very successful. Congratulatory flowers overflow the apartment; the author's agent arrives; there is a call from the publisher; guests all comment on how the author "deserves" to be fourth on the *New York Times* bestseller list and rising. Her three workshop friends fight envy resulting from their relative lack of success, and, indeed, feel the same ambivalence, the same resentment, and the same shame over being, in the words of my patient "that low kind of person". One of the three comments on how they all are wearing something of green.[6]

The man friend of one of the three women observes, "You girls must be shitting bricks."

Writing in the mid-twentieth century when Yiddish literature and the Yiddish theater were in their heyday in America, Cynthia Ozick also attacked the problem of authorial envy in a short story "Envy; or, Yiddish in America". Her protagonist envies another author for the fact that he has a good translator and hence is getting the attention that the work of both of them deserves.[7]

Ozick acknowledges: "It doesn't matter what [language] you speak, envy sounds the same in all languages."

Envy places authors, like everyone else, in double jeopardy: being envied by their colleagues or fearing it can be almost as bad as envying other authors whose work is being recognized more than one's own, especially if they are also friends. Pairs of prominent authors have been friends and rivals, but still envious. Goethe believed he had finally, at seventy-six, conquered his envy of Schiller. Addison and Pope were rivals for the esteem of readers, and one is quoted as having written in convoluted syntax the idea that his friend is lucky to be on the receiving end of his friend's envy, rather than the other way around. Hemingway and F. Scott Fitzgerald were said to resent each other's fame. Fear of envy after the meteoric success of *The Glass Menagerie* led Tennessee Williams to go into seclusion from his friends. Eventually he distanced himself even further by fleeing to Mexico, where he apparently absorbed ideas for *Night of the Iguana.*

Being envied is never pleasant, and it can endanger more than the ego, i.e., the livelihood of persons in the arts. When artists of all kinds[8] lived on the patronage of persons in high places (in contrast to the present, when, as Schoeck notes, patronage is institutionalized, coming from universities, foundations, and grants), an author faced the ever-present threat that someone would move in on his territory. Another writer might try to get the patron's ear and drive a wedge, with the view to diverting money to himself. One way to climb over another author was to persuade the sovereign that his rival's work reflected badly on the throne and should be suppressed.[9]

Spenser, whose handling of the topic of envy we have already examined, entitled his magnum opus *The Faerie Queene* to flatter Elizabeth. While writing this lengthy epic poem, he needed to stand in everyone's good graces long enough to keep getting support, financial and psychologic. Therefore he wrote several pages of dedicatory sonnets to *The Faerie Queene,* two of which appeal specifically for protection from envy, and flatter the patron.

To the Right Honourable the Earle of Oxenford, Lord
High Chamberlayne of England,

Receive, most Noble Lord, in gentle gree,
The unripe fruit of an unready wit;
Which by thy countenaunce doth crave to bee
Defended from foule Envies poisnous bit.
Which so to doe may thee right well befit,
Sith th' antique glory of thine auncestry
Under a shady vele is therein writ,
And eke thine owne long living memory,
Succeeding them in true nobility, etc., etc.

Another sonnet "To the right honourable the Earle of Northum-
berland" includes:

And eke from all, of whom it is envide,
To patronise the authour of their praise,
Which gives them life, that els would soone have dide,
And crownes their ashes with immortall baies.
To thee, therefore, right noble Lord, I send
This present of my paines, it to defend.

We conclude with envy as it afflicts authors, as portrayed at length
by two fiction writers, one writing as fiction, the other revealing
her own battle with envy.

Yuri Olesha, the Russian author whose novella *Envy* about
"Kavalerov the Envious" has been quoted earlier, wrote also a short
story called *From the Secret Notebook of Fellow-Traveler Sand.*
Although presented as fiction, it comes across to me as personal
and autobiographical, and it makes many statements about the
envy of the protagonist author for other authors and of Benvenuto

Cellini for other artists. Sand's envy is for several highly esteemed Russian authors, the French author Balzac, and one American author the Russians hold in high regard, Jack London. His story begins with the character Sand writing:

> I have a passionate craving for power.
>
> I look at myself in the mirror very often. When I'm working, I leap up every minute and rush up to the looking glass. I rivet my eyes on it and look at myself. What am I trying to find in the mirror? It is some sort of a habit and I don't know how I got into it. Well, why not. ... Perhaps it would make me feel better if I reminded myself that all writers have had their own peculiar habits which manifested themselves during their creative hours, such as Schiller's rotten apples[10] or the cold footbaths of someone or other. And so I console myself: Schiller with his apples, Fellow-Traveler Sand with his mirror. Makes me sick.
>
> When I think that I am a writer living in an era of the ascent of a new social class, when I begin to examine myself, to look back and try to appraise what I have achieved—it becomes obvious to me that my work, which at certain moments seems so all-important to me, fades into utter insignificance compared with the great events that make the history of these days and years.
>
> In the window of a bookstore there is an etching. It makes me shudder.

He describes a scene in which people crowding in the street throng to acclaim the poet Schiller after the first performance of his play *Intrigue and Love*. Sand (or Olesha) goes on:

> This is glory. He wrote *Intrigue and Love*, he created the bourgeois drama. He is the poet of the ascending class. ...
>
> Now I am a writer too.
>
> So how can I not long to write my own *Intrigue and Love*, a new type of play, a play that would stir the imagination of the

proletariat just as much as Schiller's drama stirred those burghers' imaginations?...And how could I not crave for power? How could I not crave for writing power, howling and weeping when I feel frustrated, because I need it now that a new class is rising to power.

Sand quotes from Benvenuto Cellini's *Autobiography*:

Although I was moved by honorable envy[11] and I wanted to produce a work of art that would equal and even surpass the work of such a craftsman as Lucagnolo, I did not because of this neglect my own fine art of jewelry; and so both brought me much profit and even greater honor, and in both I kept creating things unlike any made by others.

He goes on to cite another craftsman whose engraved seals Cellini admired.

I felt noble envy toward this great craftsman also although his art is far removed from other branches of goldsmithery and Lautizio having specialized in that form of art could not do anything else. So I began to study that art too although I found it very difficult; never shirking the efforts it cost me I ceaselessly tried to improve and to learn.

Cellini cites yet another craftsman, a Messer Caradosso, who engraved medals "the length of one's palm, wrought of the thinnest gold plates and so exquisitely executed that I considered him the greatest master in that domain I'd ever come across, and I envied him more than all the others."

Sand returns to literature:

And then there was an American by the name of Jack London who was a hobo, who sailed on schooners, hunted, and often had to repel those who attacked him.... This Jack London wrote stories that no one wanted to publish. But later they did publish his stories and he wrote more and more and in these stories he told of the things he had seen and other things he made up, and because he was brave and had gone through many dangers and many humiliations from which he had always emerged triumphant, other people, reading him, wanted to become bold and energetic themselves. He wrote many excellent stories and novels and, in fact, they are so well done that I consider him the greatest master in this kind of writing I have ever come across and I am full of a noble envy for him.

And I feel all the stronger because I happen to live in a country where people go out to wild places to build new towns and power stations, where they lay railroads and reverse the course of rivers, where these people display amazing daring and enterprise, just as happened once in America. And when I think of that, my envy increases because I could have been writing things just as excellent since life itself is a help to me, having created such favorable conditions.

Sand goes on to describe the work of Balzac, whose "envy" character Bette we have already seen:

He wrote day and night and as he wrote, he tore his shirt on his chest and howled and wrote on until he collapsed from exhaustion. ... He is supposed to have said that, since Napoleon had been able to achieve the supreme heights in statesmanship and the conduct of war, he, Balzac, would become the Napoleon of literature.

Balzac divided Paris into circles, in each of which were people of various occupations: goldsmiths, moneylenders, bankers, barbers, generals, shopkeepers, priests, whores, actors, adventurers, artists. ... He made them intermingle because the lot of them made up one bourgeois society and pursued one common goal—each wanted to acquire as much money as he possibly could. Balzac then proceeded to write an incredible number of novels about them, thus creating his *Comedie humaine*. He portrayed all those characters so well that we can piece together a complete picture of life at that time from his books, revealed by a magician who could see and sense how all those around him lived, what everyone was after and what he was thinking about. Well, I envy Balzac too.

Then there was that man Pushkin. He wrote epic poems and jocose verse and epigrams. He was also a tragic poet and on top of it all wrote prose fiction, critical essays and songs and was also an editor. He is really to be envied more than any other man because by the time he was twenty-four he had written the tragedy *Boris Godunov*, ... which is perfection of a kind that has never been equaled. This man, so remarkable in all forms of poetry, said that a poet must be abreast of the knowledge of his age. He seems to have lived up to that motto, for when he died, still young, he left behind a library of five thousand volumes all of which he had read with the greatest attention, for on every page of each of those five thousand books there were annotations in his handwriting.

...

There was yet another writer, a count, one Leo Tolstoy. That man was so great and felt his superiority over others so acutely that he couldn't accept the idea that there were other great men and ideas in the world that he couldn't take on and overcome in the end. So he chose the most powerful opponents, so powerful that all mankind prostrated itself before them. These were Napoleon, Death, Christianity, Art and Life itself, which is the reason why he wrote *The Kreutzer Sonata* in which he appealed to people to give up reproducing themselves, in other words, to renounce Life itself. ...

It is impossible to envy such a man because he was a natural phenomenon, like a star or a waterfall, and it is impossible to try to become a waterfall or a star or a rainbow, or to try to acquire the properties of a magnetized needle and to always point toward the North.

I am envious of everyone, though. I admit it. But that is because there is no such thing as a modest artist. If he pretends to be modest, he's faking and lying, and hard though he may try to hide his envy, it will still burst out with a hiss through his clenched teeth.

I am firmly convinced of this but not in the least depressed. On the contrary, it leads me calmly to the conclusion that envy and vanity are forces propitious to creativity, that there is no need to be ashamed of them, and that they are not black shadows left outside the door but the genius's two full-blooded sisters who are next to him when he sits down to work.

When great deeds are being accomplished, when everything around has the seal of greatness, when the word *giant* has become of current use, there is nothing shameful in my wanting to emulate artistic giants, particularly since I happen to be an artist, because the task facing me, the task of portraying the birth of a new mankind is a task for a giant.

Olesha's work escaped negative Soviet attention, and understandably they applauded his praise for Russian literature. He wrote very little after *Envy,* only a collection of dream-like short stories, and his speech to the congress of Russian authors was included in his collection.

We conclude this series with excerpts from Joan Frank's experiences in her article, "Visiting Envy", in a newspaper for authors.

Quoting several other authors on envy, she notes their agreement that even eventual recognition does not cure the damage that envy of more successful authors has done to the personality—never enough, always too late. She goes on in her own voice:

> Who among us, I wonder, has been immune to envy? Who has not felt the silent, hard internal pinch when someone we know or recognize is given the royal nod for advancement we seek—the story accepted, the grant bequeathed, the book sold, the warm blurb or review, the important award? Without warning a catch of inchoate woe squeezes us somewhere below the breastbone,[12] followed by a wormy sense of ineffectiveness; perhaps an electrical prickling of dread: *Oh, no,* we think. And who has not then instantly loathed and yet been held fast by his own meanness?
>
> ...[It] is also to be flushed with two kinds of horror: one insidiously questioning your own work; the other your natural fitness to be doing the art. Surely those who have themselves in hand don't think this way! Yet inside, a banshee howls. *How long?* cries the trapped madwoman.
>
> ... Guilt adds to dismay. ... There is a real quality of ambush in it. ... At its peak, envy challenges us to a wrestle, silent and desperate, for the life of the writing spirit. To let that be harmed or contaminated seems the worst fate of all. So we ferociously block out self-pity, a luxury we can't afford. On special occasions, yes, it might be briefly permitted—a deliciously stupefying wallow, like drinking tequila while steeped in a hot bath. ... We can practice defusing envy by inviting it in, mulling it over, waiting politely with it until it gets bored and leaves. ... What can be harnessed from raw envy, perhaps, is a kind of sour jump start.
>
> But we caution when wallowing: self-pity is also a notoriously greedy diverter of energy. And energy, my friends, is the ballgame.[13]
>
> ...Envy seems to enter the veins and travel the body like

venom; weakening, debilitating. ... [B]y weighting various external symbols of reward, envy threatens to stunt or taint the integrity of the impulse to make art in the first place.

Frank notes that being on the receiving end of envy is no picnic either. "Heaven knows envy's democratic enough; old and young, published and unpublished have eventually done their time on one or the other end of the strained congratulatory remarks; the sharp reconfigurations of the face."

Frank agrees with a "writing friend" that writers are some of the least charitable people "because a writer's product is so immutably bound up with ego and exposed self... that it stands for the self in a way that surgery or accounting or gardening or even virtuoso musicianship ... don't quite parallel."

It wouldn't matter whether there were plenty of well-paid publishing space for all: because writing's result is pure, exposed self, we begrudge the better judgment of one over another.

Surely a huge reason for petulance among writers is that mainstream venues for their work are so weirdly, competitively few—ironically, because of an Infotainment industry shifting into high gear, in which superstores, book groups, Web sites, and Oprah boosterism proliferate as national pastimes, cutting off life support for the quiet midlist titles. For writers of literary fiction—whose work editors so admire they pass it around the office for colleagues to enjoy, yet declare commercially unjustifiable—the whole business can feel like a vicious game of musical chairs....

Envy is an old, old reflex. Since before King David people have coveted each other's power, money, belongings, beauty, spouses or lovers, talent, status, and last but never least—health. But in present time, envy may be the last of the human foibles to which we easily confess. None of the writers I polled had a ready antidote for it other than a vague, troubled fatalism. ... Some claimed they only envied when they felt the objects of their envy hadn't deserved their deserts.

A wise friend ... teaches "We have a sense of fair play, and I think when that sense is violated, then we envy in proportion to that perceived violation—even though we all know life isn't fair."

Bonnie Friedman calls envy "the writer's disease," characterizing it as an insatiable demon devouring itself. ... Envy and vanity[14] are two sides of the same self-sabotaging impulse. ... Few are exempt; national and international laureates may nurse bitter resentment to their last breaths, which may baffle even their closest friends. Recognition too late? Wrong kind? Not enough? The anguish may well stem from a lifetime's "whip-saw effects of habituated envy".

Frank quotes Friedman's characterization of envy as a Chinese finger-puzzle: as you try to pull it off, its grasp tightens. It is more workable to live with it until it fades.

Frank admires a writing teacher, Donald Sheehan, who considers envy a spiritual ailment for which he proposes a spiritual remedy in his article "To Be Free of Envy". He instructs his poetry conference participants "to make—not your own art—but the art of at least one other person here better and fuller and richer. You are here to fall so much in love with another person's poems that you would give all your art over to them—freely, deeply, unhesitatingly—so that these poems, and their poet, can become more beautifully and movingly true." Sheehan finds that this approach often leads to "the first real friendships since early childhood, friendships within which—and through which—our own art grows richer and fuller." Frank is dubious about this as a panacea for envy. I agree that this kind of unselfish contribution to the art of another is an expression of genuine love, an emotion which, the recklessness with which the word is bandied about to the contrary notwithstanding, is in desperately short supply.

Frank laments, "No one is cured of the writers' disease. Envy and jealousy still lash out in unguarded moments like a hidden nest of tiny snakes, and the venom commences its awful journey to the heart."

Frank concludes with a jeremiad similar to what I have heard from other authors, a lament to the effect that if there is anything else you can do—if you are able to *not* write—be grateful, forget writing, and do the other. But, says Frank, "Each visit with envy forces us to rechoose the writing life. ... You do it because you have to."

I have Googled Frank and found two recent novels, short stories, both singly and in a collection, and several awards. It sounds as if those acceptances have helped her, despite authors' "too little, too late" reaction to writing success.

Of special interest in the present context is the fact that in a letter she told me that a collection of her short stories called *In Envy Country* has just won the Richard Sullivan Prize in Fiction and will be published in 2010 by the University of Notre Dame Press.

Notes

1. Melville died poor, unrecognized, and embittered, but recognition came in less than a century.

2. How would Schopenhauer feel about what contemporary humanism, literary criticism, and "liberal education" are doing to Shakespeare and the rest of the Western literary canon, i.e., reducing and eliminating them?

3. I don't know that "unmerited fame" often has this effect in our time, possibly not in Schopenhauer's either.

4. Life holds many disappointments, some of which lead to a feeling that it is not worth going on. Envy of another's success, associated with one's own lack, sometimes plays a role in such disappointments. Failure to be recognized, leading to depression and despair, can eventuate in suicide, which may be followed by posthumous success. One such sad case was that of John Kennedy Toole, whose *A Confederacy of Dunces* was published by his mother. William Inge's suicide also was attributed to the fact that his work did not receive the critical acclaim of that of his play-writing contemporaries.

5. I too have noticed that people, sometimes relatives, whom I would expect to read something I had written if only because I had written it, don't. I had chalked it up to our society's growing nonliteracy, as with Eric's father, but possibly envy played a role too.

6. The color green (not a verdant shade, but a sickly pallor often observed in the adolescent girls' condition known as "chlorosis") is first associated with emotions such as fear and jealousy in the year 1300, according to the *Oxford English Dictionary*. Later it was extended to include "envy" when that condition was differentiated from jealousy.

7. This story underscores the problem of authors whose native language happens to be in use by a relatively small population. It also reminds us of the tremendous debt we owe to good translators, who are largely unappreciated. A friend of mine, a literary connoisseur, has expressed the opinion that if Ibsen had written in a more prominent language

than Norwegian, he would have been as celebrated as Shakespeare.

8. Michelangelo and Bramante contended for the same patronage money, and Michelangelo left Bologna to escape the envy of other artists.

9. Artists in the Soviet Union, composers, especially, were required to keep their compositions in line with political philosophy.

10. Schiller is said not to have been able to start writing until he went to inhale the cider fumes of fermenting apples in his pantry.

11. Olesha's translator says this might be translated "honorable rivalry".

12. She locates envy, anatomically, exactly where I feel it.

13. Bertrand Russell writes, "Vitality [which he defines as "vital force"] is a safeguard against envy, because it makes one's own existence pleasant. As envy is one of the greatest sources of human misery, this is a very important merit in vitality." Russell credits vitality (or energy and the power of hard work) with promoting interest in the world. He does not comment on whether or how this vitality can be acquired, or whether he finds it innate, as I do, except for the boost of energy bequeathed by accomplishment. He observes that those who live "from within" (relatively careless of the opinions of others, like David Riesmann's "inner-directed personality type", i.e., not a mirror of public opinion) are less susceptible to envy.

14. Vanity, I add, is the first and primary of the Seven Deadly Sins, then usually called "pride" and harking back to the Greek "hubris" or "overweening or presumptuous pride". I too have observed that these first two sins of the seven often go together.

Chapter 12

Views of Scholars and Essayists on Envy

Authors from a variety of professional backgrounds, some easily classified, some not, have explored our topic of envy from their various viewpoints. Several in this chapter are clergymen (Protestant and Jewish, as it happens, and we have already looked at early Christian writings before the Eastern Orthodox and the Western Roman Catholic Churches separated). Another is a professor of business and ethics (we need more of him); some have devoted themselves full time to their literary career. The psychologists and psychiatrists are saved for the chapter on psychoanalysts. A number of these literary efforts have been of chapter or article length and meet, therefore, the usual definition of "essay". Several have produced book length works on envy, which, too long for the standard "essay", are in other ways similar. A case could even be made for classifying some with philosophers because their writing is similar to that of "accessible"[1] philosophers such as Schopenhauer or Bacon or Nietzsche, not obfuscating authors of any stripe. This chapter brings together a number of these.

Years ago I was astonished at the contemporary-sounding humor in *The Praise of Folly* by Desiderius Erasmus[2] (pen name of one baptized Gerhard Gerhards, whose life straddled the fifteenth and sixteenth centuries), a humanist, scholar, and theologian. But on current reading, I am not surprised that he sidestepped envy as too serious and painful a topic for this author's flippant and tongue-in-cheek dealing with other foibles of humankind, that are easier to joke about than the feelings and behavior of envy. [3]

Not so with Robert Burton, an English clergyman and author, who straddled the sixteenth and seventeenth centuries and completed *The Anatomy of Melancholy* [4] in 1620. (His first edition only, he published under the pen name of Democritus Junior, referring to the Greek philosopher who believed that all nature is reducible to tiny particles, "atoms". His title for this edition was the ornate *The Anatomy of Melancholy: What It Is, with All the Kinds, Causes, Symptoms, Prognostics, and Several Cures of It in Their Partition, with Their Several Sections, Members, and Subsections, Philosophically, Medically, Historically Opened and Cut Up.*)

Of the envious man, Burton wrote:

> His whole life is sorrow, and every word he speaks is satire: nothing fats him but other men's ruins. For to speak in a word, envy is naught else but *tristitia de bonis alienis, et gaudium de adversis* [sadness at others' good and joy at their harm].
>
> So often as an envious wretch sees another man prosper, to be enriched, to thrive, and be fortunate in the world, to get honours, offices, or the like, he repines and grieves. ...as he did in Aesop, lose one eye willingly, that his fellow might lose both, or that rich man in Quintillian that poisoned the flowers in his garden, because his neighbour's bees should get no more honey from them.

He quotes Marcus Aurelius who read "Greek, Hebrew, and Chaldee" authors and found no remedy for being envied except to renounce all happiness and be miserable forever. A poor preventive measure, we all agree.

Burton equates envy with emulation (similar to the way Bacon equates envy with resentment). "Honest emulation in studies, in all callings, is not to be disliked, ... 'tis the whetstone of wit, the nurse of wit and valor." He advises us "to balance our hearts with love, charity, meekness, patience, and counterpoise those irregular motives of envy, livor [malignity, spite], spleen, hatred, with their opposite virtues."

La Rochefoucauld, a seventeenth-century moralist who introduced the genre of maxims (defined as "a concisely expressed principle or rule of conduct, or a statement of a general truth"), and whose opinions on just about any subject are usually quoted by French authors, comments frequently on envy and schadenfreude.

As Kronenberger, the translator and commentator of his maxims points out, the well-to-do leisure classes had the time and energy to scrutinize their own and their friends' psychologic workings, and these maxims were the result. These, in turn, probably served as a jumping-off point for discussion and stimulated conversation, which reached a peak in the salons of his time. They no doubt sparked debate because so many of his maxims (on all topics) are anything but universal truths and immediately suggest exceptions, qualifications, and disputes. La Rochefoucauld's maxims were rarely more than a sentence or two, and several are quoted in my collection of maxims.

The British author Hazlitt admired La Rochefoucauld's style so much that he wrote his own book which he called *Characteristics: in the Manner of Rochefoucault's Maxims.* Hazlitt's were not always pithy, sometimes did not stop at a single sentence, but often went on for a paragraph or more. See my list for examples of his more pithy maxims. Here are three of Hazlitt's that are too long for my maxim collection:

> We envy others for any trifling addition to their acknowledged merit, more than for the sum-total, much as we object to pay an addition to a bill, or grudge an acquaintance an unexpected piece of good fortune. This happens,

either because such an accession of accomplishment is like stealing a march upon us, and implies a versatility of talent we had not reckoned upon; or it seems an impertinence and affectation for a man to go out of his way to distinguish himself; or it is because we cannot account for his proficiency mechanically and as a thing of course, by saying, *It is his trade*!

This goes on for another page, wandering off the subject of envy. Finally:

Envy is the most universal passion. We only pride ourselves on the qualities we possess or think we possess; but we envy the pretensions we have, and those which we have not, and do not even wish for. We envy the greatest qualities and every trifling advantage. We envy the most ridiculous appearance or affectation of superiority. We envy folly and conceit: nay, we go so far as to envy whatever confers distinction or notoriety, even vice and infamy.

A hundred years after de Tocqueville, who will be discussed in the chapter on politics, his fellow national, Eugene Raiga,[5] published *L'Envie: Son role social*. In 1933, when silence had already fallen on this topic in Western literature, Raiga's work, the first nonfiction book on our subject, appeared in French but was never translated into English except orally for me by my friend. Patton, who will be discussed, classifies and ranks Raiga with nineteenth-century "classical sociologists".

Raiga defines envy as "extreme emotion that suffers at the well-being of others". His phrase "social capillarity" implies that envy induces persons to elevate their social status. He spent a chapter on how the mother envies the father for being rewarded on his return from work by having the children jump all over him, after not seeing him all day, while she has been slaving over a hot stove and scrubbing floors for the family while the children ignore and disobey her. At the same time the father is likely to be envying the mother for not having to put up with the "slings and arrows of outrageous fortune" at work, where he must watch every word because in those days he could be fired on the whim of the boss, while the entire responsibility for food, clothing, and shelter for the family rests on him. If we could have our way, we would all like to have the benefits we already take for granted plus those we see others enjoying.

As his subtitle suggests, Raiga considers his work a "social botanical", implying that his classification of envy parallels Linnaeus' classification of plants and animals. He also relates envy to principles of equality and justice. Raiga's chapters are devoted to many personal and social situations in which envy abounds, such as the family, friends, small towns, big cities, lawyers, medical doctors and surgeons, *"petits fonctionnaires"*, literary persons and artists (painters, sculptors, musicians), critics, scientists, the military, political, government, professions, the church, and international.

Raiga cites a pattern in business and professional circles that I have also seen: a situation in which a leader envies the superior attributes of a member under him, thereby becoming conflicted between suppressing the underling's contributions out of envy or promoting them to bring credit to the entire group, including himself.

Writing in the interbellum of the two World Wars, when French society was organized along much more rigid class lines than America was then or France is now, Raiga agreed with de Tocqueville's observation a century earlier that seems counterintuitive to us, that a society with a stratified class system, like their own France, has less envy across class lines than a "classless" society with fluidity and greater opportunity to rise and fall, as in America, in both de Tocqueville's time and Raiga's. Raiga would paraphrase a working-class man in France as accepting, "I am the son of a shoemaker, so I'll be a shoemaker like my father. That's the way it is."

Like other observers, Raiga saw envy primarily between those close to each other, geographically and socially in family, work, or neighborhood, not, as we might expect, the poor for the very rich, servants for masters, or the landless for those born to prosperity.

Raiga takes issue with Descartes' belief that we envy only those worthy of their advantage; those unworthy excite only anger over the unfairness in the distribution of good things. As I have mentioned earlier, Raiga calls the reaction to both types of "envy", the former "l'envie vulgaire" (or "everyday envy") and the latter "l'envie d'indignation" (or "envy of outrage", i.e., over injustice). "Common envy" is the simple recognition that someone else has the advantage, and her superiority entails our inferiority. ("I'll never be able to beat her at tennis.") This kind of envy may inspire admiration and, perhaps, emulation. It is easier to shrug off and live with, and, wisely, to work to eliminate. The "envy of indignation" is a reaction to someone's undeserved advantage. ("She got that promotion on her back.") Either kind may include envy by proxy. ("My child is as good as hers or better and should have been given that part.") These two kinds of envy are easy to distinguish at the extremes, but in real life usually blurred in the middle.

Raiga believes that any "weakness" predisposed to envy, including feebleminded parents, depression, alcoholism, obesity, prolonged breastfeeding, female disorders, and infection (his book came out before even sulfonamides were available for treatment, and I presume he meant chronic infection, like tuberculosis, which was rampant).

He notes that the other's superiority proclaims our inferiority, and "nothing is so noxious to the happiness of man as this vice". "Envy exists," says Raiga, "in a secret hiding place."

Raiga listed a number of ways we deal with envy: pretending not to notice the advantage, joking [6], belittling, irony, malice, dissimulation, posture of indifference and/or disdain, conspiracy of silence, teasing, calumny, schadenfreude, all the way up to murder.

Raiga cites historic figures, mostly French, who admitted to envy and how they dealt with it. When Meyerbeer and Rossini were rivals, Meyerbeer enlisted (perhaps paid) friends or others to sleep ostensibly (snore loudly) through performances of Rossini's work. I am told that this strategy was not uncommon at that time, i.e., not limited to Meyerbeer.

Voltaire admitted his envy of Harvey for his discovery of the circulation of blood a century earlier, even though Voltaire was not a scientist and in no way working on problems of that kind. Raiga distinguishes two classes of scientists: true scientific "savants", or those with "love of truth" and "passion for research", and scientists competitive for priority, recognition, and fame. Most share both features. My late husband, a man at the low end of tendency to envy, would admit, at dinner, the thrill of being the first in the world to know something he had just demonstrated. He also helped me, a latecomer to science, to learn to write for scientific journals, and to identify good ideas for papers and good ways to develop them.

French symbolism portrays envy as a "toad spitting venom" by persons weak in biology [although I have recently learned from a television program that the cane frog in Florida can actually kill a pet dog by projection of venom, which was unknown when the French devised their symbol].

In his summary, Raiga anticipated Schoeck's point to the effect that there is a place in society for both everyday personal envy and envy of indignation, for the stimulus it provides for improvement of the individual and the body social. But he advises us, when we are successful, to watch our step as on a tightrope because of the possibility of envy by others following in the train of our advantage. We should comport ourselves with "admirable elegance".

His summary is worth quoting: "All the manifestations of envy that have been the object of inquiry in the preceding chapters can be summarized in a few words:

These are no more than the revolt of the conquered against the victorious, of the weak against the strong, the less endowed against the better endowed, the poor against the rich, the humble against the arrogant, various reactions, weak or strong, repressed or expressed violently, according to circumstances, the temperaments, and the characters.

All the conditions that incite envy provoke in their turn consternations, or, if one prefers, conflicts between the affected persons and, by repercussion, within the families and within society. One must be on constant guard against its deleterious effects; one fears them. The blows do not fall on empty air. They have repercussions, that is to say, on even those who are attempting to survive in society. Envy, by that fact, has a role in society.

Angus Wilson contributed a chapter on envy to a collection titled *The Seven Deadly Sins*, published in 1962, with foreword by Ian Fleming, and special introduction by Raymond Mortimer.

Both Mortimer and Fleming comment on the "seven deadly" as a group. Mortimer would preserve the term "sin" for acts against God (such as heresy or lack of faith) but use the term "wrong" for those against our fellow man or ourselves. Instead of "deadly" or "capital" Mortimer's "wrongs" are distinguished not by their gravity but by their power to generate other sins. They are, in fact, evil states of mind that tempt us into evil acts. Consider the behavior that wrath or greed or lust, not to mention envy, induces in us. But he asks, "Where would great literature be without the seven?"

Fleming offers a set of seven "new deadlies": Avarice (how is this different from Greed?), Cruelty, Snobbery, Hypocrisy, Self-righteousness, Moral Cowardice, and Malice. In contrast to the old set (which were forgiven in Dante's *Purgatorio*), the new ones represent to Fleming a passport to hell, by which he means an earthly hell. Fleming would add an eighth: being a Bore.

Wilson called envy "an affliction, not a sin, and worst among writers", an assertion we explored in my chapter on authors. He gives us a special insight into envy among ambitious British citizens of the sixties, who were expected, in the public school demand for "good sportsmanship", to jump over the net and congratulate the winner, "jolly good", rather than to be honest and drop the matter. He attributes problems stemming from envy to the unforgiving rat race up the ladder of the British examination system,[7] by which one's entire career and irrevocable status were determined by a score on a particular examination, and the successful rival's name was inescapable for life.

Wilson observed that envy would be raised to a power when the successful would elegantly brag about not having studied for the test. The doomed losers associate with one another throughout life, having been unmercifully excluded from the winners' circle by being below a cutoff on one examination.

Wilson contends that only in the event of an unforeseen and completely unpredictable "lucky break" will the loser ever be released from the social circle of the envious, from the strangling envy of which he cannot free himself.

When one's envy is all-consuming, says Wilson, that person wants to become a revolutionary and overthrow the old order; by contrast, visionaries want to change to improve the system. Thus envy is a motive force in social movement, but imitative, not creative or original.

Another observation of Wilson's is that the envious feel themselves more "interesting" and therefore "exist on their potential", not on their accomplishments. They consider themselves not who they are but who they want to be.

In British novels, underprivileged young women are shown as paralyzed by envy, unable to assert claims for recognition.

Wilson notes that in conversation, frequently his associates spew out barefaced anti-American sentiments based on envy, instead of legitimate grievances, and "one feels ashamed for the emotion that the speaker is betraying".

"Envy wears an uglier face than lust's bloodshot eyes, or gluttony's paunch, or pride's camel nose, or avarice's thin lips." "Envy is impotent, numbed with fear, yet never lessening in its appetite; and it knows no gratification save self-torment. It has the ugliness of a trapped rat that has gnawed its own foot in an effort to escape." [Is this ugly or does it evoke our sympathy as a last-ditch effort at survival?]

In the late sixties Schoeck, an Austrian sociologist, wrote a massive compendium on envy, which was soon translated into English. His interest was mainly in the social aspects of envy, and they will be addressed in our chapter on politics.

The July 1974 issue of *Harper's* magazine contained an essay entitled "Hidden Envy: The Last Dirty Little Secret", the best subtitle I have encountered, by George P. Elliott. His article had the very effect on me that Raiga's book had on my French translator: it hit me between the eyes and made me recognize for the first time the nature of my hitherto semi-buried painful attacks. This issue had never come to my attention despite my having undergone a classic psychoanalysis, which was no doubt my fault because I never was good at free-associating. Elliott's article was the first trigger that set me on the path of collecting ideas for this book project.

In three and a half pages of pure gold text, Elliott said the same things that Bacon, Schopenhauer, Nietzsche, Raiga, and other towering figures have brought to our attention, and he said it very well.[8] I have already quoted Elliott's first paragraph about advantages we envy.[9]

He says further: "When your good becomes my evil, and your

evil my good, I am so ugly I can hardly bear to look at myself."
I recommend this entire article.

In his book, *The Seven Deadly Sins Today,* i.e., 1978, Fairlie, a
clergyman, in his chapter "Invidia" [Latin for "envy", from which we
get "invidious"], observes how we have come to believe we have a
right to be, have, and enjoy everything anyone else is, has, or enjoys.
Without talent or training we can splash paint around and be an
artist by right of equality. Similarly, we can write as fast as we can
move our fingers, call the result "poetry", and by right be a poet.
"If we are not inclined to the rigors of an academic discipline, we
will destroy the standards of that discipline and pass ourselves off
as graduates. If we cannot or will not read, we will say that 'linear
thought' is now irrelevant and so dispense with reading." Fairlie
finds that "The collapse of the professions [he cites physicians and
university professors] has been largely the result of the insinuation
of the spirit of Envy into them." I agree with the idea of deterioration if not collapse of these professions, but my explanation rests
on economics, greed, and especially politics.
Fairlie stresses:

> We are giving the name of art to what is not art, of poetry
> to what is not poetry, of education to what is not educa-
> tion, of achievement to what is not achievement, of moral-
> ity to what is not morality, and of love to what is not love.
> We trivialize our concepts of them all, to make it seem as
> if we may all attain them. None of us is wholly exempt from
> the corruption.

He comments that envy makes us who are mediocre unable
to recognize that that does not make us failures, but also, unfortunately, unable to bestow ungrudging admiration on others for

areas where they excel without diminishing ourselves. For heroes we have substituted celebrities, who are admired not for talent, virtue, etc., but for their income.

One reason for this recent burgeoning of envy Fairlie lays at the door of our capitalist system, for being envy-producing out of its own drive for profit.

> Few socialist tracts are as *implicitly* and *insidiously* egalitarian as an advertisement on television; and it is an egalitarianism that, since it has no other moral or philosophical basis, must make unequals believe that they are equal in those very respects in which they are ineluctably unequal. This is one of the paradoxes of our societies: for the purposes of the economic system on which they are founded, and to that extent only, the mass market is necessarily a democratic market.
>
> The curse of the economic system, to conservatives no less than to its critics, is that it will sell anything to anyone, and it will sell any values as well as any commodities. It is commerce that sells as art what is not art, as books what are not books, as music what is not music, as morality what is not morality, as happiness what is not happiness, even as Christmas what is not Christmas. Wherever a quick buck is to be made, it will be there like a shot, and damn the consequences to society. Once licensed by a foolishly expanded interpretation of the First Amendment, commerce is not then fastidious in the retailing of pornography. As may be seen any night on television, morally and intellectually and aesthetically, its values are determined by its need for profit.

Citing what Irving Kristol calls the "new class", i.e., the *literati* of various kinds of untutored and undirected intelligence, Fairlie blames not only the individuals Kristol so designates but the envy-provoking society as causative of this "new class":

These are envious people—teachers, writers, journalists, publicists, broadcasters, dependents on foundations, dependents on grants, art students, artists, ministers, physicists, actors, directors, filmmakers—but they have been bred by Envy. For them as for others, our societies have supplied no motive for simply doing what they do well, but only the prod of envy.

In 1992, Solomon Schimmel published a scholarly analysis of how the great Western religious traditions have evaluated sin (or vice) and virtue, in his *The Seven Deadly Sins: Jewish, Christian, and Classical Reflections on Human Nature.* Refuting the notion that sin and virtue are outmoded, obsolete, and counterproductive ways of looking at human behavior, and noting that the myriad self-help groups springing up like mushrooms belie the help often sought in vain in traditional psychotherapy, Schimmel contends that the classical seven are alive, more deadly than ever, and represent excesses of normal drives (e.g., gluttony is perversion of normal appetite; lust is excessive sexual drive, etc.). Envy on the international scene leads to terrorism. The religious traditions agree that true happiness depends on virtue, which rests on impulse control.[10]

Schimmel cites St. Basil, who makes a perceptive comment about the loneliness of envy: "The worst feature of this malady, however, is that its victim cannot reveal it to anyone, but he hangs his head and is mute ... not choosing to reveal these sentiments, he confines in the depths of his soul this disease which is gnawing at his vitals and consuming them." This is the torture to which Andrei Rublev admitted when asking to be reinstated in the monastery.

This author devotes a chapter to each of the seven. While other authors have offered few specific or practical guides to help in struggling against this powerful adversary, other than to replace it with love and/or humility, Schimmel gives examples from his rabbinical counseling, such as helping a man who envies his neighbor for his sexy wife. ("She may not be as great in bed as you imagine; beautiful women are often narcissistic.") His distinctive contribution is his specific and helpful ways to combat envy, in the form of a new Ten Commandments. These are saved for my coping chapter.

Au and Cannon's *Urgings of the Heart* is written from a Jungian (the shadow) and Christian (the only unlimited thing is God's love) perspective. Their chapter "Envy: A Longing for Wholeness" states that envy is "intrinsically related to goodness...a corresponding despair of attaining it." But when hope for this advantage is lacking, we gradually come to assume the victim role, becoming angry and resentful. They cite many "defenses" to avoid recognition of envy, all destructive, including hatred and withdrawal.

"The experience of being limited, of being imperfect and incomplete, is intolerable to the envious, who feel that they have nothing because they do not have everything." As several others also have pointed out, one venue that often brings out envy is the college reunion with its inevitable comparison with everyone else's success or lack thereof.

Unlike most earlier authors, these stress as counterbalances to envy, not love but gratitude (like Klein and Berke, among others). "Gratitude and envy are mutually exclusive." Like others who cite envy as an opportunity for reassessment and redirection, these authors call envy "a valuable message that should be heeded. Envy can be a catalyst for transformation.

"When gratitude becomes our way of life, we make peace with our envy, not excusing or ignoring it, but acknowledging it as part [in the 'shadow'] of ourselves." Aware of our envy, we can reclaim our own lost potential.

✳

In 1999 Robert C. Solomon, a professor of business and ethics, edited *Wicked Pleasures: Meditations on the Seven "Deadly Sins"*, with contributions by each of seven authors.

Solomon, like others, considers "deadly" a misnomer for "capital", which he interprets to mean "supporting", like the columns of an edifice. He calls the seven the "very stuff of gossip and sitcoms", an exaggeration of normal drives, undermining by their "apparent insidiousness, subversiveness, undeniable ordinariness". They are not, says Solomon, related to damnation but to their unattractiveness, i.e., unappealing appearance, inability to attract a mate, poor health, and shortened life span. They "give us each the face that we deserve, the grimace of envy, the scowl of anger, the leer of lust, the puffy arrogance of pride, the droopiness of sloth, the hungry eyes and slight drool of greed and gluttony." Thus Solomon maintains that these are not so much sins as character flaws creating unhappiness and leading to mental and physical disorders.

In Solomon's collection, Don Herzog contributes his essay, replete with many literary examples and quotations, with the subtitle that causes us to wince, but, strangely, is not greatly pursued in the piece: "Envy: Poisoning the Banquet They Cannot Taste".[11] Herzog does cite the anecdote in Olesha's *Envy* in which the protagonist, as an early adolescent boy, tries to destroy in a little girl what would be completely inappropriate for himself.

After humorously pretending that some (including himself) are without envy, Herzog admits that this is impossible by reminding us that "To be a self, to have an identity, is already to have a story about where you stand in all kinds of pecking orders." On this incessant comparison rests envy. "Observation of others [inevitable comparison] dooms one to envy."

He begins:

> Insidious gnawing envy, the vampire vice: it creeps up
> unawares, surprises us, grabs us and sucks up our cheerful
> energy, our very willingness to get out of bed and perform

the day's allotted chores. Envy has been nominated—Lord knows it isn't alone, but the case is perfectly plausible—as not just the worst vice, but the most insistent, along perhaps with lust, relentlessly preying on our consciousness, preoccupying us during the day, making us toss and turn when we seek sweet repose, even torturing us in our dreams. Worse, it looks more or less coextensive with social life itself: or at least there are plausible, even powerful reasons to suspect it's inevitable.

Herzog quotes Hume on envy: "['T]is not the great disproportion betwixt yourself and another which produces it [envy]; but on the contrary, our proximity." He summarizes: "Rough equality enables the possibility of envy." The worker on the assembly line may envy the foreman, not the CEO.

He also addresses the egalitarian issue: "The closer people become, the more salient otherwise imperceptible differences become.... [A lot of free time to observe one another, the quality of the smile of the superior, etc.]... The social organization of devoting oneself to serving the divine is a breeding ground for one of the deadly sins.... The quintessential home of egalitarian envy isn't the Soviet Union or Sweden's social welfare state; it's the priory." [We shall later see another example of envy specific to a religious setting.]

Herzog classifies three reactions to envy. The first, emulation, is laudable, when the attitude is "I can get it too." However, Herzog suggests that sometimes the motive for emulation is base, i.e., the other's advantage is seen as an affront to be revenged. Emulation can be a way to demonstrate disdain and a put-down for the other's modest advantage that he has struggled so hard to achieve. I have apparently been spared observing or perhaps recognizing any real-life examples of such contemptible behavior.

Herzog combines schadenfreude and spite [he uses "spite" to mean hostile acting out] as a single, the second, way of reacting to envy.[12] His definition of schadenfreude is grief over the other's advantage combined with a fantasy of ill fortune befalling the favored one (the converse of joy over his actual misfortune). I would not combine this with spite. My understanding of schadenfreude has no necessary connection to envy, just pleasure in the misfortune of others, such as the pleasure some persons take when they hear about the destruction and death wrought by hurricanes and tsunamis. A friend from many years ago was always fascinated by train wrecks and seemed to collect them.

Herzog's third "reaction to envy" is "sour grapes" or downgrading the value of the advantage. I agree that taking an attitude such as "a theatrical career isn't so great after all" is a sour-grapes reaction by someone who couldn't make it in the theater (for many reasons not necessarily lack of theatrical talent). But Herzog finds this response in those, specifically, who compare themselves to others who, when faced with life-important decisions, have in the past made the better choice and the other is left with a poor one, in one case, "I'll have a family instead" and lived to be disappointed with that choice—and envy the other with the better outcome.[13] Here again, I disagree because I find that the person's envy does not necessarily involve any downgrading of the advantage at all, just dissatisfaction with the relative advantage. A woman I knew turned down dates with a man shorter than herself, but, having married the towering alcoholic football star, lived to see the short man become a physician and travel widely with his wife, half a head taller than her husband. This woman recognized belatedly the wife's superior criteria but never said the other woman's choice was bad after all. Far from it.

Herzog uses the terms "spite" for hostile acting out and "resentment" for passive, smoldering grudge, and both as integral to envy, whereas I see them both as possible reactions, but not as necessary components.

He raises a frequently asked question about envy: which is worse, resenting the rival who deserves her success or the one who enjoys success he never earned? (Adam Smith says envy is felt for those deserving, but Aristotle finds it aimed at the undeserving.) Whereas I concur with Aristotle, Herzog comes in on the side of Smith, adding that if society were 100% just and someone else got the advantage you craved, who would there be to blame? When someone deserved and got something you wanted but deserved less, that would "fester" and attack you right in the self-esteem. The envy I have noted occurred when I thought the persons I envied did not deserve the advantage, or at least no more than I did. If I had had that exact experience of believing the other deserved the advantage more than I did, I might have agreed that envying the deserving person is worse. Excessive hubris may blind me to the relative deserts of my rival and myself. Probably which configuration of envy is more trenchant depends on the person and the circumstances.

Herzog disputes going as far as Schoeck on the subject of envy in the struggle for equality: "A gargantuan and insanely repetitive conservative chorus since Tocqueville has assured us that the demand for equality, for democracy, is nothing but an expression of base envy." He observes that "liberals", who are always pushing for distributing wealth to the "have-nots", have nothing to envy, and therefore Schoeck's argument is specious. My reading of Schoeck is that Herzog has made two errors. One is that the "liberals'" fear or discomfort is not over envying (they have little to envy) but for *being* envied, similar to Dawn Powell's "consciousness of privilege" or my discomfort over opportunity. The second is that while Schoeck is aware that most sociologists, anthropologists, etc., do not accept his belief in this regard and recognize in themselves only the wish to be "fair", he specifically denied the charge that he blames "everything" on envy. He insists, however, that we do not recognize how much of our behavior results from envy, and, in fact, necessarily so, for the progress of civilization.

Herzog has two bits of advice for us who recognize our own envy. First, beware of "positional goods", or advantages that depend on having something more than someone else's with the result that their gain becomes my loss. These are intangibles, according to Herzog, successes like prizes and awards, and when they happen to someone else, they ignite the loser's envy. The problem is that tangibles can be positional too. A competitor's salary increase can make mine, with which I was hitherto perfectly satisfied, mean by comparison. His second advice is a warning to eschew the Christian suggestion of humility in favor of reasonable pride (I go along with this), since too much humility must come at the cost of self-esteem, and to adjust our standards to judging ourselves and others (we are all judgmental and rightly so) according to some kind of equilibrium between talents and use thereof, commending those who do the most with what they were given. (Kant wrote in his work on morality that the "worst sin of all" is to neglect or abuse our gifts.)

In a short essay posted on the Internet, Michael J. Hurd listed three mistaken assumptions that fuel envy: (1) the belief that one person's gain is another's loss; (2) the belief that all persons are equal; and (3) the belief that a person's destiny is outside his own hands.

Hurd believes that it is not true that another's gains are our losses. However, with this one I take exception. Many times the other's gain is truly the envier's loss, especially in the "positional goods" that Herzog discussed.

In this book we have commented on the obvious differences between individuals, and Hurd reminds us not to confuse our individuality with *political* equality, which, though imperfect in our society, is our ideal and our goal.

Though acknowledging the many givens in any person's life, Hurd stresses how we all have the ability to think about our situation, make decisions and plans, and alter our environment.

He believes that a correct take on these erroneous beliefs goes a long way toward relieving envy, and he advises parents to take care to avoid passing the wrong assumptions on to their children. ("We are all different: you have some talents that others don't; and they have some that you don't. We must all do the best we can with what we have.")

We walk a fine line, however, between reinforcing a realistic interpretation of talents and abilities in our children and promoting a false image of their potential when we try to ensure their self-esteem. Even in the earliest years we must all earn our own self-esteem by effort, and that can be reinforced from the outside by recognition of accomplishment, even the accomplishment of effort. Praise and encouragement should place self-esteem on a realistic basis. "You tried very hard, and next time you'll probably be better at it."

Hurd believes further (and I concur) that envy is the most under-diagnosed of psychologic problems, and therapists, themselves often envious, may reinforce their patients' false beliefs.

Bob Sorge, a Protestant clergyman, in 2003 published a book entitled *Envy: The Enemy Within*. He cites two reasons for writing the book: (1) "The power of envy is broken when it is confessed", as he does in his book, and in this way he found writing it a form of therapy (as I did with mine), and (2) he wants readers to know he's not "preaching" at them but a fellow envier, i.e., "not speaking from the aloof position of someone who is beyond envy's tentacles". His first awareness of his problem with envy came when he noticed his intense competitiveness going back to childhood.

He draws attention to many more examples of envy in the Old Testament than I do.

He rather wittily identified envy in the title of chapter one as "The Most Common Problem That Nobody Has". When he would inquire, he would invariably get the standard response. "Envy? Not a problem for me, as best I can tell." They didn't know how truly they spoke. He would ask his parishioners to read his book anyway.

Given his profession, he observed envy between ministers and between parishioners. "How large a congregation do you have?" "How fast is it growing?" "We're building a new church." Within the congregation, the most jockeying for position comes from the musical performers, who are often disgruntled when someone else is selected for solo parts.

Sorge refers to Foster's anthropologic concept of "Limited Good", cited in my anthropologic addendum. He contrasts it to Christianity's unlimited supply of love.

He considers one of the best ways to deal with envy is simply to admit its presence. I would agree that that must at least be first, but the hard part comes next.

He urges us to be realistic about our strengths and weaknesses, and to enjoy others' talents that we lack. Like others, he is concerned with the spoken and unspoken messages parents convey, and he would like to see parents make a point to teach their children to enjoy each other's talents that they lack and to do the best they can with what they have.

Joseph Epstein's *Envy* appeared in 2003, as one book in a series of seven, each based on a lecture at the New York Public Library. His book contains many funny cartoons and abundant references to the works of others. I was attracted to his book by the good review it received in our newspaper.

As advantages for us to envy, Epstein indicated that "wealth, beauty, power, talent and skill, knowledge and wisdom, and extraordinary good luck come close to completing the list." F. Scott Fitzgerald is reported to have acknowledged that while he lacked the two most important advantages, strong animal magnetism and wealth, he had the next two, good looks and intelligence. Except for beauty, Epstein's many examples lack advantages that are specifically female, just as my book shows a dearth of male examples, but a spate of female instances. Nowhere in Epstein's or anyone else's list have I seen self-esteem, contentment, and a sense of humor, which I would include. Epstein himself is not lacking in humor. And he notes, as have we all, that "sometimes the distinction between schadenfreude and justice hunger is a tough call".

Epstein identifies the core features of others' observations on envy: Melanie Klein's stand that envy is insatiable; the Marxists' impossible promise to the proletariat to put an end to all the conditions making envy possible. Epstein calls greed the sin of capitalism, envy the sin of socialism. He notes that the advertising industry is "a vast envy-creating machine". And he, others, and I agree that envy is most prominent in pursuits of art and the intellect.

Envy of the old for the young includes not only their health, vigor, and libido, that is, issues that cut across both sexes and all stations in life, and includes, for the creative and talented, the sorrow and regret we invariably feel, as we age, for not having made more of our life, as we observe in the young "their chance still to write an impressive record on the many days of life remaining to them".

A unique contribution to the subject of envy by Epstein is his belief that anti-Semitism is fueled by envy: envy of the disproportionate representation of the professions in the Diaspora, and envy of Jews' cohesive belongingness.

As I am completing my book, the first chapter of Thomas Patton's *ILL WILL: On Matters of Envy, Resentment, and Schadenfreude* appeared on the author's website and previews the rest of his book. The book itself is not in print, but the author offers to send chapters to interested readers.

Patton expounds on the universality of envy and its role in driving our political and economic systems. "Envy powers our appetites and advertising fuels envy." "Notwithstanding the passion of apologists for communism and capitalism, envy is the biosocial dynamism that drives both systems."

He cites one of my favorite authors, Neil Postman, who, back in the sixties, recommended a required high school course in "crap detection". (This is reminiscent of a chapter on "propaganda analysis" my husband wrote for his English professor's book.) Needless to say, Postman[14] was ignored, as was Marshall McLuhan, and advertisers had nothing to fear.

As a counterpoise to envy, Patton recommends a massive revamping of our education system, to what would certainly enrich life for those who pursued it: orientation to lifelong coordinated education and meaningful work. "In my mind, American education must proceed from an entirely different concept, one that expresses the unity of life-long learning and authentic work. ... We can begin by considering both work and education as the same life-spanning activity."[15]

Patton concludes: "Ordinarily, people are not aware of their envy, neither its intensity, its vast dominion in daily life, nor its implications for good and evil. To become cognizant of one's own envy and its ruinous effects can liberate dormant creative energies that are experienced as a spiritual rebirth, as a new, powerful, adequate identity. So much needless time and effort go into camouflaging our resentment; so much pain and humiliation reward our efforts. When we begin to realize the immensity of our secret envy it becomes imperative we put it to rest."

Due in part to the millennia-long non-recognition of women, women's names do not appear in the envy literature apart from psychoanalytic literature, recent fiction, and Joan Frank's honest demonstration of her own struggle with envy, explored in my chapter on authors' envy. For this reason, because of being female myself, and the fact that most of my patients (and friends) were and are female, my exposure has been slanted toward envy as experienced by women. One large area for this we have already seen in "Reproductive Envy".

Notes

1. This is the current euphemism for "easy to read".

2. "Erasmus" is a play on one of the Greek family of words for "love".

3. As a young woman I was strolling through the cathedral in Basle and literally stumbled on Erasmus's grave. Therefore I considered him Swiss until we read him in Great Books, where I learned that he was Dutch. Later yet I pursued the fascinating novel surrounding his life, Charles Reade's *The Cloister and the Hearth,* which portrays Renaissance life in colorful fashion. It had been recommended by my high school English teacher and recalled her maxim: "History records, but fiction vivifies."

4. This enormous compendium of beliefs by classical writers and Burton himself on all aspects of psychology, has been called by Orlan "the greatest medical treatise written by a layman".

5. Raiga had already written in a variety of fields, including the economics of war, diplomacy, and public administration. We have not found reference to him after *L'Envie,* and, his publishing house sounding Jewish, Raiga himself may have suffered a Jewish fate in World War II.

6. A "light" jokester, says Raiga, makes fun of himself too, but not an envious one.

7. I understand the system has now softened to some extent. But suppose an adolescent girl had to take such a test while suffering from dysmenorrhea. A premed student I dated in college failed for some reason to take his Graduate Record Examination (predecessor of the MCAT) and therefore never went to medical school. Any no-second-chance system is cruel.

8. I envy Elliott his rhetoric.

9. He gives us a chance to laugh at what others envy—"new sneakers, ... a Stutz Bearcat", and my book gives others, among other things, a chance to laugh at some of the things I envy—wanting to find my own trilobites.

10. My contention is similar, that happiness cannot be chased and tackled but will sometimes, when we are lucky, catch us while we are doing something worthwhile.

11. That title, which is reminiscent of Melanie Klein's "wish to spoil" as integral to envy, is taken from Dr. Johnson. "Most of the misery which the defamation of blameless actions, or the obstruction of honest endeavours brings upon the world, is inflicted by men that propose no advantage to themselves but the satisfaction of poisoning the banquet which they cannot taste, and blasting the harvest which they have no right to reap."

12. Although I would agree that "spite" is the wish to harm someone, it is not necessarily part of the envy configuration, nor is it necessarily acted upon.

13. Herzog makes interesting comments on choice: "Every time we make a choice, we renounce indefinitely many other possibilities." "[S]culpting one's life means murdering thousands of counter-factual selves one could have become but has chosen not to." The large choices—mate, career—are obvious, but, according to one school of philosophy, every possible alternative occurs in another multiverse. If so I am a lawyer somewhere else. It boggles the mind.

14. Postman once wrote to me, "Can you explain how you seem to be the only person who understands/agrees with me?"

15. I have evolved my own version of Patton's suggestion: attendance at a Great Books Discussion Group that exposed us as lifelong students to the seminal literary works of Western civilization, along with attending conferences and congresses as all physicians wish to do and are required to do, to keep abreast of the extreme changes in psychiatry over the years of my career.

Chapter 13

Envy As Interpreted by Psychiatrists, Freudian Psychoanalysts, and Experimental Psychologists

G iven the foregoing, one would expect envy to be a fertile field for psychologists, psychiatrists, and psychoanalysts. I was therefore surprised to learn that while envy had been of interest until early in the twentieth century to other disciplines (sociology, anthropology), it was not of particular interest to psychiatrists during the first half of the twentieth century, w hen psychiatric study and writing were taking their place in modern medical literature. Even in the second half of the twentieth century, as a student and resident and later as a psychiatrist practicing psychotherapy, where feelings of a negative nature of all kinds are discussed with a view to helping the patient understand and handle them better, I noticed in retrospect that envy had come up so rarely that I remembered the specific instances. By the mid-twentieth century the topic attracted attention by the psychoanalyst Melanie Klein and her followers, to be discussed presently, in chronologic sequence.

The early psychiatrists, or "alienists" as they were called, can be credited with recognizing persons with psychiatric disorders as members of the human family,[1] though mentally ill, and after centuries of abuse and cruelty, began treating them humanely with compassion and good diet, even though they needed to be confined and sometimes restrained to avoid self-harm. Charcot ran his clinic at the Salpetrière in Paris, famous for giving paper knives to women with "grande hysterie"—fits of total body flailing and paralysis—but their rational selves knew that the weapons were fake. Observing these and returning to Vienna, Freud pursued his search for the unconscious and conflicts called "neurotic".

Envy never occupied a prominent place in Freud's thinking, although he anticipated a connection recognized much later when he wrote: "The demand for justice is a modification of envy." He believed envy to be behind *esprit de corps*, as a device to assure that peers would have little reason to envy one another because they could demand the same treatment for all, while all deferred equally to the leader. "The demand for equality is the root of social conscience." This *esprit de corps* concept was probably more prominent in Europe in Freud's time than it is now in Europe or ever was in the New World.

The most prominent place of envy in Freud's theoretical constructs is his much-touted "penis envy", which he felt to be unconquerable in women.

Appleby (and others) have reminded us that Freud believed envy to be the overarching feature explaining women's psychology. And not just any envy, but envy of men's definitive organ. Freud has been mocked for his "blind spot" regarding women. But if we hold the penis to be symbolic of the sociologic advantages men are given without necessarily earning them—status, influence, freedom, preference at work—the idea is hard to dispute.

Envy also surfaces in Freud's case study known as "The Rat Man". Note his formulation, which includes fear of the malignant power of one's own envy:

> The patient had a charming little niece of whom he was very fond. One day this idea came into his head: "If you indulge in intercourse, something will happen to Ella" (i.e.,

she will die). When the omissions have been made good, we have: "Every time you copulate, even with a stranger, you will not be able to avoid the reflection that in your married life sexual intercourse can never bring you a child (on account of the lady's sterility). This will grieve you so much that you will become envious of your sister on account of little Ella, and you will grudge her the child. These envious impulses will inevitably lead to the child's death."

Freud's follower Abraham considered envy as involving two persons and setting the stage for jealousy. He identified a feeling of deficiency compared to another (equated with wounded narcissism), resulting in envy (consisting of spiteful impulses, and likely to result in acting without thought of consequences), and often leading to jealousy. He dated envy to the oral phase of life, and considered generosity and magnanimity its opposites. But he equated envy with hostility associated with anyone's attempt to deprive the envier of what he possesses or thinks he possesses, for which we now reserve the term "jealousy".

Three other types of envy of anatomic parts and physiology follow Freud's "penis envy". Jones introduced the concept of "birth-giving envy", while Boehm called it "womb envy" (both found in little boys), and later the Freudian psychoanalyst Melanie Klein devoted the latter part of her lifetime to study of "envy of the breast" (in infants of both sexes), as we shall review later.

Alfred Adler,[2] a follower of Freud's, left Freud's organization because of a disagreement over the role of "drives" (Freud) versus "environment" (Adler) as critical in psychologic development. A third of Freud's supporters followed Adler. His theoretical construct comes close to our take on envy, even though the word "envy" is rarely used in his work. He begins with the undeniable observation that we all begin weak, helpless, and dependent on others for life support. (Even Darwin found mankind, in nature, a "weak being" relative to many other newborn animals much better able to fend for themselves.) Adler believed that the child, recognizing himself as weak, feels inferior, cannot bear it, and strives to remedy this situation and become "superior".[3] "The level of psychologic adjustment is to be found in feelings of inferiority." Adler's term "inferiority complex" has entered the language.

Unlike Freud, who believed that "drives" are, in fact, the driving force in behavior, Adler sees the newborn with certain biologic givens on one side, and on the other, whatever the environment is bombarding him with. (Adler's dispute with Freud was over Adler's insistence on the importance of the fact that we are all "socially embedded".) In between, and working with his heredity and his environment is the newborn, using his own creativity. The infant is not like a filing cabinet into which the environment dumps data; rather, Adler's position is more like "soft determinism" and the biologic and environmental givens are only possibilities with which we work. "The growing infant takes into account all the impressions he receives, those from his own body and those from the environment, and under their influence creatively forms his opinion of himself and the world, together with his idea of his individual [dimly envisioned] goal of success." By the latter, Adler does not mean, e.g., "to become a teacher" but either positive ways to behave so as to benefit others as well as himself, or various negative possibilities such as "always to get others to do everything for me". (This is a possibility, for example, when a child discovers that his pampering mother always jumps at his slightest whimper.) The latter types of life goals that do not aim at the common weal, Adler maintains, are what lead to neurosis. The important thing is what the child does with what he inherited, and Adler believes this is shaped by age five[4] into his "life style" (long before that expression came into popular use). Yet the individual has a high capacity for self-repair and selectivity.

All behavior, Adler contends, is shaped by the individual's intended rise to "superiority", involving a striving for "power and dominance", which promotes security and self-esteem. The growing child is constantly "gauging and balancing" the advantages of others. Some consequences include ambition, competition, and rivalry, which give rise to avarice, envy, overcompensation, and belligerence. "All human activity moves from a felt minus situation to a plus situation, from a feeling of inferiority toward superiority." "Inferiority feelings are not in themselves abnormal. They are the cause of all improvements in the position of mankind. All our human culture is based on feelings of inferiority." These ideas are similar to Schoeck's, about envy driving progress, as will be discussed.

(In the early twentieth century a British professor, Stephen Potter, published several humorous books with "advice" about maintaining a relatively superior position. These became popular in our country by the 1950s and contain more than a grain of truth. He exaggerates and carries to an extreme many devices [he calls them "ploys" and "gambits"] to define our status as "one-up", since, as Potter points out, "If you're not one-up, you're one-down." His work introduced at least three words into the language—"lifemanship", "gamesmanship", and "one-upmanship". One example I remember at this distance is that, in a period when "all" British middle- and upper-class men belonged to clubs, Potter advised everyone to belong to two clubs as disparate as possible, such as a retired army officers' club and a poets' society, and to arrive at each dressed for the other.)

Adler's position is similar to Nietzsche's "will to power" and to Maslow's "self-actualization". Our translators and editors of Adler's work note that a number of so-called "neo-Freudians" hold beliefs that come closer to Adler's than to Freud's. They include Karen Horney, Eric Fromm, Frieda Fromm-Reichmann, Harry Stack Sullivan, and Franz Alexander.

Harry Stack Sullivan, a mid-twentieth-century psychiatrist, offers another explanation for the phenomenon of envy, which he defines as "an acute discomfort caused by discovering that somebody else has something that one feels one ought to have". Persons much at the mercy of envy, according to Sullivan, have learned to appraise themselves as unsatisfactory, inadequate human beings. This self-assessment may have been simple and direct: they may not have met parents' and teachers' expectations. These expectations may have been realistic relative to their natural gifts. Or parents may have held unrealistically high expectations relative to the child's natural gifts. In either case they conclude that they simply do not rate (similar to Adler's "inferiority complex"). Therefore the envious person experiences more than usual thwarting of life satisfactions. Thus such an envious person is happiest around others without particular evidence of success along the lines the envious person seeks. However the envious person rationalizes his lack, and he easily assumes that he would have whatever it is, if life were just. This ongoing dissatisfaction may be accompanied by unrestful sleep because such a person takes the day's unfinished business to bed. As he ages, according to Sullivan, he often develops hyper-tension. He may look for others who will agree that those who have the desired traits are no good and acquired them by foul means.

For reasons different from de Tocqueville's, Sullivan also believes that Americans are particularly prone to envy. With educational opportunities unparalleled in America, he suggested that wave after wave of immigration put the newcomers into the role of "targets of hostilities". This encouraged an upward mobility that precluded a more settled life with friendship and intimacy, as in Europe.[5]

Sullivan concludes by suggesting that competition and "morbid ambition" (as in sports and intellectual pursuits) is relatively juvenile, and is explained because the other fellow gets in the way, not by envy.

✳

By the mid-twentieth century Melanie Klein gave envy a central place in her constructs, in articles and one book, *Envy and Gratitude*. Her focus is the origin of envy in infancy and the infant's relationship to the mother's breast. Conflating her two half-definitions, we have "Envy is the angry feeling that another person possesses and enjoys something desirable—the envious impulse being to take it away or to spoil it...[and] implies the subject's relation to one person only." Her "wish to spoil" criterion makes her definition more stringent than Webster's [and our] "feeling of discontent and ill will because of another's advantages". But Klein also finds envy more basic than covetousness: "To look maliciously and spitefully, wanting to spoil something, is more integral than wanting to have." On the other hand, our "negative comparison" component is too advanced for the infant stage Klein analyzes. In her view, the only *sine qua non* for envy is the infant's realization that the breast is external. She identified it variously as the infant's innate "feeling" or "impulse", not a reaction to frustrating external events, but a "motivating force" (cf. Schoeck's reference to envy as another kind of motivating force, i.e., one that drives civilization). She did not call it "envy of the mother" but rather "envy of the feeding breast", thus relating it to primitive necessities of life and to the first collaboration of all of us. Thus envy results when the infant is evicted from Eden and required to work for a living.

Believing the capacity for both love and hate to be constitutional and of different intensities in different individuals, Klein asserts that the capacity to love makes gratitude possible, while the potential for hate gives rise to envy. Thus she found envy to be self-generated, innate, its source inherent in the child, not a result of the mother/child interaction, although varying from child to child in innate strength. Klein looked at the origin of envy in terms of her so-called "positions", the more primitive paranoid-schizoid position and the later depressive position. Some of her followers found that envy deriving from the earlier stage was the more entrenched and closer to psychotic. Klein notes also that later in life envy can be considered a conflict between the real and the ideal self, to which the real self is not living up.

She writes: "I consider that envy is an oral-sadistic and anal-sadistic expression of destructive impulses, operative from the beginning of life, and that it has a constitutional basis." Elsewhere she hedges, calling envy "not entirely constitutional". Most of her followers contend that envy cannot occur as early as Klein believes because what they and I agree to call envy is predicated on a comparison with another's advantage, and the newborn is unable to make such a detrimental comparison, a comparison that Klein does not consider integral to envy. On the other hand, Klein adds "wish to spoil", whereas we find that a frequent accompaniment to envy but not essential. Klein's "envy" is also not—comes before—covetousness, i.e., wanting the breast on or for oneself.

Furthermore, besides not including a comparison to the disadvantage of the envier, Klein denies that envy is a reaction to frustration and anger that the breast (proxy for the mother) is withholding or not providing enough milk, or even fear of loss of the breast, called by some psychoanalysts "the nameless dread". On the other hand, the idea of envy being a very early phenomenon (but not so early as Klein's) is picked up by her followers to the effect that the greedy, solipsistic infant fantasizes a perpetual fountain of milk of his very own, believing that what he gets is always too little and too late, but this is frustration, not envy. (Imagine what would become of an infant who was constantly filling herself with milk.)

Klein believes that the infant's innate capacity to love makes it possible to lose the breast over and over, prior to any ability to hope, and still retain faith in its return, developing in time a counterbalance for envy, which is gratitude for another's goodness. In this way repeated satisfaction permits growth of confidence in the self. ("If I can handle the all-powerful breast, I can handle anything.") The innate capacity for hate is what translates into envy, in Klein's construct. Hence primordial envy is an expression of the infant's counterproductive rage, wanting to spoil exactly what he needs the most from the all-powerful mother who from his per-spective can do anything she wishes. Klein admits that there are inherently different potentials for different levels of envy in differ-ent infants, and we all know that there are different degrees and kinds of imperfection in the mothering of infants. It is the balance between how imperfect the mother and how envy-prone or resil-ient the infant, that minimizes or stimulates the child's ongoing envy reaction in the course of development.[6]

So-called "survivors" who manage to reach a fairly comfortable adulthood through natural endowment plus luck, and also, perhaps, external help, professional or other, despite being deprived of the normal mothering and supplies of warmth, love, care, etc.—people like Antwone Quenton Fisher—these people put the lie to the idea that the child takes nothing to the equation. Regarding the vast majority of infants we have derived the idea of the "good enough mother", at least "good enough" for this particular infant, though not necessarily so for the next child. If most of our needs as infants are met most of the time, most of us can develop self-esteem and trust that we can control or at least channel hate and envy, as well as handle other aspects of our lives and what the world does to us. On the other hand, a baby with a high potential for envy could have experienced a good mother/child feeding experience but go through life with much discomfort from excessive envy regard-less, and even suffer a shackling of his potential for *joie de vivre*.

Klein notes that in adults a relative lack of envy makes for seren-ity, whereas the envious are insatiable. (This can be interpreted as illustrating the frequent correlation of greed and envy, which one of our later authors will comment on.) Klein finds envy both destructive and difficult to analyze, holding the patient in thrall and producing attacks on well-intentioned friends' and even the analyst's attempts to help. Examples from her analysands focus on her efforts to help them learn the use of gratitude to free them-selves from the worst of their envy.

Formerly it was believed that in mother/infant dyads there is infinite variety in mothers (loving, giving, grudging, rejecting, hateful, abusive, etc., etc.) whereas infants have been produced in a cookie-cutter fashion, or emerged into the outside world, each, in Skinner's term, a "tabula rasa". Now it is recognized that infants also come in infinite variety, but their differences cannot be observed, since they are in obscure, rudimentary form until they evolve over their lifetime as their natural endowments interdigitate with their reactions to the environment. Whereas in the former theoretical construct, the outcome of the child rested solely on the mother (and hence placed her under an intolerable burden), now the outcome is raised to the power of two infinities of variety, which is exactly what we see in the real world. Randomness and chance hold good cards in this high-stakes game.

But why should all this translate in the child into what Klein calls envy? Why not some combination of love, appreciation, gratitude, anger, resentment, determination to retaliate, compensatory greed—all in body feelings, long prior to language? Using the more inclusive definition to the effect that envy is not just a sense of looking spitefully and wishing to destroy but a feeling of disadvantage based on comparison, and granting that we surmise infants are not yet capable of comparison, their frustration can be equated with their powerlessness, but not with the comparison necessary for what we call envy. What Klein is calling envy is something more primitive that what we call envy, an affect that perhaps we should call, as some have called it, "proto-envy".

One of the main objections to Klein's formulation by many of her followers is the question of whether envy is innate, as she argues, or reactive to the insults and assaults that we all encounter in the best of circumstances. The infant has plenty of opportunity to feel imposed on, neglected, made to wait too long, given too little and too late. This can be felt by the body as angry resentment that she (mother) or it (breast) has the milk and is keeping it from the screaming infant. He needn't necessarily hate his mother for the delay (or having all that milk and keeping it for herself, as he sees it), just wish to get that comfortable feeling in the stomach that follows his feed (and in some formulations is comparable to the blissful feeling following an orgasm in adults). The infant's caregiver, imperfect as we all are, does her best with love-conveying caresses, supportive holding, and other body language, as well as vocal reassurances and food itself, but she must remember that the infant takes his own innate resilience, and besides help him be comfortable and satisfied, she should help him learn to tolerate and deal with life's inevitable frustrations. (But frustration does not equate with envy.) Still, the mother should not do too much, should not avert every need, because the infant must learn, little by little, to tolerate frustration and to accept the inevitable conclusion that others have needs that sometimes preempt his and that he cannot be the center of the universe.

Thereupon, in the envy sequence, follow impotence, inferiority, and humiliation. Whether this is severe enough and chronic enough can affect the individual's ongoing reaction to life's endless frustrations, with envy or with creative problem-solving to circumvent the obstacle.

Although they wrote decades later, we mention Etchagoyen, et al., next because they are even more insistent than Klein that envy is innate, not reactive or explicable by frustration reactive to the environment. They quote Rocher to the effect that envy requires a prior moment when what the other has and oneself lacks is painfully obvious, and this sets in motion an envy attack. Agreeing with Rocher, who, as we noted, dubbed it an "exquisitely irrational phenomenon ... no serviceable end [other] than that of attacking what is valuable in the other", they insist that in therapy, envy and frustration must be accurately delineated and differentiated. Furthermore they hold that envy must always be interpreted immediately and without consideration for tact or timing. The analysand must not be permitted to place or to continue to place the blame on the envied one, i.e., (s)he must "own" the envy and work with how to relieve or modulate it. They go so far as to contend that if the analysand be permitted to sustain his belief in an outside cause for his envy, the analysis has been downgraded to "supportive psychotherapy". Despite his lowered self-esteem, anger, humiliation, feelings of inferiority, compounded by shame over being "that low kind of person" in the words of my teacher/patient, and other confounding emotions, envy is the analysand's emotion to make something of, and that something can be good. As he learns better ways to handle impulses (including envy), the fact of the analyst being unperturbed, despite often being the object of the patient's envy, strips it of its presumed omnipotent destructiveness, as it sometimes feels to the patient (cf. Freud's "Rat Man"). He can then go on to learn better strategies. (In my experience, a more frequent painful component of envy is not a feeling of omnipotence but just the opposite, one of impotence to compete and the shame that goes with powerlessness.)

Klein, Sandell (*vide infra*), Etchagoyen, and others are the hold-outs for a constitutional basis for envy, while most students of envy cite the external world as operational in the genesis of envy. Most find negative comparison and its attendant frustration sufficient to produce envy when that invidious comparison attacks the envy-prone individual in a domain of importance to him. Certainly the world offers each of us ample exposure to others who outrank us in those areas we hold dear, to light the fire of envy.

Back in the 1960s (soon after Klein's death) when the London psychoanalysts were debating the nature-nurture question of envy, Joffe reviewed the then current beliefs on envy, beginning with Klein, and summarized his findings and his own belief. He found envy "a complex object-related attitude or tendency, made up of different component parts, and a certain level of ego development is necessary for its existence".

Also:

> The concept of envy as a primary inborn instinctual drive is completely rejected [i.e., Joffe rejects Klein's concept]. It is seen rather as a complicated attitude which occurs as part of normal development and which is closely related to such other attitudes as possessiveness. It is linked with aggression and destructiveness, but the aggressive component and the fantasies linked with it can be drawn from all phases of development, and is not only oral in nature. Rather than being seen as a primary drive, it can be seen as a secondary motivating force which may have positive and adaptive consequences in ongoing development, or may lead to the most malignant pathology. It has an intimate relation to the state of the individual's narcissism and self-esteem, and the essential stimulus to its development lies in disturbances within that domain.

Bion linked envy in the first instance almost to the opposite of frustration, to the inability to accept what the good mother has to give (and, as a later character trait, what the envied one has to offer). He calls the absent breast the infant's "first thought". He too relates envy to narcissism, with "subtle disguises, may be confused with jealousy, greed, frustration produced by the environment. It can produce a confusion of good and bad; it may be confused with a demand for justice; and, used most productively, it can be deployed into admiration and emulation." It is the therapist's job to help the envious analysand take charge of envious and other hostile impulses, including those directed against the analyst, and learn to deploy them productively.

Bion notes that defeat may produce envy "with its cartage". On the other hand, the analysand may envy the analyst's success with him and sabotage it.

Hanna Segal calls envy and narcissism two sides of the same coin, and she considered envy a form of narcissistic defense. By this I think she means that it is better to envy than to find oneself worthless. Narcissism can be considered, for our purposes, a kind of excessive self-orientation. To the envier, his attack on the one he envies feels legitimate and he is guilt-free, since he considers envy the fault of the envied one.

Segal offers several strategies the envious one uses to try to escape the pangs of envy: (1) denigrating the envied quality ("It's not so great after all"); (2) projection of envy ("I'm not envious; she is"); (3) idealization of the envied person (put on a pedestal); (4) identification with the envied person ("She's a colleague of mine"); (5) emotional withdrawal from the envied person and stifling of love. This latter strategy has the unfortunate result of shrinking the emotional world of the envious person.

Segal finds envy the worst when we are dependent on the one we envy, and there is no escape.

An apologist for Melanie Klein, Segal wrote an introduction to her work and also a chapter on Klein's technique in Wolman's book on various psychoanalytic techniques. She stresses Klein's insistence on the early appearance of envy, along with greed. "Greed aims at the possession of all the goodness that can be extracted from the object, regardless of consequences; this may result in the destruction of the object and the spoiling of its goodness, but the destruction is incidental to the ruthless acquirement. Envy aims at being as good as the object, but, when this is felt as impossible, it aims at spoiling the goodness of the object, to remove the source of the envious feelings. It is this spoiling aspect of envy that is so destructive to development, since the very source of goodness that the infant depends on is turned bad, and good introjections, therefore, cannot be achieved. Envy, though arising from primitive love and admiration, has a less strong libidinal component than greed and is suffused with the death instinct. As it attacks the source of life, it may be considered to be the earliest direct externalization of the death instinct. Envy stirs as soon as the infant becomes aware of the breast as a source of life and good experience; the real gratification which he experiences at the breast, reinforced by idealization, so powerful in early infancy, makes him feel that the breast is the source of all comforts, physical and mental, an inexhaustible reservoir of food and warmth, love, understanding, and wisdom. The blissful experience of satisfaction which this wonderful object can give will increase his love and his desire to possess, preserve and protect it, but the same experience stirs in him also the wish to be himself the source of such perfection. He experiences painful feelings of envy which carry with them the desire to spoil the qualities of the object which can give him such painful feelings."

This can go on through life, and severe envy often leads to interminable analysis. Segal shares two cases, one more severe than the other, in which envy going back to the family of origin sabotages the attainment of life's goals.

The woman whose envy was less severe, near termination of her treatment, cited an old Spanish proverb: "If envy were ringworm, how many ringwormy people would there be in the world!"

Referring to the "complex affective experience of envy", Rosenblatt posits that a *sine qua non* for envy is the ability to imagine an end state relieved of the envy itself, but that "this conclusion that what is desired cannot be obtained evokes feelings of helplessness, accompanied by varying degrees of lowered self-esteem and anger. Combined with the feelings of entitlement, this complex feeling state constitutes the envy experience."

He lists the prerequisites for and constituents of envy: (1) the perception that a desirable object or attribute is possessed by another; (2) the perception that the envier does not possess it; (3) the feeling that the envier is entitled to it; (4) the appraisal that it is unattainable, resulting in helplessness; (5) a resultant feeling of inadequacy and inferiority; and (6) anger at the possessor.

Rosenblatt explores possible defenses against the many components of envy, component by component. Regarding the seemingly unattainable desire, for example, one might relinquish the desire as unimportant, or perhaps realize that it is attainable after all (cf. the advice to Frederick Bastien, "Make your own name famous"). One might appreciate her other better attributes (cf. the intelligent sister in *Picnic*, who envied her sister's beauty but consoles herself with her own intelligence) or that the advantage is ill-gotten ("He cheats on his income tax"[7]). One might denigrate the attribute ("That five-carat rock is in terrible taste") or the person ("She may be smart, but she's fat"[8]). One might implement the feeling of possibility ("I can get it for myself"). Finally (and in some ways best), one may identify wholly or in part with the envied one ("That football star is from my hometown") or brag, "My brother is a professor at Stanford" or take pride in, e.g., her child's accomplishments and bask in her albedo.

Sandell defines envy as a "temporary or transitional affective state characterized by destructive hate, with cognitive [knowing] and conative [willing] processes of mind, partly conscious and partly unconscious, with specific contents of phantasy, and dependent on experiential and situational factors for their realization. It is dependent on experiencing subjectively a realization of relative deprivation, compared to another, and this 'other' can be a single person, a group, a category of persons [e.g., young people[9] or generalized 'other']". Furthermore, he sees admiration as a positive facet of envy, which can lead to gratitude. In this case judgment is not impaired, as it is in other expressions of envy. The "other" has two aspects, the good and giving of whatever one lacks for oneself (in the infant's case, milk) versus the mean and grudging aspect, (i.e., the bad will of nature). Agreeing with Klein, Sandell believes the capacity to hate is innate and the basis for envy, which can go on to include humiliation. Hence, for the infant, envy is an admission of inferiority and (like jealousy in later life) is a triangular affair, but the two others are not whole persons but part-objects (or trait objects), the good loved part and the bad hated or envied part. In later life, envy is predicated on admiration of an attribute of the other, though not necessarily admiration of the whole other. The envier, also, can be represented by two parts: when the actual ego resents another person's attribute because of its own relative lack, but the ideal ego appreciates it, those two aspects of the ego are dyssynchronous. Part of therapy and analysis consists of bringing the two ego aspects together, i.e., by combining learning to appreciate and enjoy the other's admired advantage, with developing one's own deficient aspect. Sandell also echoes the refrain about the demand for justice being "a reaction formation against envy".

Lopez-Corvo uses the term "self-envy" to refer to different parts of the ego in conflict.

The condition of self-envy results from, among other things, the interaction of different elements forming the Oedipus complex—for instance in cases in which a serious increment of envy has taken place during childhood between a child, who felt excluded, and the parental couple. This is an envy usually related to different aspects of parental harmony, power, control, creativity, capacity to reproduce, and so on. Those envious feelings experienced by children toward their parents will remain inside as foreign and active objects, without ever being assimilated within the ego. When these children grow and become adults like their parents, they will then envy in themselves their own capacity to establish a harmonious relationship, as well as to create, or to exercise control, etc., just as they envied their own parents in the past. Because of the severity of the splitting, these feelings are not experienced as one's own, and it is this impression of extraneousness that allows envy to take place. I believe that self-envy is a more common conflict than we have thought.

Clifford Scott says much the same thing: envy results from a conflict between a depreciated part of the ego and an idealized part.

Shengold contends that envy relates to what one is only relatively deprived of, and within range of aspiration, not, e.g., some film star's beauty. He believes that primal envy is a kind of destructive aggression that later becomes differentiated into envy, hatred, and greed. One's deficit may be temporary and transient and only partly conscious. It relates more to the conative (willing) than to the cognitive (understanding) mental processes. It can have good outcomes: gratitude and admiration. Shengold notes also that the envied one may be a "generalized other" (professional athletes, career women). It can cut across borders of real time (e.g., envy of one's own children for their greater opportunities and for their longer and, presumably, better future, as one of my sons admitted feeling vis-à-vis his little daughter, whom he dearly loves and for whom he is trying to assure a better future than his own, by avoiding what he perceives to be my mistakes, as most of us try to do for our children).[10] This kind of envy has been felt and sometimes controlled (sometimes not) in immigrants, who, recognizing soon after arrival the grinding labor with trivial rewards offered in this "Land of Opportunity", accepted the reality that their own lives had to be sacrificed to buy opportunities for the next generation. My highly intelligent late father-in-law came to this country with the intention of attending night school, but we smiled when he explained that shortly after his marriage his wife "got pregnant" with my late husband and his responsibilities rapidly escalated. He helped his sons attend college and offered to help his daughters, but they declined. This generous man, realizing that his sons needed educated wives, offered to borrow against his steel-mill pension to pay my final year's tuition, when my father threatened to withhold it. But my father came around.

✳

Collaborating between Israel and Argentina and publishing in 1994, the psychoanalysts Feldman and de Paola consider envy as a "compound affect or a complex feeling, not an impulse or a drive derivative". After an extensive review of the psychoanalytic literature on envy, beginning, of course, with Klein, and including many authors not included in my review, their position was that to experience envy or even its preliminary manifestation, an infant must be able to feel some sort of differentiation of himself from others, the breast in the first instance. "Envy seems to be related to ... when and how the human subject develops a knowledge of himself as separated from other subjects." Although they reject Klein's favoring of the instinctual mode (hence constitutional), they acknowledge that constitutional factors affect the intensity of the envy reaction. They date proto-envy to about six months, at which age they believe there appears a limited ability to delineate the self from other persons, but long before a comparison becomes possible. They agree with Spillius' (*vide infra*) assertion that envy should be considered in the light of the giver/receiver—mother/infant—situation, with both conscious and unconscious factors in both, and in each case a correct or an incorrect interpretation of one's own and the other's attitudes. Too much dissonance (e.g., infant wrongly attributing grudging miserliness to the breast, i.e., keeping the milk to itself) can be felt not as frustration but as being robbed by the breast and can tilt the balance toward an envious predisposition in the growing child. These authors see the good other (breast) as not permanently lost but at least retrievable over and over. When the breast is perceived by the infant as an unattainable ideal, this gives rise to envy (angry hatred). "One major derivative of the capacity for hate is the feeling of envy." Thus these authors find envy as the outcome of a complicated interaction beginning prior to the infant's ability to differentiate himself very well from the outside world—and finding himself impotent.

Their summation:

We propose, avoiding moral, religious, or cultural biases, that instead of considering envy the result of frustration or the direct expression of instinct, we consider it as a complex feeling, fully developed only around the establishment of the depressive position [about six months]. This feeling would stem from the loss of an identification (total?, partial?) with an omnipotent-idealized object (breast/mother), which we call a *nameless loss*. It would occur at a time when, we suggest, there would be a (relative) self-object undifferentiation and no real feeling of frustration. Rather, the infant's feeling would be in the nature of a *lack* of something, meaning that the self was 'robbed', forcefully torn up by the object. This would lead to a breach of self-idealization, security, well-being, goodness and the blissful state of mind. ... We think that at these periods there is a mixture of strong feelings: some terrible, such as smallness, impotence, complete dependency, humiliation; others awesome such as admiration, passion, craving. All these feelings are stirred up by the infant's situation, and point towards the unbridgeable gap between the baby and the mother, which turns the mother's (breast's) capacities into an *unattainable* gift. ... The most crucial aspects of envy seem to be the feelings of loss, lack (incompleteness), and the unattainability of the qualities of the idealised-omnipotent object ... a process that we call 'precocious mourning' ... the search to recover the fusion of the idealised-omnipotent object (Klein's description of the phantasy of an inexhaustible breast), and the destructive measures that are meant to eliminate the source of feelings of anger and persecution (the sense of being robbed) triggered by the perception of the unattainability of the desired ideal-omnipotent qualities of the object, which simultaneously mirrors the 'extreme poverty' of the infant's ego.

These authors' perception of infantile envy is that it is directed against an idealized mother, one who appears to perform with impunity what is forbidden to the rest of us—and get away with it. This configuration often gets linked up in later life with the demand for justice, which is often tied to envious motives. Thus the highest ideals become confused with the worst feelings, and they can be difficult to differentiate.

In the analytic setting, the therapist can observe in the same individual idealized aspects of the personality and depressive feelings of worthlessness and humiliation.

Working in the opposite direction, feelings of shame and humiliation in a patient point to the possible presence of envy in the patient. It behooves the therapist to be aware of the patient's envy so as not to become entangled, with the goal that interpretation can strip envy of its destructive potential. As always, the therapist must recognize and assess his own envy in order to keep the countertransference clean.

In a panel discussion on "Envy, Jealousy and Shame" chaired by Herrmann and de Paola, a novel comparison was made between envy and contempt (both comparative and self-conscious emotions), with "shame[11] lying downstream from each".

The currently practicing London psychoanalyst Spillius entitled her article "The Varieties of Envious Experience", in deference to William James's book *The Varieties of Religious Experience*. After acknowledging Klein's contribution to our recognition of the importance of envy and its destructive potential in the emotional life in general and the analytic process in particular, Spillius goes on to propose a giver/receiver model. Since envy exists in a two-person context, it is important to tease out how much of the envy is rooted in the envier's constitution, how much is a reaction to experience, and how much is derived from the interaction. In the early months of life, not only are there two individuals (mother and infant) with giving and receiving needs and perceptions, but these perceptions can be in accord or not, and there can be multiple interpretations and misinterpretations of the unarticulated feelings of both. Spillius believes envy can result whenever the complicated mother/child consonance becomes distorted into "malignant dissonance". She holds that the mother's job is to maintain the infant's illusion of power and omnipotence long enough to develop psychologic resilience, and to have developed the ego strength to cope with the inevitable misadventures and disillusionments of life. This seems to me such a difficult assignment that I would ask how many mother/child pairs would ever get it close to right. Still, most outcomes are not as bad as all this would warrant.

Spillius differentiates two kinds of envy. The first is akin to Klein's attack on a good object, a breast flowing with milk. This envy is ego-dystonic, unconscious, well contained, and guilt-producing due to failure to recognize the injustice in a destructive attack on a good object on whom the subject is dependent, i.e., the breast. The envier fights envy and buries awareness. This counterproductive (cut-off-your-nose-to-spite-your-face) kind of envy is primitive. The envier in treatment needs help to recognize it, face it, and overcome the guilt.

It is even worse when the envier not only suffers the lack of whatever advantage the envied one has, but is also dependent on him and beholden to him. This situation the helpless infant feels in spades vis-à-vis the apparently omnipotent mother, and it is recapitulated in the patient/analyst relationship. In this kind, the patient and analyst can at least agree that the issue is envy.

Not so with the second kind, which Spillius calls "impenitent". This brand of envy is already close to consciousness. The envier feels wronged, the fault is attributed to the envied one, and hence the envy is perceived as legitimate, but the envier perceives this not as envy but rather as justifiable grievance and resentment of injustice. Thus the patient and therapist are in disagreement over whether the emotional reaction is even envy. If excessive, this type, involving the giver/receiver relationship, is found in later life in sadomasochism and preoccupation with power.

Spillius lists defenses against envy: (1) denigration ("It's no good anyway"); (2) projection ("I'm not destructive; she is"); (3) idealization of the envied object and identification with it ("My doctor is the best");[12] (4) identification with the envied objects so that comparison becomes irrelevant; (5) stifling of love, intensification of hate, indifference, and withdrawal ("Who does she think she is anyway?"); and (6) hopelessness ("No point in going on with this").

In the tangled interrelationship of patient and analyst, the envious patient experiences difficulty in receiving whatever help the analyst offers. To be beholden to the object of one's envy stokes the envy fire. When this is overcome, receiving help is an improvement for the envier as well as a gift to the giver. Not that the analyst should be given a gift, but the analysand needs help in being comfortable while both giving and receiving.

Spillius concludes that since we cannot know what an infant thought or felt decades earlier, or what his or her "true" experience with the mother was, and to what extent current issues with envy result from the infant's maternal interaction, the only material available for the analyst to work with is how the patient experiences envy in his world now, its severity, its expression, and his defenses against it. We strongly concur.

While Spillius postulates a giver/receiver model, the Australian analyst Maizels offers an active/passive model for envy (comparable to but not identical with the life/death instincts of Freud and Klein). Maizels believes that from earliest years, the urge to be active and the urge to be passive are counterbalanced in a kind of psychic tango, each aspect envying the other when it is in dominance. When the infant can introject parts of the giving mother, bringing together the active and passive aspects, it helps reduce feelings of envy and contributes to his growing appreciation for the nature of goodness.

✳

In the 1990s, a nurse psychoanalyst, Sheila Rouslin Welt, wrote a paper (later published with Herron as a chapter of a book) in which she defined envy in the standard way, as requiring a comparison that finds the envied other as having or being something better, thereby inducing humiliation. According to this author, "Envy is a universal phenomenon experienced by all persons at one time or another…that is automatic and that is not always consciously recognized by its holder. By outsiders, it is observed through behavior, often indirectly inferred only through defenses against it." After citing definitions and attributes of envy by earlier psycho-analysts (Ernest Jones, Harry Stack Sullivan, and Neubauer), which emphasize deficiency, self-devaluation, and humiliation, she goes on to add her own observations on the subject. Thus she finds it a phenomenon both intrapersonal and interpersonal, pervasive and enslaving. By focusing on the attainments or attributes of others, and evaluating the self as "not good enough", it "gives rise to resentment and contaminates relationships, which are colored by obsessional preoccupation with comparison and guided not by a wish for closeness but by discontent with the self." Associates are selected to be devalued, rather than admired. The fact of the envy may add insult to injury by resulting in shame over being a "low kind of person". Jealousy may be (usually is) an outgrowth of envy when a third person is seen as the "interloper who got what I should have had", and the envier seeks parental supplies, later shifted to parental surrogates. There is usually a parental figure (often God, as with Salieri) "hanging around in the background".

   Rouslin Welt calls the universal comparison of the self with others "normal envy" and sees it as an impetus for attainment and repair of deficits, a stimulus to close the discrepancy gap, a motive for emulation, and a way to share in the enjoyment of what others have. Thus her "normal envy" is a good and positive thing.

   Though acknowledging that the roots of envy come from early

in the infant's relationship with the mother, this author, like Spillius, does not get embroiled in the nature/nurture argument but focuses on the expression of envy in life, as exemplified by what goes on in the therapeutic relationship. In the consulting room envy is often expressed through anger, which may attach to the disparate statuses (social, economic, educational) of the patient and therapist. Her advice to the analyst (or psychotherapist) is that, although recognizing that a patient's envy is anxiety-producing in the therapist, she must nevertheless be alert to it: (1) when the patient idealizes you, don't be flattered, and don't try to avoid uncomfortable issues; (2) expect to be devalued and the patient to become grandiose because these are frequent defenses; (3) expect the patient to have to deal with envy by devaluation of the self, denial of envy, and punishing the self for it; (4) expect the envious patient to have difficulty taking what the therapy has to offer, and therefore expect defensive aggression, interpret it, and drop it; and (5) expect envy of yourself and do not try to sidestep it. Another reminder is not to try to woo the envious one with acts of kindness because they do not work and usually backfire.

She recognizes "circumscribed envy", a form in which someone who is not generally an envious person focuses envy in a particular area. Her example is the "excruciating envy" felt by women who have lost a child; they cannot look at pregnant women or babies without experiencing it (cf. my chapter on reproductive envy).

She shares a fascinating case of envy in a woman whose father was absent or inaccessible in her growing-up years. In a relatively good marriage, this woman envied her daughter for having a good father, the patient's own husband.

Rouslin Welt urges the therapist to help the envious one to learn to use envy as an impetus for his or her own development. What is seen and envied (for example, something of the therapist's) can become a sort of "transitional object" with which to identify and be proud. The use of a room in the therapist's own home as a consulting venue (as is sometimes done) makes the patient aware of aspects of the therapist that analysts usually would not share. Her new home and redecorating project offered aspects of herself with which female patients identified and compared in their own homes. This had the positive outcome in group therapy for several women to undertake their own redecorating. For a time I used a remodeled porch in our home for seeing patients, and it became increasingly cluttered with books, papers, letters, earlier drafts, and other flotsam from various writing projects. I apologized for this mess to a young man I was working with, and his positive transference reaction was "That's just the way a guy would do it!"

Finally, Rouslin Welt offers a much more extensive analysis of *Amadeus* than mine, including the fathers of both composers, and Salieri's envy of Mozart expanding into rage against God for withholding the talent Salieri craved and had bargained for, but that God had granted instead to the obnoxious youngster.

Two authors have drawn attention to the envy felt specifically for women by one or other of the sexes. Noting that the psychoanalytic literature contained at the time only two case reports devoted exclusively to pregnancy envy in men, Kato van Leeuwen reported a case illustrating how a young man's therapy was influenced by envy of the pregnancy of his analyst.[13]

Janet Rodgers, a nurse and professor, wrote that women fear being envied more than do men, particularly women in the nursing profession. She believes that two situations set nurses up as special targets of envy: (1) as the nurturing profession par excellence, its practitioners are in the position of mother with its baggage of "envy of the breast" (more primary even than the envy of the mother we just discussed); and (2) members of the profession are already in a subordinate position, and this, plus the nurturant role equating them with the milk-giving mother, sets them up for envy by physicians and patients alike. I suggest that both these would be less likely to make the nurse envied, more likely to make her denigrated. In fact nurses have complained to me about just the opposite, the condescending and superior attitude of many physicians of both sexes. Physicians may resent the fact that patients, a little afraid of doctors, are often more willing to confide in nurses, who must then relay the information to the doctor.

Rodgers questions the belief that envy flourishes only in near-equals (of course how near is near?). She finds that fear of envy, usually subconscious, is a factor in her colleagues' rejection of the mentor role with younger nurses, who are themselves studying to go into nursing education. Rodgers believes that as soon as the need for help is past, the now colleague turns against the former mentor, whereas the older woman would prefer that the two establish a comfortable collegial relationship. Rodgers distinguishes the (sometimes) bad outcome of emulation, i.e., devaluation and contempt, from the (sometimes) good outcome of gratitude, which can help detoxify envy. It has long been recognized that those in superior positions live under the constant possibility of being dethroned, and this threat also makes them wish to avoid a position in which they may be envied.

Until this point in this chapter, we have presented psychoanalytic contributions chronologically. At this juncture we no longer use chronology as our criterion but change to an arrangement based on concepts concerning the pathogenesis of envy in infancy and childhood.

Recently psychoanalysts have shown a recrudescence of interest in envy and have taken another look at whether and how Freud's "penis envy" or other early experiences with envy affect the development of sexuality. In general they have concluded that female sexuality has a very complicated evolution, involving envy, but earlier, so-called "pre-Oedipal envy", more importantly envy of the mother. Harris, for example, believes that women suffer more problems with ambition, competition, and aggressiveness than do men because of their early identification confusion over object relations with their mothers. Envy being particularly a province of the powerless, females are primed for it. The effects of early envy in girls often result in later mother/daughter stress that Harris compares to low-grade debilitating fever. Women frequently fear that success must be bought at the price of relationships.

Dahl believes that the concept of "penis envy" gives way to our understanding of "primary femininity" as resulting from "gender identity" acquired by age three by interactions with the mother, and that "penis envy", observed later and on the surface, has little mutative effect.

Willkinson draws attention to the fact that children of both sexes must come to terms with the fact that they both lack something, little boys grieving over their lack of procreative ability. At least little girls can console themselves with the idea that they will eventually develop birth-giving ability like their mothers'. For both, this is a pre-Oedipal task.

Burke sees envy as one response to feeling overwhelmed or impinged upon. Finding oneself not omnipotent is bad enough, without being dependent on someone else (caregiver) who seems to have the advantage of unlimited power. Thus envy antedates the struggle with sexuality. The problem Burke sees is to develop trust in "relationship constancy" even while learning to acknowledge that caregivers and others have other relationships of their own, external to the child—and trust that they will return again and again and the adult/child relationship survive. If this is not successful, a borderline personality results, with incomplete relationships.

Lax looks at the specific problems of boys' envy of their mothers and their procreative powers, which he calls "woman envy". Unlike their sisters, boys will never attain the ability to have a child. They must learn to "live with it". Unlike women's "penis envy" which is relatively conscious, understandable in light of men's superior position in the world, and therefore accessible to treatment, male "woman envy" originates earlier in infancy, is deeper-rooted, and less accessible to help. Its cost to the suffering individual is painful enough in gender-related issues and narcissistic wounds, but its cost to society is greater, often demonstrated in devaluation of women, machismo, abuse, and violence.

Lax cites many examples of rituals of primitive peoples in which males imitate females in their rites of passage, including Herdt's fascinating work in New Guinea, which I have mentioned earlier and also cited in my own review article on mental illness in primitive peoples.

To complicate the issue further, a recent study has shown that genetic factors affect clitoral response. We are far from the solution to this problem.

Moving on to envy in older, preschool children, and referring to it as the "envy constellation" ("a complex state of mind composed of ego, affect, and drive components"), Frankel and Sherick believe envy is a part of normal development and a reaction to narcissistic insult. They subscribe to the idea that the ability to make clear distinctions between the self and others is necessary, and that this is not possible until about the middle of the second year. Observing normal preschoolers with their mothers in a psychiatric hospital nursery school (mostly the children of students and staff), they studied the methods such children employed to get what they wanted, from age 1½ to 5. They observed both behavior and bodily and facial expressions as the children learned, over time, to negotiate and to use more sophisticated ways to satisfy their wishes, e.g., for adult attention. Many of their observations seemed to me to represent jealousy rather than envy, and to be similar to what would be encountered in a multi-child family. They noted that both sexes, by the age of four to five, display envy for the sex-related traits of the other, including boys' anatomy and girls' organs and future procreative ability.

Piers and Singer (like the popular belief) contend that envy comes from sibling rivalry. They find that the "oral aspects of sibling rivalry" are accompanied by resentment, depression, and dissatisfaction that can color the entire personality, and hence experiences with siblings are a major cause for envy. I cannot accept this generalization because if it were true, adult only children would stand out by virtue of a non-rivalrous, non-resentful personality, and one cannot pick such persons out of a crowd. (And I as an only child would have had less envy to battle over the years.) Besides, only children have every opportunity to envy neighborhood children, and, for that matter, either parent for the attention (s)he gets from the other, as well as grandparents and cousins. Like Frankel and Sherick, Piers and Singer see envy as a stimulus that can lead to constructive ways to get attention, become competent, and enjoy admiration. This requires a level of intelligence and ability to experiment that vary from one child to the next.

In an article devoted to constructive uses of envy, Smith and Whitfield draw attention to the fact that children in a play situation will flaunt skills or possessions in such a way as to attract the envious attention of other children, whom they are hoping to entice to play with them.

These authors also present an adult case illustrating envy for the analyst and all her obvious advantages, i.e., professional life and good income. This analysand gradually learned to tolerate the unfairness of life, regarding the fact that the good things are so unevenly distributed, but not to let that deter her from using her natural positive attributes such as intelligence to acquire by small increments some of the good things herself.

Psychoanalysts agree regarding the difficulty that patients pose whose envy is a major part of their problem. Moser-Ha illustrates these problems in her description of when and how to introduce painful envy issues silently operating beneath the surface. Waska

displays the relationship between the patient's envying the analyst and his demandingness (seen as greed) but unwillingness to
be forthcoming (giving and sharing of himself) while the patient
must remain dependent again, as in infancy. This imposes a more-
than-average difficulty for the analyst.

A psychoanalyst Harold N. Boris (who cleverly shortens his work
by using the abbreviations of P for patient and ψ for psychoanalyst,
meaning himself, whenever he quotes interactions with patients)
has collected eight earlier papers and added two chapters into his
book, *Envy*, and has continued writing on the topic in other papers
all subtitled "Unconscious Envy". His organizing principle consists
of two ways we experience a dyadic relationship: as a PAIR and as
a COUPLE (not necessarily meant romantically).
He writes:

> I have particularized two fundamental states of mind—one,
> the COUPLE, following from and embodying the pleasure
> principle and involving the discovery and use of differences;
> the other, the PAIR [also expanded into the GROUP], fol-
> lowing from and embodying what I have called the selec-
> tion principle and involving the need to discover or invent
> likeness in order to facilitate, through identifications, the
> formation of pairs and of groups. This is true of the rela-
> tionship one makes with one's self and those relationships
> others seem to make with one's self. That this duality is
> paradigmatic means at one and the same time that choice
> is necessary and impossible. Accordingly, the dialectics
> of paradox become the *lingua dicta* for the study of envy.

The "pair" aspect of dyadic relationships is more primitive and
narcissistic than the "couple". It looks for similarities and expands
into groups, and this makes it possible to cope with envy. The therapist must expect to be a target of envy in the "pair" relationship

with the analysand. The "couple" way of relating is complementary (the earliest being infant mouth and mother's breast) and looks for reciprocity and differences that make for pleasure. Boris asks, "What is group stuff needed for our identities and sense of belonging and which is couple stuff to foment innovation and discovery?" Boris believes that homosexual couples, lacking the difference in sex, more often look for other "couple" differences, such as wide age disparity, race differences, and occupational differences, than do heterosexual couples.

In one of his later papers Boris proposes "to deal with the maneuver by which people try to mitigate their envy by converting differences into similarities".

As one reviewer, Peggy Hutson, observed, one must suspend usual expectations about psychoanalytic writing to follow and benefit from Boris's analysis.

At least one author, Rachel Wahba, has picked up on Boris's idea of pairs and the need for similarities. She studies patients who look for "twinship" in selecting their therapist, in terms of gender, orientation, class, status, ethnicity, even income, in order to feel comfortable in their therapy. This should minimize envy in those patients who are primed for it, but the issue must be faced regardless in other, if not the therapeutic, relationship.

As interest in envy grew, another book came out by a practitioner in the mental health field. Berke, a British psychotherapist, in 1988, wrote about greed, envy, and malice in *The Tyranny of Malice: Exploring the Dark Side of Character and Culture.* "Envy is a state of exquisite tension, torment, and ill will provoked by an overwhelming sense of inferiority, impotence, and worthlessness. It begins in the eye of the beholder and is so painful to the mind that the envious person will go to almost any lengths to diminish, if not destroy, whatever or whoever may have aroused it." In his book Berke analyzes together three hate-related, malice-expressed affects (envy, jealousy, and greed), in literature (including fairy tales), in his patients, and in life (in both individuals and larger social groups). "Salieri [in Pushkin's play *Mozart and Salieri*], Iago [in Shakespeare's *Othello*], and Ivan Babichev (envious along with Kavalerov) [in Yuri Olesha's novella *Envy*] all demonstrate the essential criteria of unrestrained envy.... It is an intense, implacable, irrational, irreconcilable, spiteful passion solely concerned with spoiling, corrupting, defaming, and begrudging." Later he credits envy with eliciting the self-analysis and discipline to grow and surmount.

Concerned with "malice", this author considers those three emotions (envy, greed, and jealousy) together, as, in fact, they often occur in life. Indeed, his colleague, Nini Coltart, even conflates envy and greed into the portmanteau word "grenvy". I like Berke's lattice analogy, which is reminiscent of the Medieval attempt to balance the seven deadlies with seven virtues. Berke finds those three hate-related affects opposed by three growth- and joy-producing and love-related: gratitude, generosity, and compassion. After extensive exploration of the feelings of darker texture, the malice-related trio, he advises "tipping the lattice" toward the healthy and loving ones.

He notes three damaging effects of envy: changes in perception (it becomes exaggerated and selective, sometimes leading to projection), painful feelings (agony and anger), and hostile impulses (hatred and aggressiveness). He observes also that fear of envy produces an increased sensitivity to malevolent intentions, real or imagined.

Looking at "grenvy", Berke quotes Money-Kyrle's categorization of wealth: (1) necessities (food, clothing, and shelter); (2) luxuries (what we want because others have them); and (3) nontransferable commodities (beauty, intelligence, good education, and distinguished heredity). The third category is the one most envied because "these [attributes] are unique and convey a crushing sense of superiority".[14] "Status is a nontransferable blend of position and prestige, in contrast to class, which denotes wealth and power." Thus status is hard if not impossible to acquire and hence ripe for envy, whereas the nouveaux riche have been successful in making inroads into wealth.

Berke also recognizes malice at a societal level, in the same way as Schoeck recognizes societal envy. "The politics of malice is the transformation of envy, greed, and jealousy from personal events to social processes." Similarly with envy, "Institutionalized envy is the expression of spite, grudge, vengeance, and venom by corporate bodies, political parties, and other established entities."

Berke notes the methods Schoeck describes for societies to contain envy and exploit it to serve societal needs: (1) attempting to eliminate it (in all kinds of leveling methods, i.e., communism, transfer of wealth, Christianity, which offers equality of value in this life and equality of status in the hereafter); (2) detoxifying it by attributing advantages to blind luck; and (3) taking steps toward restoration of self-esteem by tipping one's lattice from the negative affects (envy, greed, and jealousy) toward the good love-related affects (gratitude, generosity, and compassion). He comments how throughout history, religious leaders, philosophers, and authors of other kinds have urged love as the remedy.

Psychologists approach the problem of envy from a different (and typically psychologic) perspective, based on standard psychologic tests that are scorable and quantifiable, performed mostly with student subjects.

Peter Salovey, a clinical psychologist, has compiled and edited a collection of essays, *The Psychology of Envy and Jealousy*, by twelve psychologists (mostly social, some clinical) and two sociologists. Of the twelve resulting chapters, just three deal with envy, the rest jealousy (an affect obviously much more studied by psychologists). In his introduction, Salovey considers envy (and jealousy) "mental states of individuals resulting from the appraisal of certain provocative situations".

Referring back to *Nichomachaean Ethics*, in which Aristotle interprets emulation as a good kind of envy, involving an intention on the envier's part to improve, W. Garrod Parrott (in his essay in Salovey's book, "The Emotional Experiences of Envy") refers to what other authors have called "admiring envy" or "emulating envy" or "benign envy". Parrott reserves the term "nonmalicious envy" to encompass all the nondestructive reactions of "envy", including emulation, intention to improve without any thought to harm another, etc., but notes that "malicious envy" focuses on the hard-core, gut-wrenching, hostility-engendering feeling of inferiority, that we define as envy and are studying. Only the latter, says Parrott, qualifies for inclusion in the Seven Deadly. With or without hostility, envy involves the painful comparison, as we all use the term. One purpose of this book is to look for ways to help us convert that genuine hostile envy to nonmalicious emulation, which I do not define as envy at all but as a health-giving way of dealing with envy.

Crediting an earlier work by Richard Smith, himself, and Diener, Parrott finds envy-proneness to rest on three factors: (1) the frequency and intensity of envy-provoking circumstances; (2) the intensity of feelings of inferiority; and (3) resentment and preoccupation with unfairness.

Parrott studied "envy episodes" by having subjects write accounts of incidents in their lives, which Parrott then scored for various situational and emotional components. The feelings he found in these vignettes included intense longing for the advantage, inferiority (including distress, anxiety, and despair), agent-focused resentment (anger and hatred for the envied person whether or not (s)he is realistically to blame), global resentment ("Life isn't fair"), guilt (what Parrott called "enlightened malicious envy"), and admiration (emulation).

These feelings clustered in certain configurations, depending, largely, on how the subject interpreted the situation. Parrott concluded:

> I have consistently found that inferiority and admiration tend to occur most frequently when agent-focused resentment is absent, and vice versa. Global resentment and longing seem to be consistent either with inferiority or with agent-focused resentment. Reports of intense guilt about ill will do occur, but are fairly uncommon.
>
> These findings suggest that two basic determinants of the quality of an envious experience are whether one believes one has been unfairly treated and whether one believes that one's disadvantage is one's own fault. Our data suggest that when one's own qualities are seen as being responsible for one's poor showing by comparison with another, the most salient responses are those concerning feelings of inferiority as well as motivation to improve oneself. When unfair treatment is perceived, feelings of anger and resentment predominate.

That "unfair treatment" causation of envy is the focus of "Envy and the Sense of Injustice," Richard H. Smith's chapter in Salovey's book. Smith analyzes the sense of injustice in Cassius' envy of Caesar's undeserved advancement and arrogance in Shakespeare's *Julius Caesar,* and the injustice Salieri (in Pushkin's play) feels for God's preference for Mozart. He describes an experiment in which subjects were asked to respond to first-person accounts of envy; their responses were studied with regressive analyses under three variables: (1) subjective unfairness; (2) objective unfairness (as assessed by an impartial observer); and (3) subjective feelings of inferiority. He concluded that if the envying person felt hostility, this implies that he is interpreting the problem as one of injustice (regardless of how an objective observer would interpret it). When the envious person senses unfairness (rightly or not), he feels the most anger, even though he may know that his assessment of unfairness is not shared. The envious person who perceives that others do not agree with his assessment of unfairness realizes that it is the better part of wisdom to hide this feeling of unfairness by behaving in such a way as to forestall envy being attributed to him. The reason so few people admit to envy is that so doing would betray hostility that observers would find unwarranted. [It is my belief that another reason to hide envy is so as not to draw attention to the inferiority that occasioned it or to the impotence it proclaims.] When the world shares his feeling of unfairness, or when it is a matter of chance or fate or something beyond his control, the envious person is much freer to share it with his friends. When the envious one is preoccupied with his feeling of inferiority, he may turn his hostility inward on himself and become depressed.

Smith concludes with an analysis of Claggart's envy of Billy Budd, where there is no issue of unfairness to explain Claggart's envy and no possible excuse to justify Claggart's acting on his feelings.

Salovey himself with Alexander Rothman wrote the concluding chapter of Salovey's book "Envy and Jealousy: Self and Society". They find two "processes" regarding the successes of others: reflective (which makes you feel good) and comparative (which makes you feel terrible). Beginning with the understanding that envy occurs only in domains of importance, they report a study in which subjects assess envy in areas such as beauty, wealth, etc., and another study manipulating apparent success by the subject in areas of the subject's career choice. They show and quote from other work that the reason envy is critical in domains of importance to the envier is that it "evokes the comparison process". We can tell when someone is envious because his behavior is calculated to maintain his prestige in an important domain. Furthermore, what is defined as an important domain is related to culture, as in the professor/graduate student culture, where success by upcoming students can be a source of trenchant envy. These authors quote William James, who admitted that as a psychologist he couldn't abide observing that another psychologist knew more psychology than he, but he was unconcerned about a co-professor's facility with Greek and was willing to "wallow" in his own ignorance of Greek.

Where does all this leave us? We've covered a lot of ground but haven't yet even reached a consensus on a classification under which to subsume envy, not to mention an agreed-upon definition. Our experts all have their terms and definitions: emotion, feeling, attitude, motivating force, state, impulse, reaction, affective state, sin (second of the Seven Deadly), "envy constellation", "envy attack", "complex feeling, not drive derivative nor impulse", "attitude, linked to other attitudes such as possessiveness", "complex affective experience", "temporary or transitional affective state characterized by destructive hate, with cognitive (knowing) and conative (willing) components, dependent on experiencing subjectively a realization of a relative deprivation, compared to another, and this 'other' is an idealization of the self, i.e., what one expects of oneself and falls short of realizing", "mental state resulting from the appraisal of certain provocative situations", "part of normal development", even "exquisitely irrational phenomenon". Obviously, the only consensus about definition seems to be a lack of consensus. Envy is a complex, slippery phenomenon, difficult to pin down. We recall Kant's observation that whatever has a history cannot be defined because it changes over time. (His example is "punishment".) We cannot even use the old phrase applied to pornography, "I can't define it, but I know it when I see it" because neither the envier nor the envied nor the observer is always aware of being in the presence of this hidden feeling.

Now I enter the fray with a definition: Envy is an ego-alien, self-castigating feeling of dissatisfaction within the self, resulting from realizing oneself lacking compared to another individual or group in a domain of importance to the envier. This dissatisfaction is an analytic assessment, thus cognitive, but the feeling of belittlement on which it is based brings with it concomitant feelings of humiliation, thus emotional components. Layered on this complex can be another level consisting of shame for experiencing a feeling beneath one's personal standards, for being envious in the first place.

If this happens frequently, it may lead to an "envy constellation", consisting of low self-esteem with a chronic sense of not being up to the mark and a feeling of global failure, and the envier often counterproductively gives up. This may result from a disparity between one's self-assessment and realistic goals, i.e., the tendency to expect more than the self can deliver, having set unrealistically high, unattainable standards. Inappropriate evaluation of one's strengths and weaknesses may result from hubris (overweening pride), which in Medieval times was considered the Deadly Sin Number One.

The cause of envy is also in dispute. Is it innate or reactive to the environment? Some still hold that it is innate. I believe it to be reactive to an experience with the outside world, though originating in the individual who is making a comparison and finding herself lacking. Hence it results from something we find negative about ourselves in comparison with someone else. But we need to take responsibility for it, to move forward and make a better adjustment by integrating our goals with our self-assessment and our self-esteem.

At yet another level, envy, like all other affects, is transmitted by neurons in the brain. At this moment neuroscientists are studying how different parts of the brain function during different mental operations, such as memory or mathematical problems, and in different circumstances, such as stress. Geneticists are studying genes singly and in combination for their effects, e.g., on an individual's susceptibility to depression. The time is coming when an individual's reaction, based on his genetic inheritance, to the many inputs from the outside world will be understood, and one of these bio-psychosocial reactions to be studied will be envy.

Notes

1. Pinel: "They are our brothers."

2. Even as an undergraduate, before becoming involved in medicine or psychiatry, I learned of three giants of modern psychiatry: Freud, Adler, and Jung. Freud's name is still in common parlance, and, in fact, a few years ago *Time* gave him top billing along with Einstein as the two thinkers in the twentieth century whose ideas have been most instrumental in expanding our horizons, one concerning the universe and the other the inner self. Jung went into eclipse for a time but has recently sparked a resurgence of interest, based, mostly, on literature and mythology. Adler's name is virtually unknown.

3. Cf. Herzog regarding how it's not long in our lives before we observe we are in several "pecking orders". Raiga calls them "ladders" with persons above and below us on each.

4. I was astonished to learn of a boy who entered first grade at age five and already stole thirty dollars a few dollars at a time from his trusting mother's wallet to impress the other children, despite his having been taught the usual rules of right and wrong.

5. My husband's nephew from Eastern Europe, now naturalized here, and I have discussed this, and his point is that back in Europe, people are "friendlier", and I realize that he means what Sullivan referred to fifty years ago.

6. An interesting question arises if one subscribes to the importance of the first mother/child collaboration (feeding) as critical in character development. Throughout history (until recently, with artificial infant formulas), babies had to learn quickly to work with the mother (or wet nurse) in order to survive. In some mothers, particularly with the first child, establishing good milk flow can take several days. Breastfeeding can be painful from engorgement and sore nipples, and the first breast product, colostrum, is less nourishing than subsequent milk. The screaming infant often frightens the inexperienced mother into abandoning her breastfeeding attempt (rather than, for example,

augmenting with formula until the breast flow is abundant). A very common story from a young primipara is "I tried to breastfeed, but she wasn't getting enough, so I had to go to the bottle."

With my children, my intention was to breastfeed in order that they would benefit from maternal antibodies in breast milk as well as psychologic bonding with a mother/breast. With the eldest I too had difficulty establishing a good flow. But I knew that my full-term infant, weighing over seven pounds, had both the good masseter muscles and the sucking reflex necessary to do his part. Realizing that infant formula by bottle is less work for the infant because the rubber nipple holes are larger, and fearing that he would take the easy way, not doing what had to be done to get the better breast milk, I gave him water by bottle so he would not dehydrate, while waiting for abundant breast milk to come in. In other words, I made him work for his dinner. This strategy succeeded, and soon there was enough milk that I could pump the excess and refrigerate it to leave with the babysitter. His healthy constitution and the antibodies from breast milk permitted him to enjoy a very healthy childhood.

But I have often wondered whether his body somehow translated those first hard days of fighting hunger into a kind of sense that the extrauterine world is a demanding place where you have to struggle for everything you get. Might his experience be paraphrased, "Why must I work so hard just to be fed? Why does the world/breast withhold my sustenance? Why is life so hard? Why do I experience this strange rage some call 'envy'?"

Of the many positive and negative traits the flesh is heir to, envy is not one that this son displays. He exhibits genuine pride in his brothers' accomplishments. Yet identification with the envied one is a strategy for dealing with envy.

7. Told that someone's money was "tainted", Mark Twain replied, "Twice tainted. 'Tain't yours and 'tain't mine."

8. An eating disorder specialist once drew my attention to the fact that whereas anorectics are usually somewhat above average in intelligence, the Mensa Society is overrun with morbidly obese women.

9. Envy used to be targeted in the opposite direction, i.e., envy by children for adults, who were perceived as having prerogatives denied them. I vividly recall as a child being shamed by my father for being "only a child" (the implication being "so what did I know?"). Therefore I yearned to be "big" so as to merit respect and to share the secrets that adults seemed to enjoy, including even the privilege of staying up late (in days when children were put to bed at a non-negotiable time, so their parents could rest or enjoy adult time together). Years ago I was astonished to hear one of my young sons saying that he had no wish to grow up, the implication being that he preferred never to take on adult responsibilities. I believe that with the enormous increase in privileges and "rights" for the young, there is no longer much incentive to mature, and the goal of taking one's place in adult society is often replaced by the "Peter Pan complex", or intention never to grow up. We have made childhood too enjoyable for some children.

10. In my practice I worked with two women who came of age in the mid-century and whose mother in one case and father in the other had deprived them of a college education (at no cost to the family, in either case). The father of one would not let his daughter take advantage of a full scholarship, with room and board at the home of a coreligionist, in exchange for housework. The other woman's best friend's well-to-do father had offered to send my patient to college with his daughter, an only child, so they could room together and share college experiences. That patient's mother would not let her accept this generous offer. Both women recalled that their growing-up years were times when obedient daughters did not go off on their own in opposition to parental mandates. The word "envy" never came up in their recollections of their experiences, but when I suggested envy as a possible cause for their parents' obstructionism, they both jumped on this possible explanation. We have seen in various contexts that the envier may conceal his feeling from others, and often even from himself.

11. Shame has recently entered the limelight in the interest of psychoanalysts.

12. Spillius' patient would argue thus: "Her doctor may respond to calls, but mine could probably solve problems hers couldn't."

13. Years ago I entertained an idea to write an article on how my patients' therapy was influenced by my pregnancy, and that not a normal pregnancy but one under constant threat, requiring me to lie on my own couch and seat my patient at my desk. The birth of my healthy son shelved my writing project, as I sprang into action taking on this second simultaneous full-time career of motherhood.

14. I agree with Berke, that these are the most envied, but only in the case of those persons who do not suffer deprivation in the first two categories. People envying those tangibles probably experience not only envy but covetousness, as I distinguish the two, but Berke does not.

Chapter 14

The Politics of Envy

The Wealth of Nations by Adam Smith, the eighteenth-century Scottish economist of "invisible hand" fame and considered the father of modern economics, is on the lips of economists, CPAs, MBAs, and, in fact, everyone who has been through a Great Books program. Most of us (including myself) had not been aware that Smith wrote an earlier book, *The Theory of Moral Sentiments*, in which he first introduced ideas about the role of competition, envy, and rank or status in economic life. He believed this early book would establish his fame. We should all be so lucky as to be remembered for the wrong book.

Smith believed that every kind of society (with a single exception) requires a power structure to protect citizens from the envy of others, thus making possible economic growth. The exception he cites is one based solely on hunting, in a climate without natural refrigeration, because envy resulting from the hunter's skill or luck is short-lived and dissipates after two or three days, by the time the leftovers stink.

Smith observes, further, that while an orderly society requires stratification, i.e., with ranks and levels, "Wealth and greatness are often regarded with the respect and admiration which are due only to wisdom and virtue; and that the contempt, of which vice and folly are the only proper objects, is often most unjustly bestowed upon poverty and weakness, has been the complaint of moralists in all ages." In this early work he writes:

> Our respect for the great is most apt to offend by its excess; our fellow-feeling for the miserable, by its defect. Moralists exhort us to charity and compassion. They warn us against the fascination of greatness. This fascination, indeed, is so powerful, that the rich and the great are too often preferred to the wise and virtuous. Nature has wisely judged that the distinction of ranks, the peace and order of society, would rest more securely upon the plain and palpable difference of birth and fortune, than upon the invisible and often uncertain difference of wisdom and virtue. The undistinguishing eyes of the great mob of mankind can well enough perceive the former: it is with difficulty that the nice discernment of the wise and the virtuous can sometimes distinguish the latter.

Jean-Jacques Rousseau, a political philosopher almost exactly contemporaneous with Adam Smith, famed for *The Social Contract* as seminal in revolutionary thinking in France, also wrote an earlier work, *A Discourse on Inequality,* which the editor of my edition, Cranston, reports was more influential in pre-French Revolutionary times than the better known *Contract.* Like other Enlightenment thinkers, Rousseau evinced a nostalgic belief in a Golden Age of prehistory, in which our species lived without ambition and competition, each dependent solely on his own efforts to secure a living and without any permanent ties to mate or children.[1] With the advent of agriculture and metallurgy, however, came specialization, and with it class and status.

Civil society was founded, he contends, when the first human fenced off land, claimed ownership, and kept others from sharing in the crop grown thereon. With civil society, according to Rousseau, came human misery. (Voltaire pointed out the folly of expecting anyone to cultivate land and then not prevent the confiscation of the resultant crops by human or animal predators.) First came barter, later a money economy because of the difficulty of trading equal values when the units were large, like domesticated animals.

Rousseau held that a universal desire for reputation, honor, and promotion devours us all, excites and multiplies passions. In making all men competitors, rivals, even enemies, it causes everyday failures, successes, and catastrophes of all kinds. Thus primordial equality disappeared, its place taken by the inequality of talents (what can you do about that?). As possessions became disparate, humankind developed status, rank, and power (based on riches) with their attendant cascade of troubles (successes, failures, and, of course, envy), a function of the constant jockeying for position.

> Finally, a burning ambition, the burning passion to enlarge one's relative fortune, not so much from real need as to put oneself ahead of others, inspires in all men a dark propensity to injure one another, a secret jealousy which is all the more dangerous in that it often assumes the mask of benevolence in order to do its deeds in greater safety; in a word, there is competition and rivalry on the one hand, conflicts of interest on the other, and always the hidden desire to gain an advantage at the expense of other people. All these evils are the main effects of property and inseparable consequences of nascent inequality.
>
> It [universal striving to get ahead of one another] is responsible for what is best or worst, a multitude of bad things and a very few good ones.

Rousseau does not see the strong dominating the weak, but the rich the poor (actually these are usually the same), and this discordance evolves into masters and slaves. Nor does he plead for universal equality but that all should be honored and favored, and their position in society correspond to their merits and services. Justice does not require equality but in placing everyone where he ought to be by merit and contribution to the general good.

> There is something in freedom, as there is in heavy and succulent foods and rich wine, which fortifies robust constitutions used to it, but which overwhelms, ruins, and intoxicates [the rest]. Free time has bad outcomes too. Singing and dancing lead to the vice of vanity and scorn [in the talented], to shame and envy [in the untalented].

With specialization came different and varied talents resulting in opportunities for offense, necessitating restraining laws. All this welter led to envy and the necessity to protect oneself therefrom. Rousseau recognized the omnipresent slippery slope between envy and fairness. Fairness and justice lie ultimately in the eye of the beholder. "Since wealth, nobility or rank, power and personal merit are generally the four principal qualities by which one is measured in society, I would prove that harmony or a conflict between these several sorts of distinction is the surest indication of the good or bad constitution of a state. I would show that as between these four kinds of inequality, personal qualities are the origin of all the others, and wealth is the last to which they are all reduced because wealth, being the most immediately useful to wellbeing and the easiest to communicate, can be readily used to buy all the rest." [While wealth can buy tutors and SAT workshops, how can it buy personal merit, the fourth "quality by which one is measured in society"?]

"*Liberté, egalité, fraternité*" was the rallying cry in the Enlightenment. After centuries of enormous inequalities, this movement hoped to make men equal as well as free, and the hope was irresistible in France, in America, and in a third polity, which converted a five-class to a classless society without shedding a drop of blood—in Poland. Later Marx and Engels and Communism in Russia and elsewhere and socialist movements in England tried to equalize.

In America our founding fathers also tried the egalitarian[2] experiment, with equality for all and no one with a handicap at the starting line (and hence, presumably, no occasion for envy). No handicap, that is, except for the very limited sense and specialized meaning by which persons may be considered "equal". But how can equality at the ballot box (forget equality in court with Justice blindfolded) preclude envy in all other spheres of life? Then, as now, we are all born to wealth or poverty or something in between, to loving parents or no parents at all or some intermediate kind of caregivers, with good or bad physical traits, including beauty of body and strength of mind or its converse. [Even now, some believe that strength of mind can be legislated, with "no child left behind". But I digress.]

Little more than half a century after the establishment of our new federation, a Frenchman, Alexis de Tocqueville, wealthy, highly intelligent, a shrewd observer of human nature, spent a year in North America, studying, talking to people of widely diverse backgrounds, interpreting, and predicting the likely future of the States, which he saw as much more powerful than the infant federation. Although he made a brief foray into the South, he spent most of his time in New England and New York, and thus his view is one of Yankee America. Some of his predictions were right on target—e.g., that Native Americans would be squeezed to the margins and largely eliminated. Others were wide of the mark—e.g., that not only was there no solution in sight for the slavery problem, but that blacks and whites would never integrate.

He identified "equality" as an important part of our federation's experiment: "The first and most intense passion which is engendered by the equality of conditions is, I need hardly say, the love of that same equality."

Germane to this study, de Tocqueville found Americans riddled with envy. Occurring frequently in his work is the French word "*ressentiment*". More than "resentment" in English, this word means a recurrent recollection of past wrongs, envious anger, and long-lasting grudge, or in the *Petit Larousse* "being reminded repeatedly of an injustice and wishing for revenge".

Like John Stuart Mill's worry over the cultural consequences of egalitarianism in the form of lowering of standards, de Tocqueville feared that in an atmosphere of egalitarianism we would not have the resources to combat public opinion as the test of morality and virtue.

In a country touting not only liberty but equality, de Tocqueville saw resentment of the rich by the poor despite intended equality of opportunity. He wrote "I never met in America any citizen so poor as not to cast a glance of hope and envy on the enjoyments of the rich or whose imagination did not possess itself by anticipation of those good things that fate still obstinately withheld from him."

Elsewhere, "It cannot be denied that democratic institutions strongly tend to promote the feeling of envy in the human heart; not so much because they afford to everyone the means of rising to the same level with others as because those means perpetually disappoint the persons who employ them. Democratic institutions awaken and foster a passion for equality which they can never entirely satisfy.... [T]he people are excited in the pursuit of an advantage, which is more precious because it is not sufficiently remote to be unknown or sufficiently near to be enjoyed. ... Whatever transcends their own limitations appears to be an obstacle to their desires, and there is no superiority, however legitimate it may be, which is not irksome in their sight." The proximity of social classes increases bitterness and envy, he believed. "It must be admitted that man's hopes and desires are oftener blasted, the soul is more stricken and perturbed, and care itself more keen."[3]

The situation in America, he wrote, was in marked contrast to that in his own homeland, revolutionized fifty years prior, where citizens apparently accepted easily the station to which they were born ["My father was a shoemaker, so I'll be a shoemaker"] and worked for and under those in high positions without apparent resentment. This observation held true almost a hundred years later when Raiga wrote.

Hear de Tocqueville:

> All revolutions enlarge the ambition of men. This is more peculiarly true of those revolutions which overthrow an aristocracy. When the former barriers that kept back the multitude from fame and power are suddenly thrown down, a violent and universal movement takes place towards that eminence so long coveted and at last to be enjoyed. In this first burst of triumph nothing seems impossible to anyone: not only are desires boundless, but the power of satisfying them seems almost boundless too.[4] Amid the general and sudden change of laws and customs, in this vast confusion of all men and all ordinances, the various members of the community rise and sink again with excessive rapidity, and power passes so quickly from hand to hand that none need despair of catching it in turn.
>
> The first thing that strikes a traveler in the United States is the innumerable multitude of those who seek to emerge from their original condition; and the second is the rarity of lofty[5] ambition to be observed in the midst of the universally ambitious stir of society. No Americans are devoid of a yearning desire to rise, but hardly any appear to entertain hopes of great magnitude or to pursue very lofty aims.
>
> I believe that ambitious men in democracies are less engrossed than any other with the interests and the judgment of posterity; the present moment alone engages and absorbs them. They are more apt to complete a number of undertakings with rapidity than to raise lasting monuments of their achievements, and they care much more for success than for fame.

> All are constantly seeking to acquire property, power, and reputation; few contemplate these things upon a great scale; and this is the more surprising as nothing is to be discerned in the manners or laws of America to limit desire or to prevent it from spreading its impulses in every direction. It seems difficult to attribute this singular state of things to the equality of social conditions, for as soon as that same equality was established in France, the flight of ambition became unbounded. Nevertheless, I think that we may find the principal cause of this fact in the social condition and democratic manners of the Americans.

One reason that de Tocqueville identified for the difference in this regard between France and the young United States was a function of the laws of inheritance. With primogeniture (in France) a large estate could remain intact over centuries unless and until squandered by a scion with little ability or interest in managing it. When property is divided among heirs (as in America), it usually does not remain intact, and each new generation must start afresh, albeit usually a little ahead of their fathers. Immigration to this country in the nineteenth and early twentieth centuries was stoked by the fact that repeatedly dividing a farm in the "old country" among the sons did not leave enough for any of them to make a living, and other arrangements had to be made. In my late father-in-law's case, one brother got the land, the second joined the army (and was killed), and they put the third, Wasil, on the ship.[6]

> What chiefly diverts the men of democracies from lofty ambition is not the scantiness of their fortunes, but the vehemence of the exertions they daily make to improve them. They strain their faculties to the utmost to achieve paltry results, and this cannot fail speedily to limit their range of view and to circumscribe their powers.
> Another thing that prevents the men of democratic

periods from easily indulging in the pursuit of lofty objects
is the lapse of time which they foresee must take place
before they can be ready to struggle for them. 'It is a great
advantage,' says Pascal,[7] 'to be a man of quality,[8] since it
brings one man as forward at eighteen or twenty as another
man would be at fifty, which is a clear gain of thirty years.'
Those thirty years are commonly wanting to the ambitious
characters of democracies. The principle of equality, which
allows every man to arrive at everything, prevents all men
from rapid advancement. [And, of course, fifty was the life
expectancy for most males in those times.]

De Tocqueville underscores the downside of equality: the greater
the equality, the harder it is for anyone to achieve much on his own.
Thus democracy has drawbacks and imperfections. For this reason,
de Tocqueville recognized the need for associations in American
societies, since it is through banding together that persons who are
weak individually can make their demands felt. Cooperating in trade
unions can strengthen workers' demands for material advantage.
We see the principle of strength in numbers in more esoteric areas
today: persons who as individuals can do little to alleviate ills in the
larger community hope to make an impact by engaging in one or
another of the many organizations promoting causes dear to their
hearts, in areas such as child welfare, environmental issues, problems of health and disease, and social change.

De Tocqueville notes that equality helps everyone a little, no
one very much:

> As wealth is subdivided and knowledge diffused, no one
> is entirely destitute of education or of property; the privileges and disqualifications of caste being abolished, and
> men having shattered the bonds that once held them fixed,
> the notion of advancement suggests itself to every mind,
> the desire to rise swells in every heart, and all men want to

mount above their station; ambition is the universal feeling.

But if the equality of conditions gives some resources to all the members of the community, it also prevents any of them from having resources of great extent, which necessarily circumscribes their desires within somewhat narrow limits. Thus, among democratic nations, ambition is ardent and continual, but its aim is not habitually lofty, and life is generally spent in eagerly coveting small objects that are within reach.

De Tocqueville makes the same point that has been raised earlier in this book that democracy seems to promise more than it can deliver. At this juncture, envy enters because the promise seems to have been broken, and for many citizens this is worse than for it never to have been made. De Tocqueville again: "It must be admitted that man's hopes and desires are oftener blasted, the soul is more stricken and perturbed, and care itself more keen."

"Ressentiment" is the term frequently used by de Tocqueville, and by it he means a nagging hostility toward those who have acquired what has eluded the grasp of the envious one. Thus it is almost the opposite of what one might expect, i.e., the greater the promise of opportunity, the greater the ressentiment when, like Tantalus forever reaching for the fruit, success comes too little and too late, or never.

A century and a third after de Tocqueville wrote about envy in our infant democracy, and thirty-five years after Raiga's book was published on the ubiquitousness of envy, an Austrian sociologist, Helmut Schoeck, conducted an extensive study and wrote in German a clear, comprehensive scholarly book, *ENVY: A Theory of Social Behavior* (translated into English in 1969), on the sociologic and political implications of envy.

Schoeck saw envy as not only a pan-human phenomenon[9] for which social groups must devise ways to protect their members, but also a driving force in civilization without which we would not strive for the good things we see others enjoying and without which civilization itself could not progress. At the same time, a balance must be found for the control of envy. Schoeck writes:

> Few concepts are so intrinsic a part of social reality [as envy], yet at the same time so markedly neglected in the categories of behavioural science. ... I do not wish to give the impression ... that I consider envy as a universal ultimate cause: envy does not explain everything, but it throws light on more things than people have hitherto been prepared to admit or even to see.

Schoeck makes several salient points about envy. He finds it "a silent, secretive process, not always verifiable"; it is "concealed, proscribed, repressed". There is no litmus test, no Rorschach for envy. Schoeck admits that its presence cannot always be validated; it can only be inferred and surmised from the behavior of the envious one. But, contrary to the common belief of the envier, envy originates in the person who envies; we are chasing the wrong cause when we look for the cause of genuine envy outside the envier (i.e., in the envied one or in society). Another point unique to Schoeck is that envy can sometimes be the hidden basis when we fail to warn someone of a danger, when such warning would be the only decent thing to do.

Schoeck asserts that (1) fear of envy from others deters competition, which is needed for any culture to grow and progress, whereas conversely innovation is possible only when an individual is free to act without fearing the envious retaliation of the lower echelons left behind, and therefore (2) each culture must devise (evolve? stumble upon?) mechanisms (usually beliefs in primitive societies) to detoxify envy as a deterrent force by helping the envious tolerate it and the envied one feel protected from depredation, in the event that he has an idea and the ambition, courage, and willingness to take a chance and perhaps succeed, even marginally, beyond the envious rank and file, and (3) when a social improvement is made to a condition that the envier has been criticizing, instead of rejoicing or even looking pleased, the envier acts as if he would rather complain.

"Every man must be prone to a small degree of envy; without it the interplay of social forces within society is unthinkable." For civilization to progress there must be status distinction as well as division of labor that inevitably cause envy.[10] At the same time, such envy must be regulated. The premise of Schoeck's book is: "In society and in private life, the ability to act as if there were no envy accelerates growth, progress, and innovation." For this to happen, "Both envier and envied have to come to terms with inequity."

One early such device for the regulation of envy was belief in good and bad luck (the "blind goddess Fortuna"[11]), whose gifts are distributed randomly, thus helping the loser lacking the desired advantage feel that the cause of his failure was not his own inadequacy or fault.[12] Belief systems involving the importance of day of birth or influence of the planets and stars (such as the Wise Men's star) have also helped people tolerate the success of others. Widespread belief in the "evil eye"[13] (which was interlinked with the idea of witches) was another envy-coping device. It was more face-saving for the have-nots to believe that someone had cast bad fortune on them than to have to accept the reality that they were less competent than those whom fortune, intelligence, or talents favored. For coping they sought counter-charms to discourage the negative attention of the evil eye. The fact that those likely to be envied also believed in this power made them conclude that the better part of wisdom would be to hide their advantage. Thus a logical extension would be secrecy about their accomplishments, and, as Bacon pointed out, protection against envy is one good reason for modesty. Before investigating envy, I would never have suspected that superstitions like the evil eye, though widespread across time and cultures, would have persisted well into the twentieth century, and perhaps even to this day.

Whereas many ancient religions involved deities who ridiculed failure, a major reason for the overwhelming success of Christianity was that it moved in the opposite direction: it legitimized progressive inequality and thereby amply protected the envied from the envious by offering to the long-suffering individual willing to accept with patience his lot in this life, equality and eternal happiness in the afterlife, compared to which all disappointments, failures, and injustices in this life were less than trivial. This belief made it possible for a few to deviate from the average without too much fear of retaliation, and for the have-nots to accept their lot without too much resentment.

Schoeck writes: "In the West, the historical achievement of this Christian ethic is to have encouraged and protected, if not to have been actually responsible for the extent of, the exercise of creative power through the control of envy." (Kant, Nietzsche, Feuerbach, and others have also credited Christianity's phenomenal success to its offering true equality and bliss in the afterlife, compared to which all current tribulations are insignificant, thus helping the oppressed underclass endure envy in the here and now.)

Another approach to an idealized envy-free society is to strive for a classless society of equals. This was offered by Karl Marx, but Schoeck documents that whenever communism has been tried (as in Israeli kibbutzim), envy does not vanish but becomes a worse problem. Envy was notorious in the old USSR society, as was addressed in Olesha's fiction. Herzog (discussed in the chapter on essayists) contends that envy reaches a pinnacle in religious societies of presumed equals, and Sorge also presented his observations on envy in Protestant churches.

Contradicting the idea commonly held by both the general public and many sociologists and anthropologists that preliterate peoples live in poor but loving harmony, Schoeck cites evidence that they display envy over advantages that to us seem marginal at best. His observation is confirmed by the anthropologist Foster (cf. my anthropologic appendix).

Having shown that envy goes back historically and culturally, he goes on to draw attention to a remarkable phenomenon that occurred a century ago: envy went underground. Whereas formerly envy had been freely discussed and written and preached about, the pendulum slowed, stopped, and reversed. Suddenly there was a sea change: a widespread pall fell on the subject. Almost overnight the word and the concept of envy went into eclipse, as documented by counts of titles in anthropologic and sociologic literature. (Our society's sudden reluctance to address the topic of envy has been compared to the silence, a century earlier, on the topic of infant sexuality. The difference, however, is that prior to the early twentieth century, envy was commonly discussed, whereas sexuality, particularly in children, had never been in the open.) During the twentieth century, at the same time that search of relevant indices in the social sciences produced little on the topic, instead of "envy" we began to find "justice", and now, when we do hear the word "envy", it has come to be used almost exclusively in a trivialized way. "We use the word Envy only when the situation excludes genuine, destructive, malicious envy," in Schoeck's words. His explanation for our silence is that the demands of the envious, both legitimate and specious, have become increasingly accommodated (although not under that opprobrious term). The focus moved from "envy" to "justice", and the presence of what would formerly have been considered envy has come, more and more, to "prove" social injustice. Schoeck is well aware that the weight of all liberal opinion is against him on this, that liberals as a rule insist they are talking about true justice, and that Schoeck is wrong. Schoeck writes, "Instead of Envy we talk about Justice or lapse into sour and bitter silence." At the same time, some persons who are advantaged and believe themselves to be envied may become embarrassed[14] and sometimes even ashamed of their advantages, and if in positions of power, attempt to equilibrate.

Schoeck observes that many have come to accept almost any cavilings, legitimate or specious, as something that must be rectified. This has encouraged the "victim mentality". Envy has become the implicit/explicit basis of social policy, as we have come to see the mission of government to prevent the prosperous from annoying the rest of us. Envy of the rich is generally recognized to be the basis of many jury awards. Schoeck takes care, however, to acknowledge and differentiate legitimate complaints, such as exclusion from unions for reasons of race or nepotism, i.e., only relatives need apply.

As a society, we have come to take a broader view of justice and to see more and more commodities as people's "rights" and look for ways to provide them. All this has paralleled the shift from "envy" to "justice".

While Schoeck's description of envy is similar to others', he adds an additional feature. He cites studies (possibly European) in which persons polled would choose to have less (e.g., income), if that meant everyone else had less also, rather than to have more themselves if it meant that a few would have an even higher income. This attitude is remarkably similar to the *esprit de corps* described by Freud, of which the hallmark is that the leader must treat everyone precisely the same. A lower status for all is preferable to mixed statuses.

We see an example of similar reasoning in our Americans with Disabilities Act. A new facility cannot be constructed unless it includes access for the handicapped, with the result that if everyone cannot use it, no one can. An example of unforeseen (?) problems created by this law was presented on *Sixty Minutes*. A group of nuns in New York City wanted to buy and renovate a condemned building to be used as a shelter for the homeless. Their plans met all the requirements except for an elevator to the second floor. Since the second floor was intended as living quarters for the vigorous nuns planning to run the shelter, an elevator would have been a luxury. After a year of struggling with the bureaucracy to try to find a way around this legal provision, they finally had to abandon the entire project because of being unable to run the obstacle course of the superfluous elevator. Therefore the shelter was never accomplished for anyone.

Schoeck subscribes to the idea that some of us (I include myself) who are blessed with a combination of many good things of life, whether earned or by lucky accident (such as intelligence, good education, interesting, well-paid work, comfortable living circumstances, supportive spouse), may sympathize with those lacking these advantages and feel uncomfortable about this, perhaps even "guilty" and ashamed, especially if they were partly given to us (while I studied hard in medical school, my father kept writing tuition checks). We may impute envy to these persons, and some may feel it, others not. It is a small step to suspect envy on the part of others, whether they really experience such envy or not.[15] If they do envy, it may be only the tangibles, not the intangibles, such as education, and the tangibles can range from the most basic human needs, such as food, to the luxuries, such as automobiles not as transport but as status symbols. These conflicting feelings led to the privileged haves (often the "liberal" elites) to try somehow to equilibrate, to lessen the gap between themselves and those without. Thus many intellectual liberals have become the self-proclaimed mouthpieces of the masses, according to Schoeck. Sometimes the "haves" have recognized injustice and legitimately shared their prerogatives. It was white men's vote that gave suffrage to all men, including black, and later men's vote that gave suffrage to women.

But not always. The fulcrum of social policy has often been, according to Schoeck and others, to attempt to assuage envy by replacing the old god(s) with the new god of equality. Their utopia is a classless society of equals. One utopian idea has been to eliminate inequality and hence envy by universal education. This fails, of course, because of unequal intellectual, academic, and motivational qualifications. When the perceived gap consists of material things, the principle of economic redistribution has been applied by progressive taxation, even negative taxation. Politicians are quick to take advantage of this discomfort with inequality, for the benefit of their constituents, as well as their own benefit in the form of votes. Schoeck states:

> [T]he agnostic[16] twentieth-century intellectual seeks a new god, promising the same protection as the Christian God's against the next man's envy (often only suspected) and the same freedom from the consuming sense of guilt engendered by his personal superiority. This substitute god is progressivist ideology or more precisely, the utopia of a perfectly egalitarian society. It may never [cannot] come true, but a mere mental pose of being in its favour helps to bear the guilt of being unequal.

Elsewhere Schoeck observes:

> We are least capable of acting sensibly in economic and social matters when we face, or believe we face, an envious beneficiary of our decisions. Allocation of scarce resources is rarely optimal when decisions are based on fear of their envy.

He points out that trying to equilibrate (in contrast to trying to behave justly) is a fool's errand for several reasons. One such is that there can never be an envy-free society (under communism as Marx proclaimed, or in kibbutzim in Israel, or in any other system) because there will never be enough of anything for everyone to have all he wants (although Sorge sees an exception in the love of God). Contrary to expectations, whatever the envied one shares fails to quell envy but effectively opens the door for the envious one to complain about other disparities and demand more.

Also, Schoeck sees such efforts to accommodate to envy as a

hindrance by encouraging the envious to assume a helpless stance and discouraging working for and earning one's own. Finally, "Few arbitrary actions, especially those of a legislative nature, are so thankless, and few are so fraught with undesirable consequences, as an attempt to balance the scales of fate in order to assuage envy." We see this in unpleasant perspective in the matter of foreign aid, where, apart from the fact that aid is often stolen from the needy by the fat cats, it often seems to have the counterproductive effect of perpetuating our image as "the ugly American". Most of us, at different times, are benefactors and recipients, and when recipients, we may be aware of our own resentment toward our benefactors. Continued benefaction in the face of ingratitude can make the giver come across as more magnanimous and unbearable.[17]

One interpretation (and hope) for the "all men are created equal" doctrine is that since ideal equality cannot be universal, hoped-for equality could at least be realized in the realm of opportunity. According to Schoeck, even this is impossible:

> In an achievement-oriented society there cannot be equality of opportunity,[18] there can at most be adequate opportunities for different kinds of people: person and opportunity must be complementary, but the result of such a system is a society stratified along socio-economic lines in which classes or status groups, professions and prestige are clearly discernible. This will provide occasion for envy, but it is more honest and more healthy socially, in the long run, to acknowledge this fact than to behave as though equality of opportunity were really feasible.

Think about it: common sense maintains that we can't send the whole cohort to Stanford.

Schoeck believes that inequality is accepted in persons who know each other intimately and appreciate each other's true individual essence.

With these arguments, Schoeck disputes those who try to achieve a "just society" or utopia by creating a society of equals and thereby removing envy:

> There is only one group of authors who really deserve to lose their reputation and who moreover, should be regarded as having been empirically refuted: those who have used envy for the stuff of their social and economic philosophy, and who dream of reorganizing social life in terms of a society devoid of envy—free from either the need to envy or the possibility of being envious. ... The dividing line between vulgar [he means "ordinary, everyday"] envy and justifiable indignation-envy [Raiga's distinction], so vital for an ordered social and national life, has been blurred by an increasingly fervent egalitarianism, the misunderstanding and exaggeration of the idea of equality. Further, a dimension of time was lost. 'Justice' must be attained this very minute: its postponement until tomorrow or the next day is now considered inconceivable. If ... the idea that a higher status or standard of living must be acquired by work, and earned, falls into disuse, [i.e., "instant gratification" takes the place of responsibility] if, that is, the idea of equality becomes identified with complete immediacy, it will no longer be possible to distinguish between the two forms of envy. Thus every privilege, every superiority of rank, every difference in property and prosperity and every authority, no matter how legitimately elected, is basically open to attack from the street whenever people, their faces distorted with envy and hatred, gather to protest against it.

Today we can state on a better empirical basis than would have been possible fifty or a hundred years ago that the world cannot belong to the envious, any more than the causes of envy can be eradicated from society. The society devoid of all traces of class or status, and similar refuges for wits'-end thinking and uncomfortable feelings, should no longer be considered worthy of serious discussion. ...

Even those who have never taken seriously utopias of classless societies and pure socialism have been seduced in the course of the last hundred years into falsely concluding that the critical role in society is the prerogative of envious dispositions whom a single concession would supposedly placate. ... [H]istorical observation and rules deducible from basic human behaviour would seem to suggest that there is something like a hardening towards exaggerated sensitivity to envy. Francis Bacon had already realized that nothing is more calculated to exasperate the envious man and to feed his discontent than irrational action, an abdication from a superior position with the removal of his envy in view. The time has surely come when we should stop behaving as though the envious man was the main criterion for economic and social policy.

Finally, yet another thirty years later, in the USA in the 1990s, Doug Bandow, in his *The Politics of Envy: Statism as Theology,* made several points germane to this inquiry.

Although writing from a different (a Christian) perspective, his observations are remarkably consonant with Schoeck's, to the effect that envy drives politics.

> Politics, in the United States, at least, has increasingly been based on envy, the desire not to produce more for oneself, but to take as much as possible from others. Of course, all the proponents of the politics of envy proclaim themselves animated by public-spiritedness: who in Washington would admit that the higher taxes he advocates will be used to pay off the interest group of the day, whether

farmer, corporation, or union? Who would suggest that he has anything but good will toward those whom he is intent on mulcting?

To get votes, Bandow says, one's plank should be the destruction or confiscation of someone else's assets, nothing constructive, just "redistribution".

Addressing the problem of poverty in the light of equity and fairness, he writes: "Poverty is a complex phenomenon because it has more than one cause. Its causes include not only personal infirmity and imperfect social structures; much poverty also results from poor individual decisions—drug use, criminal activity, premature pregnancy, excessive spending.[19] And individual differences play an even greater role in generating income inequality."

He questions the moral ideal we champion of equality: "Income will inevitably be unequal because people are unequal. At issue is not just natural ability but ambition and personal preference. If the larger social order, particularly the economic rules of the game, are just—and admittedly this is an important and controversial "if"—then the resulting economic distribution should not be regarded as morally suspect. Where inequalities result from injustice, the injustice should be addressed because it is unjust, not because there are inequalities."

Distinguishing between need and envy, Bandow favors aid to the needy (food, clothes, and shelter) but not attempts at equilibration. "Complaints about income distribution inevitably end up resting on envy. And redistributing wealth for the purpose of satisfying envy—where the issue is not that people lack shelter, but that their home isn't as big as someone else's—would seem to run afoul of the Tenth Commandment against covetousness." He favors meeting people's genuine needs but calling this by what it is, "charity", not some kind of "entitlement".

He points to big government as the culprit (citing statistics to the effect that between 1950 and 1990, corporate profits rose 757 percent, personal incomes rose 1870 percent, and government spending grew 3163 percent). Like Schoeck, Bandow sees government as the successor of religion in people's lives, encroaching in areas of life that should be left to religion.

> Ours is a secular age. But faith has not disappeared. Rather, the gods have changed. Today the reigning theology is statism: government has become god, charged with the people's salvation.
>
> ...There are, I believe, more important things in life than politics. That is not a widely held view in Washington and the capitals of most other nations, however; American opinion leaders spent months in 1993 debating 'the politics of meaning', a philosophy, held by some people of enormous influence, that government can fill people's every need, spiritual as well as material. This epitomizes the theology of statism and is ... pernicious, aiding and abetting the expansion of the state into precisely the areas of people's lives through which they should find meaning.
>
> The more subtle [politicians and social leaders] seek support by endorsing 'change', proposing to 'reinvent' their institutions, and pledging to offer 'meaning' to people's lives.

This is not—and should not be—their job, according to Bandow. The '80s have been called "The Decade of Greed", and Bandow proposes for the '90s the epithet "The Decade of Envy". He cites another author, Jay Johansen, who contrasts the politics of greed ("let's do things that make us all richer") with the politics of envy ("I don't care what happens to me, as long as my neighbor suffers"). He finds the latter more pernicious because, unlike greed, which harms only the greedy, envy expressed in politics contaminates the larger community.

Schoeck and others have noted that *Homo sapiens* has been called, depending on the originating discipline, Homo other adjectives—*H.*

faber, H. ludens, H. economicus, and now, at Schoeck's suggestion, *Homo invidiosus.*[20]

Another area that invites envy and greed, along with hubris, for analysis as motivating forces, is war. The ancient Greek historian Herodotus in *The Persian Wars* quotes the Persian emperor Xerxes as calling a council and deciding "It's time to enlarge our empire." With more than a million and a half foot soldiers (according to Herodotus' count), that drank whole rivers dry, and a navy, Xerxes set out to invade green, well-watered southeast Europe. In one of the most celebrated defeats in military history, the 300 Greeks under Leonidas held the pass at Thermopylae against the hordes of Asian infantry until it was hopeless. Then, in Xerxes' arrogance, he was outwitted when the Greek naval commander Themistocles sent a message to the effect that he was Xerxes' friend and that the best place for a naval battle was Salamis. That was true: it was the best place for the Greek navy with smaller, faster ships, though vastly outnumbered. At the renowned battle of Salamis Themistocles turned back Xerxes and his horde and kept the Asians out of Europe.

Two millennia later, the British saw no reason why the sun should ever set on their empire. *Plus ça change, plus c'est la même chose.*

We conclude our look at envy in politics with a delightful and thought-provoking novel, *War with the Newts*, satirizing everyone from Napoleon on, written in the 1930s by the Czech author Karel Čapek, who, in another work, with his brother, gave us the word "robot". Although not dealing directly with envy as such, Čapek creates a very homogeneous society, drab, colorless, but powerful, composed of intelligent amphibians who eventually overthrow our heterogeneous society. One of the author's points is that without diversity, the newts' strength comes at the cost of emotional and cultural life. Homogeneity is too high a price to pay for an envyless society.

There is a great deal of truth in what Schoeck and others propound on the subject. Their interest, however, is envy in the macrocosm of society, where it concerns itself mainly with wealth and power and blends into covetousness and greed. My main interest, on the other hand, is envy in the microcosm of the individual, particularly envy of intangibles such as talent, intelligence, position, and recognition, as well as the not-so-easily-transferred tangibles, such as beauty.

Heterogeneous societies with a diversity of opportunities, like ours, afford avenues to many varieties of envious experience, but also avenues to personal satisfaction for those willing to pursue them.

We return now to envy in the microcosm.

Notes

1. Rousseau is justifiably castigated, however, for having left his own five children in an orphanage.

2. Defined as absence of unearned or inherited deference; unwillingness to acknowledge self as a social inferior.

3. This is hardly the democratic utopia we were taught in school to believe in.

4. In a recent letter on the op-ed page of the Cleveland *Plain Dealer*, a correspondent paraphrased de Tocqueville as saying that democracy can work until we all conclude that we can vote ourselves a big raise. Which is what we have been doing by borrowing from China until we are up to our eyeballs in debt.

5. Repeatedly the translator uses "lofty", usually in the context of "lofty ambition". By this adjective, I think he means that de Tocqueville meant something close to "ambitious to make a lot of money and become a Rockefeller", not "struggling to go to Harvard Divinity School". Like Adam Smith, de Tocqueville was focused on pecuniary gain, and thus envy was entwined with covetousness.

6. Interestingly enough, that ship was the *Carpathia,* which, in April 1912, went to the rescue of the *Titanic,* and Wasil watched them haul terrified passengers out of the icy waters. The chilled survivors were given the warm beds, and the steerage passengers completed the passage out on deck.

7. Although de Tocqueville's—and Pascal's—point pertains to making a fortune, the old "from rags to riches", the same is true with persons whose ambitions require education. If they must devote time, energy, and effort to earning the education, more years will have passed before they can attain career or life goals they set themselves. This problem is compounded if in the meantime, they have assumed other obligations, such as a family to support, financially and psychologically. Life is not long enough if you have to start at square one, or even before

the starting point, although educational loan opportunities and additional years of life expectancy in the twentieth century compensate somewhat. Traditionally, immigrants to our country came with hopes for success, financial and other, but soon realized that their dreams would, in most cases, have to be delayed a generation. My father-in-law's plans to go to night school had to be shelved, permanently, when his responsibilities increased because his wife conceived my husband-to-be.

8. Defined, cynically, by Trollope in his novel *Barchester Towers,* "as the upper classes in rural districts are designated by the lower with so much true discrimination".

9. The closest I have come to an exception to the universality of envy is reflected in the remark of an author/friend of mine who, as a child, was incessantly put down and degraded by her parents: "I had never felt envy. I would just have assumed I didn't deserve whatever it was." That is worse than envy.

10. See the description of the film *Murderous Maids* in my modern fiction chapter.

11. An Aristophanes play entitled *Plutus (Wealth)* makes the point that when the blind god Wealth is cured of his blindness and distributes his largesse to the worthy rather than randomly, then persons with skills and talents, no longer pressed for money, stop working, and wealth does no one any good. I did not interpret this as a play about envy, as one of my sources (Berke) did.

12. By the time of my upbringing the pendulum had swung to the opposite extreme, to the effect that "you" can have anything you want if you only strive hard enough. Running counter to the recognition of any role of chance or luck in life, or even the vast array of human traits and talents, this belief must be found to be untrue, sooner or later, and the result can be bitter disillusionment. There is such a thing as happening to be in the right or wrong place at the wrong or right time, with the right or wrong aptitude, and, always, with or without the necessary capital.

13. Recall that even such thinkers as Francis Bacon believed in the evil eye. Thomas Frederick Elworthy, originally a linguist, while studying English dialects encountered so many examples of this superstition, along with counter-charms and protections, that he wrote a compendium, *THE EVIL EYE: An Account of This Ancient and Widespread Superstition*. Examples piled upon examples make this author's work reminiscent of Frazer's monumental twelve-volume anthropologic work *The Golden Bough*.

14. This is the kind of discomfort I admit feeling when I travel in the Third World.

15. I find it hard not to imagine Olga, our cleaning woman, not being envious when she hears about our travel and sees interesting things we have brought home, as I am sure I would be in her place. But her occasional comment, "I just love working here because I always learn something" would seem to preclude envy.

16. Recent secularization of society has trended away from the erstwhile Christian protection against envy. Doug Bandow will comment on this presently.

17. My friend cites an Italian saying: "I don't know why that man hates me; I never did him a favor."

18. Attempts to equalize opportunities in education have been made in this country, as, e.g., in the "No Child Left Behind" legislation, but of course no legislation can equilibrate ability to be educated. As has recently been observed in public schools facing their standardized tests, gargantuan efforts to save the schools' showing by "teaching to the test" have resulted in many superior and gifted students becoming progressively more bored and disruptive. Families that can afford it apply to private schools.

    Even with "free" education for gifted students, many are unequally able to compete because of family and prior obligations. As Pascal and others have pointed out, when we all start at the starting line, no one can get very far, whereas those with an added boost from family, money, connections, scholarships, loans, etc., will go farther. Those who "stand on the shoulders of giants" will see farther, be off to a head start, and, it is to be hoped, use their advantages for the benefit of others as well as themselves. *Sagesse oblige.*

19. He might well have included "lack of discipline, refusal to be educated or trained for productive employment, and failure to take responsibility", the latter, another word dropping out of the language.

20. Man the Toolmaker, Man the Playful, Economic Man, and now Man the Envious.

Chapter 15

Good and Bad Ways of Coping with Envy by the Envied One And by the Envier

Returning to envy in the microcosm as it affects us one by one, we remember that, like fire, it can serve good or bad ends, depending on how it is used. So let us look at ways to cope by both the envier and the envied one.

First I suggest we make a conscious effort to become less prey to envy. We need to learn to read the subliminal messages from Madison Avenue. Another gown so outré as to look ridiculous by next year? Another candidate who promises to tax everyone else but me? Yet another status symbol when this one gets me where I need to go in safety and relative comfort?

On the one hand, what if all those envious people are someone else, and we are the target of their envy? How do we handle that? Our reaction to being envied ranges from blissful ignorance of the pain we are inadvertently inflicting through efforts to elude or defuse their envy, all the way up to glorying in being envied. Nothing (or little) is more maddening to the one wishing to be envied than having no one seem to notice.

Either the envied one or the envier or both can be unaware of the situation. If it is the envied one who is unaware, he has no way to address the other's envy. But if the envied one has an inkling of what is wrong, he can at least begin by giving the envier more space, perhaps moving away from the suspected envy problem.

Some even avoid being envied by arranging not to achieve or by actually making a point to fail. Factory workers on the line have refused promotion to foreman so as to remain one of the gang, and comradeship trumps possibly inflicting envy. In the military, avoiding promotion to a higher rank is sometimes attributed to unwillingness to bear responsibility for decisions that could affect a comrade's safety or life, in other cases to fear of envy.

To be envied is ordinarily not as bad as to envy. At least we have whatever that advantage is. Yet being envied is not without its own set of problems, different, opposite, sometimes posing genuine threats. But not always. Again, the envied one herself may be happily unenlightened, while the envious feelings may be apparent, or at least surmised, by persons at the periphery of the coterie or even onlookers. Sometimes only the envious one is aware and manages to hide his envy, as in the case of the pre-seminarian's envy of me, which did not surface until decades later at the class reunion. One subject I interviewed suggested that if he thought someone wished to be envied by him, he might play along by pretending envy, to gratify the other. He might "confess" to envy he did not feel, as a form of flattery.

When fully cognizant of envy as the cause of the other's discomfort, the envied one has two types of ways to deal with it intentionally: (1) to try to minimize the unintended hurt; or (2) to enjoy it, rejoice in it, gloat over it, use it to hurt even more, try to inspire even greater envy. Which avenue is chosen depends on the character of the individual with the envied advantage. Robert Solomon refers to the "delicious" feeling some experience when they are aware of being envied. This is often in the area of tangibles, like showy clothes or jewelry.

When the envied person is not particularly introspective or ana-lytic, he may be aware only of a general tension and the setting in which it occurs, but not the reason for the discomfort. But if the target of the envy surmises the reason, he would need a very spe-cific reason to try to bring it into the open. Instead, nine times out of ten, he would do better to back off. Epstein relates that when a colleague called him "enviable", he immediately cut back on dis-playing or admitting his literary successes. I was fortunate to have attended a prestigious medical school. Years ago I noticed that whenever I would mention this in a medical circle, a sudden hush would fall, and I quickly learned not to bring this up unless asked directly, and if possible to dodge the question.

Often the envied one is aware, dimly or poignantly, of the uncom-fortable feelings the other individual is suffering and perhaps acting upon in hostile or retaliatory ways with or without knowing why. Some such envied persons, whom I would consider deficient in charity for their fellows, glory in being envied, flaunt their advan-tage, are flamboyantly ostentatious, gloat over it, and sadistically watch the other's pain, as they rub their opponent's nose in his disadvantage. In an article on gloating, Whitman and Alexander identify gloating as a reaction to knowledge of one's own superi-ority (with or without envy on the part of the other) by a flash of a particular kind of unpleasant smile (perhaps a smirk or sneer) suppressed in a split second. This immediate reversal to a neutral expression may acknowledge that the reaction is personally unac-ceptable to the gloater, or that at least he doesn't want it known, so he tries to hide his fleeting look of superiority.

Flaunting the advantage with haughtiness or condescension is not a recommended strategy, not because it doesn't work, but because it does. Only in exceptional circumstances is the estab-lished superiority worth all the costs, worst of which is detriment of the envied person's character, with downgrading of the esteem in which he is held by others and by himself.

Bacon, we remember, recommended a modest demeanor, even

"false modesty" as a protection against envy, advised us "not to boast", and to "hide prized possessions or skills" to minimize the envious reaction of others. And so did Petrarch. Worst of all was the plight of ancient Athenians who could be banished for ten years if they looked too superior to envious fellow citizens, and so they had good reason to downplay their advantage.

I am reminded of the advice given intelligent young women when I was growing up: we were coached to pretend to admire young men's opinions in order to ensure that they felt superior, which most of them felt was their male prerogative.

Schopenhauer pointed out that persons with high self-esteem hate to be envied, not wishing to be even the innocent cause of another's unhappiness. Persons who are sensitive to their own envy and do not wish to cause others the same kind of suffering do well to collude in pretending the envy does not exist, so as to avoid shaming the other.

Alternatively, we may look for a way to alleviate the envy. Unfortunately there is no good one. Often the impulse of envied persons who are sympathetic to the plight of others is to try to help the envious by sharing the largesse, e.g., teaching the admired skill. Reassurance in the form of "You're a pretty good photographer, after all" is a mistake because the envious one knows it's a lie and is likely to increase her sour resentment. No one can really give value to someone who is devalued; he must do something to create genuine value in himself. One possibility is "Shall we go out and practice sometime?" Both may benefit and become better tennis buddies. Unfortunately, many attributes most envied cannot be transferred, such as beauty.

But most such attempts are unsuccessful. For example, a woman considered beautiful may try to help someone less attractive by teaching her better use of makeup or how to dress to better advantage ("Don't wear magenta with your carroty hair"). Such an attempt not uncommonly provokes anger in the envier for being shown up and patronized, and thus doubly belittled (but if she's smart, she'll remember it, think about it, and test it against reality). While many enviers prefer to have the consolation of believing that the one they envy is at least arrogant, condescending, or personally repugnant, of course no one is obligated to be obnoxious because someone else would prefer it.

If tried at all, this approach should be circuitous and done with finesse, drawing attention to and praising someone else for not making the same mistake ("That ultramarine suit is striking with Gloria's auburn hair") or even drawing attention to how the problem is handled in art, as in a Titian painting. But offering help cannot equalize the score.

Often the only or best way to cope with the other's envy is to collude in pretending it doesn't exist, so as not to embarrass her.

I have found that a good way to help those who are psychologically needy, whether envious or not, is to do something counterintuitive, i.e., to take graciously and with appreciation what the other has to give, thus conveying a sense of my belief that she is a worthy peer with something valuable to share. The late Mr. Rogers of children's television fame made the same point: he thought the greatest gift you could give someone was an honest receiving of what that person had to offer. We see this when a child brings you a gift of her artwork.

Large differences in financial circumstances often make friendships difficult, including the case when one suddenly experiences an upturn in wealth, inherits money, or marries into it, especially if the other is of an envious disposition. The richer one may try to downplay her advantage, as Bacon and others have recommended, or she may try to "pick up the tab" for her friend. Both may be uncomfortable.

In very special circumstances the envied one may be able to help. When I have traveled in the African wild, I have noticed the dark looks on the faces of many locals, even while they need—and subsist on—tourist dollars. The only Africans with whom the language barrier permits a foreigner like myself to enjoy a human kind of relationship are the guides. I have had the good fortune to become relatively close to and relatively open with several highly intelligent guides, who were largely self-educated in natural history and in English, and pursued their career in difficult circumstances, often supporting an extended family, educating younger siblings, and even trying to save with the view to eventually owning a house and marrying. I have experienced a surge of respect and warmth for those whose primary orientation was not passive envy but active struggle against overwhelming odds to earn a living while accomplishing something of value for themselves, their families, and their community. Around the campfire at night, I have leveled with several such people. My opening gambit would usually be to ask whether they found many American travelers arrogant and obnoxious, as they sometimes seemed to me, and they were usually willing to agree to this. Then I would ask about the unpleasantness and ambivalence they must feel when working for and with privileged travelers ("not in our present group, of course"), and this reaction also they were sometimes able to acknowledge. On separating at the end of the trip, instead of the usual tip, I would give them something to further what they were trying to achieve, such as a subscription to a relevant publication. For strategies like this to work, there had to be a high level of fellow feeling, mutual respect, and, usually, a relationship that terminated with the goodbye at the end of the trip.

In Madagascar we had a guide who had been sent to England by his mother's Episcopal Church (his father was a witch doctor) to be educated as a social worker. This thirtyish man[1] conducted tours, ran two boys' orphanages, and "read law" at night (a self-educated lawyer just like Abraham Lincoln). Working under the draconian Napoleonic Code (dating in Madagascar from the period when the British and French colonial powers would confer and decided, in this case, "You take Madagascar and we'll take Zanzibar"), he had been successful in freeing several prisoners who had been thrown into jail for minor offenses and forgotten. One had, literally, stolen a head of cabbage[2] and was lost in the prison system until our guide represented him and effected his release. As we prepared to board ship at Diego-Suarez, the world's largest harbor, I was negotiating with women on the pier to buy some shirts embroidered with lemurs, but all banks were closed because it was the Easter weekend. Because we were on our way to the Seychelles, I was carrying British pounds, so I bought the guide's local currency with pounds sterling, illegally, at a good rate, and he was delighted that I tipped him also in British currency, helping his larger mission that involved dealings with England.

Returning to dealing with the one who envies you, sometimes a good possibility and one more likely to succeed in most circumstances is to enlist the help of a third person, not herself involved in the envy snare, to come to the aid of the person who looks as if she is feeling disadvantaged. Such a strategy requires a great deal of finesse on the part of the person trying to help.

One critic reading a draft of this book worries that this strategy can easily backfire by confirming in the mind of the (somewhat paranoid) envious person a conspiracy in which the other two are not only more advantaged but more sophisticated than the envier. Instead, he suggests, on an occasion when this is not an immediate problem, attribute the problematic taste to an unknown other, as in "I know a woman who always tries to match shades of red, and since this is virtually impossible, the result is always jarring."

In most cases, it is best not to ferret out and work with envy, but just to be unostentatious and in an unobtrusive way to give the identified envier more space. Unfortunately, when friends have similar goals and one achieves several small successes or perhaps one big accolade, the other may not be able to rejoice for her friend, and this may preclude the friendship's continuation on the same terms. Persons who have won large jackpots in the casino or the lottery often find that not only are the relatives' hands all out for their share, but their relationships with both family and friends deteriorate as a result of envy, or when they think the winner didn't share enough, or because they are no longer interested in bargain-chasing.

A time comes when hiding or playing down one's assets is the better part of wisdom, to forestall not only envy, as Bacon suggested, and Foster noted, but also the kind of admiration that can be off-putting and preclude normal social give-and-take. My favorite story of this kind comes from a time when my husband and I were on shipboard with one of our sons, then a medical student, whom we encouraged to socialize with other shipmates. One evening early in the trip, when our son was eating with the ship's young doctor, my husband and I found ourselves at a table for six, with two elderly women, who were chatting privately and paying no attention to us, and another older couple. Introducing ourselves, my husband caught their somewhat unusual surname and asked, "Didn't your father or a brother at the University of Michigan back in the fifties win a Nobel Prize?"

Whereupon the husband became flustered, shushed us, and half-whispered, "That was me, but please don't tell anyone. I don't want it to get around the ship."

We assured him that his secret was safe with us.[3] Privately I advised our son to make the man's acquaintance and inquire about his research. I promised that on the homebound flight I would tell him something of interest. While on shipboard, our son had even had the laureate sign his medical text on the page that related this researcher's discovery, before I shared the news on the plane, "Now you've met a Nobel laureate."

A special case of being envied, as discussed in the chapter on envy in psychoanalysis, is a patient's envy of the therapist. Envy is particularly difficult and painful in a setting where the envier is dependent on the one he envies. The therapeutic handling of this problem has already been discussed.

Once an individual is aware of being envied, he should be aware also of the range of possible spiteful actions on the part of the envier, and take steps to protect himself from the effects of gossip, slander, sabotage, or other types of attack, direct or devious, that the envious person may employ consciously or unwittingly. Sometimes the only effective strategy is distancing.

We may even just presume that others envy us for our advantage that we hold dear, which in fact they may not actually even consider important. As in all other considerations of envy, the boundaries are not sharply drawn between envy, self-esteem, ambition, rivalry, competition, and greed.

As has been discussed at some length in the chapter on politics, a large murky area exists between societal changes we who are conscious of our own privilege work for in an effort to move toward a genuinely fair and just society and changes we work for because we (with status or some kind of power) are envied—or think we are—by those without. Those who esteem such things as education expect others also to hold them in high regard, and wish to share them, which was the reason for earlier cohorts of benevolent women to become teachers and social workers. Current generations may learn, however, that those with whom they are trying to share may disdain the same advantages, as witness the enormous dropout rates in our "free, universal, compulsory" education system (some, but not all, of these dropouts relating to contempt for the education that society is trying to provide). At the same time, others without educational opportunities may be asking, "Why should education be wasted on people who are trashing it?" Years ago, when college courses were taken in to penal inmates in a rehabilitative effort, I saw a woman on television asking, "Why should my taxes reward criminals by educating them when I have to come up with my own tuition dollars?" As with everything else touching envy and fairness, rarely are the motives unmixed. Good and generous motives to help others are snarled up with glimmerings of uncomfortable and denied or repressed feelings that one is envied. As Bandow and others have pointed out, the natural differences in individuals in physical, emotional, and intellectual traits, not to mention values and self-discipline, vary all over the map, imposing a daunting task on anyone who seeks to "equalize". The best we can do is what Schoeck advises: to try to make available what we believe is an appropriate match for a vast diversity of people, and we may disagree among ourselves about what that might be.

Our laudable efforts to help those with physical (and other) disabilities, who, we believe, would understandably wish they could find themselves in that broad, hazy category without sharp boundaries, of "normal",[4] find expression in our Americans with Disabilities Act. But this legislation has had consequences that not everyone foresaw, like the loss of the shelter for homeless, resulting from implementing the idea that if everyone can't have something, nobody can.[5]

Worldwide, citizens of developing countries consider us Americans privileged, and we are, with even our poorest citizens better off than almost everyone in the Third World.[6] This makes us targets of their envy-induced resentment. Our efforts to help developing countries help themselves have often backfired in a number of ways and for a number of reasons, one of which is that envy is rarely quelled by the other's altruism. Attempts to address the enormous problems of the Third World by advising, sharing, and offering a helping hand often only stoke their envy. Instead of using our help as a launching pad, their hands are often out for more. Unfortunately, our help may even find its way into the pockets of the fat cats. It is said that our country goes about aid to developing countries in the wrong way, but what is the right way? A German politician interviewed recently on television regarding the low opinion in which the US is held abroad said, "We don't teach history the way we should. Most people in Europe don't realize that Europe would not be where it is today without post-WW II help in reconstruction and the Marshall Plan, and that help not only to the allies but to the defeated as well." [And even, I add, to non-combatant collaborationists like Iceland.]

Terrible strategies have been employed by persons and groups with power, who arrogate the right to destroy those they envy and resent. Schoeck documents how revolutionaries, once having seized power, slake their envious thirst by eliminating their own educated and previously privileged classes. Schoeck tells us that in one African country, after a recent military takeover, the revolutionaries killed everyone with more than a sixth grade education, leaving the country with no citizens with skills requisite to start rebuilding. In another shakeup, a university student home in Africa on vacation after one year on scholarship at an American university was beheaded in the public square with the explanation that he was an "intellectual". These examples illustrate how the envious will often destroy someone with something they cannot incorporate into themselves, even though it is a skill they need. Those envied have little protection from others with the awful combination of envy and power.

The same behavior is explored in fiction. In the recent French film, already mentioned, *How I Killed My Father,* the physician father flees for his life when revolutionaries destroy his clinic in Algeria.

In the 1960s, the Chinese tried to equilibrate their population in a maneuver called the Cultural Revolution. Their educated classes were brought down by sending them to the hinterland where their training and skills were used less if at all. This period and this strategy form the backdrop of a novel, *Balzac and the Little Chinese Seamstress* by Sijie Dai, in which two high school boys are deported to work on a remote farm because their parents are educated and professional.

A real-life example of this same envious backlash in the Chinese Cultural Revolution is the experience of a Chinese classmate of my husband's and mine from medical school. On graduation, this gifted young man was offered opportunities in the United States, but, an idealist, he wished to return to serve his own country's future, unlike many other expatriates who, once educated in our country, do everything possible to remain. Our classmate became a professor of genetics in China's premier medical school. Several decades later my medical school roommate was traveling in China and contacted him with a view to getting together. He told her that he could not entertain her at home but they would need to meet in her hotel lobby and talk apart from listening devices. He related to my friend the following appalling story:

At the time of Mao's bloody tyranny, this physician was separated from his wife (also a professional), and they were sent to different remote areas, where our friend served as a "barefoot doctor". Their infant was taken from both of them and sent elsewhere, later reported to have died in an unexplained way. Our friend was eventually returned to the medical school in Beijing.

One may ask how we know that the motive for Mao's program related to envy. Actually, as with almost all other envy configurations, it is never acknowledged as such. Envy must be surmised by inference as the best explanation. Protecting ourselves from the envious in power is very difficult, as citizens of ancient Athens learned who were exiled for looking too fortunate to their envious voting peers.

You will recall that both Hartley and Vonnegut satirically addressed the problem of envy by creating fictitious societies in which the envious destroy the highly prized, nontransferable enviable advantages in others (beauty, strength, talents, intelligence) since they cannot be redistributed. These stories may be considered cautionary tales.

In our society we perform a milder analogous device in the enormous gray zone where fairness and envy interdigitate, but where we prefer to set our sights on the fairness issue while closing our eyes to any possible envy aspect. We set test-score bars at different levels for those perceived to be socially disadvantaged or not, personally privileged or not. For veterans who have lost years of their career life, in appreciation we give them a handicap in the form of point preferences on civil service, postal service, and national and state park examinations in partial payment for their service to our society. We move white males back in the line as retribution for centuries of preference given to their ancestors. They understandably resent being penalized for something done years before they were even conceived. There is another, usually unrecognized, effect of this tare on the scales. Originally intended to be temporary until true equality of opportunity is achieved, it is observed not only to be ongoing but often to escalate. Such preferential treatment says, in effect, "You can't compete on a level playing field."

We turn now to the reverse of the coin, ways for us, as the envying person, to cope, good, bad, and questionable, both at the moment of envy's surge when our impulse may be to lash back, and over the long haul. They range from developing strategies to conceal both the envy and our shame over it, to overcoming it, to developing similar or other advantages within reach, to destroying the envied person.

First, however, the envy problem, like any other, must be defined with the utmost specificity. We know that, despite being called *Homo sapiens,* we are not necessarily rational beings, but as we learned in Psychology 101, we tend to "think" with our emotions.[7] A general rule is: the more difficult the problem, the more important it is to bring logical, intellectual, planned strategies to bear over unthoughtout emotional reactions. If we have experienced envy in the past, we are wise to anticipate its recurrence and be prepared to put into action previously designed plans, and, it is to be hoped, handle the problem better than the last time. That is, we need to change from impulsive to controlled, from emotional (right-brained) to analytical (left-brained) strategies.[8]

But before that, there are times when, as with the envied one, the envier cannot even begin to problem-solve because she is unaware of the precise cause of that highly uncomfortable feeling often located under the sternum, as author Joan Frank noted. The envier may think, "I just can't stand that woman—she thinks she's so great", when the truth is that the other person has conducted herself in an unpretentious manner, has treated everyone with appropriate respect, and has done nothing for which to be resented except having some advantage dear to the envier. Is it really the rival's poise and self-assurance or the favorable attention it brings that the envier finds so galling? Perhaps the other woman is wearing a beautiful engagement ring, while the envier is no closer to a "commitment" than she was five years prior. This might be the time to take unhappy stock and make hard life decisions.

In times past, the opera was the prime venue to evoke envy for costly jewelry and the skins of other mammals.[9] According to Veblen, writing in the latter part of the nineteenth century, "conspicuous consumption" was the way for the "leisure class" to demonstrate that it had so much wealth that it could indulge in "conspicuous waste". Whether envious or not, or angry over the fairness issue, one can find ways to make the ostentatious woman forever less comfortable in her mink. My friend, who is a defender of wildlife, has her retort ready for whenever another woman bids for admiration if not envy by flaunting skins that should have been on jaguars: "It makes you look a little chunky, dear."

We have surveyed many reactions that the person envious of us may demonstrate, and we may try the same array of attacks when the envy problem is ours. We may give vent to impulsive aggression, denigrating, lashing back, putdowns that make no sense, attempts to bring down or destroy the envied one, ridicule (think how ridiculous this makes the disadvantaged one look, i.e., "Look at so-and-so. I just won the prize and *she's* ridiculing *me!*"). Yet all these forms of attack come into play in other situations as well and therefore cannot be considered pathognomonic of envy. All these reflex vengeful ways to handle envy offer no more than transient relief, if that, and are usually unsuccessful and counterproductive. Furthermore, they do nothing to address the wished-for advantage.

Longer-term expressions of envy and modes of attack when one is out of the presence of the envied person include criticism, gossip and lies or calumny, attacking her reputation, or "back-biting", a term that in some of the older literature came close to being synonymous with envy, being such a frequent concomitant (in the same way that Bacon used "resentment" as synonymous). My French translator friend, already in his sixties when working on Raiga's book, belatedly identified his own use of sarcasm as a signal to himself that he was envious. Similarly, I recently noticed myself ridiculing someone's incorrect use of a particular word as resulting from my own envy. Epstein's book shows a cartoon of an editor studying a manuscript that he obviously wishes he had written himself, and over his shoulder a horned individual advises him to "damn with faint praise". (In the Middle Ages, envy was often personified as a mean woman with a snake coming out of her mouth as her tongue.)

All these devices may have the desired effect of hurting the envied individual. But they are more efficacious in eroding the mental health and the character of the envier.

A person who suffers frequent attacks of envy and permits herself to develop patterns of this kind for coping may have unconsciously bypassed identification of envy as the original cause of the discomfort.

Whether or not the envious person correctly assesses the reason for her "bitchiness", she is likely to start casting blame inappropriately on all and sundry. This is the point at which to remember that while we did not choose to be envious and therefore are not to blame for suffering it, still the envy is ours to handle. Envy is primary and internal (although secondary to the inciting trigger), whereas our reaction is secondary and either contained internally or expressed externally. What we are responsible for is how we handle it, and that is responsibility enough.

If the envious person generally has a spirit of agape or altruism toward her fellow humans, she will feel doubly compromised—not only for lacking the advantage but also for being so petty as to envy.

Recall how Schimmel pointed out that if "sin" seems an inappropriate categorization for envy in the twenty-first century, "suboptimal mental health" sums up the case nicely.

Efforts to deal with envy—fighting back recklessly with any weapons at hand to bring down the other, to eliminate her advantage, to punish her and make her suffer—all these may actually serve to harm the competitor or they may not. This frontal attack is not generally recommended. At least it should not be unpremeditated but should be employed only after weighing and being prepared for all the risks: the envied one is likely to be more powerful and able to retaliate, thus making the envier not only disadvantaged but exposed as weak, defeated, humiliated, and without the prized advantage. Once recognized as this kind of vindictive person, she may suffer the shame of being not only inferior and déclassé but also mean-spirited enough to try this defense. This could give the envied one the ultimate advantage of being too "big" a person to retaliate, making the envier look even worse by comparison. For all these reasons, this array of tactics is not recommended.

A more important—in fact the main—reason to avoid expressing our own envy is for the harm it does us, the envier. If focusing on some form of retaliation does nothing more than distract the envier from looking for a more constructive way to live, that is bad enough. But if an honest appraisal results in a realistic assessment of strengths, weaknesses, and options, it has helped move us toward achievable goals.

Meanwhile, when a person is aware of the part envy is playing in her behavior, she may be willing to reassess and consider other strategies to reduce or eliminate the sting of that devastating emotion. Various philosophic and religious thinkers have advised us to learn to rejoice in the happiness of others, i.e., to stand schadenfreude on its head. The very truth in the opposite of schadenfreude is caught in a quotation of Goethe's: "Who is the happiest of men? He who values the merits of others, and in their pleasure takes joy; even as though it were his own." I do not suggest that this is easy, but we experience this joy most whole-heartedly in the happiness of our children.

We need to identify the circumstances in which we are vulnerable and recognize the old enemy when we see it coming, as that armchair philosopher Pogo pointed out, "We have met the enemy, and they is us." We should immediately drop a flag on the play. This requires controlling the mouth[10] while working on longer-term intentional and planned ways to deal with that treacherous emotion.

In general, it was—and is—better to recognize our vulnerabilities, to stop "thinking" with the right (emotional) side of the cerebral cortex, and to move to the left side of the brain, anticipate the problem and have an advance plan for how to handle it when it happens again, as it surely will. Often the best strategy is something between utter silence and impulsive talk. No solution is perfect. If I had a perfect solution, I would probably patent it.

A sudden silence on the part of the envier is an improvement over blurting out something to regret later, but a silence of this kind is still a message to astute onlookers about the envious person. Recall how my mother noted that her sister would clam up when the conversation moved to a part of the world that my peripatetic aunt had not visited. In a case like this, a better way to handle the situation is to affirm the envied one, but not too effusively, or it will appear hypocritical, and be so. In the longer term it pays to learn to replace envy with admiration, perhaps followed by emulation.

An "envy attack" of this kind may make one wish to run and hide, often with a thinly veiled excuse, like my reaction to the laureate fingering her medallion. Yet astute onlookers would have asked, "Why did she take off like that?" and probably come up with the right answer as the dust settled. To the pain of envy would be added the pride-damaging shame for it to be known—or surmised—why.

Sometimes envy is so painful that we sidestep the risk of repetition by avoiding the envy-provoking person altogether. The problem, if one leans on this strategy of breaking off with the target of our envy, is that we will deprive ourselves of other good features of that person and even her friends, and the cost-benefit ratio may not be worth the loss. If we do this too often, we soon will find we have narrowed the horizons of our entire life. It is better to cultivate friendships with people to admire and emulate, rather than, as the envious often do, persons to devalue. On the other hand, if we find it politic or impossible not to break connection with someone we envy but also find abrasive, we might keep a reserve of responses with which to trump her next boast, e.g., "My brother-in-law just got promoted to partner in his law firm."

Another ill-considered reaction to envy is to try to steal what the other has that the envier covets. One mode of theft is grabbing credit for someone else's accomplishments, as is often done in corporate life, a strategy frequently employed along with adroitly shifting blame for one's mistakes to someone else. Again, anyone considering this strategy must be prepared for the consequences of exposure. In the literary world this type of theft is plagiarism, although one author friend tells me that plagiarism is due more often to laziness than to envy. Even if we get away with any form of theft, the pleasure is sullied or spoiled by the internal awareness of being a fraud. The envy account is not squared because the recognition is not for one's own accomplishment.

A better way is to "steal" legitimately, by devising ways to share in the other's advantage and enjoy it, by observing, learning,[11] and emulating, as recommended by many thinkers on the subject of envy, such as Rosenblatt, Rouslin Welt, and others.

In Alexander Pope's *Essay on Man*, one couplet advises:

Envy, to which th' ignoble mind's a slave,
Is emulation in the learned or brave.

Herzog distinguishes two kinds of envy. He quotes Aristotle's usage of "honest envy", meaning a determination to equal or exceed the other's "virtue" for legitimate purposes. Herzog's second is a desire for revenge, exemplified in the sentiment "Who does he think he is? I can do better than that. I'll show him." As Herzog notes, and as in all the other aspects of the murky subject of envy, these extremes are easily distinguished on paper, but mixed and blended in real life.

Herzog questions (and so do I) Aristotle's usage of "honest envy", since emulation is not envy at all but a reaction to it, and among the best.

On the other hand, Smith and Whitfield devote an entire article to turning envy in a positive direction, toward emulation, the partial cure we have also noted, striving in other directions, and satisfaction with partial achievement. They reported a case in which a husband overcame what is many a spouse's problem, envy of the other's achievements. Their patient learned to bask in his wife's accomplishments. With more women in the competitive world, envy of spouses for each others' achievements has become more common than formerly. Recall the wife in *Brooklyn Boy*, the play in which the fact of both spouses being writers, the husband successful, the wife not, dripped poison into the wife's wound.

Many good ideas are out there free to be incorporated. Learning from and copying what one envies sometimes results in becoming, in time, comparable to the envied one, and perhaps a better tennis player or good bridge partner. At worst, one may have to accept that the other has superior talent and decide to be satisfied with accomplishment at a lower level ("I'll never have a singing career, but at least I can sing around town"), and still have the kind of family life that you can't have in the lonely life of professional concertizing.

Alternatively, having accepted one's relatively minor talent, a person may decide to find another asset to develop, in a completely different arena. Once an advantage is clearly beyond one's grasp, it can be a kind of relief to stop struggling and look for other satisfactions. I have a friend with a son who spent several years as a ballet danceur, who made it to the final cut and lost in his audition. He is happily pursuing computer servicing, to his (and his mother's) relief.

We have seen the strategies tried by Joan Frank, who admitted to suffering an especially severe form of writer's envy. With each new envy attack, she permitted herself a short period of feeling sorry for herself for the envy to dissipate, but not too long a time to prevent her wiping her eyes and returning to her own work so as not to delay or jeopardize her future efforts to achieve her own literary goals. While it may help Frank, wallowing in self-pity is not time-cost-effective in this or any other endeavor. The strategy of my journalist friend of "buying off" her envy with that congratulatory telegram freed her of any face-to-face congratulations or responsibility of further notice of the envy-inducing accomplishment. Congratulations of this nature are what I recommend for anyone plagued with envy for a competitor's specific success. At the same time, she might benefit by analyzing how the competitor made the difficult transition from visualizing a book to getting a contract.

Life can be a series of maximizing the good, reducing or detouring around the bad. I like the advice from the old song, "Accentuate the positive; eliminate the negative; latch on to the affirmative; don't mess with Mr. In-Between."

Alexander Pope's most quoted couplet advises:

> Know then thyself; presume not God to scan.
> The proper study of mankind is Man.

To know oneself intimately is basic advice for persons with envy problems (as well as everyone else). Odysseus is quoted as saying: "I have traveled among the nations of mankind and have come to know myself." I wish I had said that.[12]

Enviers, like everyone else, are wise to avoid self-deceptions about their strengths and weaknesses, to be honest and accepting of the fact that there will always be others with more or better whatever it is they crave. There are longed-for advantages that we can do something to acquire, but others that we cannot. It is wise to acknowledge the difference, adjusting our priorities around our strengths. The reverse of this coin, however, is to be prepared to do just what we were taught as children to eschew. In addition to admitting our weaknesses, we should feel free to be forthright about our assets. We might say, for example, "Yes, I'm pretty good at handling money and keeping books, so I'll run for treasurer." The other side of this is "No, Doris is more of a people person than I am; get her to head up that committee."

As with solving any other problem, the first step is to define it with the utmost exactness. Do we crave the advantage itself or the attention it brings? (There are many, often easier, ways to get attention by doing something worthwhile in the family or community. On the other hand, if you've been doing this and they don't notice, quit suddenly, and you'll be surprised at the attention it generates.)

The second step is to begin to minimize the deficit or look for other avenues to satisfaction. How bad is the disadvantage? Can it be rectified, improved, sidestepped, eliminated, ignored? Francis Bacon noted that some disadvantages[13] that he called "incorrigible" can sometimes be used as motives to succeed over adversity. (I have often wondered whether my husband would have become a scientist of repute if he had not had the handicap of one bad leg, and therefore been accepted by his jock contemporaries.)

A friend from high school told me that at her "aunt's" funeral, her "mother" had said, "I hope the papers were all in order." In this way and at that emotional time she learned that she had been adopted by her birth mother's sister.

She told me, "I felt just terrible for the next day or two, but then I realized 'This is ridiculous; I'm the same person I was yesterday.'"

"Good for you!" I agreed.

Are there other parallel attributes that you can develop? If your sister is a singer but you are tone-deaf, investigate art or theater. If you would like to be artistic but can't draw, take a course or try photography or collage or ceramics. If your physical attributes are only average, move on to developing the traits of personality that make you the kind of person you and others admire and enjoy being around. Remember to compliment those you envy, sincerely, but not too effusively; it makes you look better. If others have more intellectual gifts, develop yours by listening and learning formally and informally, by seeking out enriching experiences, and by using them conversationally so that people will find you interesting.[14] If your means are modest, look for free resources in most communities, in public libraries and community and other colleges.

If you want things that money can buy but don't have the money, go back to school for salable skills. If you wish to be talented in some form of performance but are not, learn to enjoy the accomplishment of others in that art. As Goethe and others advised, learn to enjoy the happiness of others. This is easiest with the happiness of our children because we are usually not competing with them.

Very few of us win the big prizes, and most of life's pleasures are the little ones that we are alert to seize when they are offered. Learn to be receptive to the little jewels, a beautiful rainbow, a snuggle and kiss behind the ear, a crayoned Mother's Day card, a good book in front of a fireplace fire, a walk on the beach. *Carpe diem.*

Earlier I promised Schimmel's Ten Commandments for combating envy:

1. Reconsider the underlying assumptions you have about what makes you a worthwhile individual.

2. De-emphasize the value of the envied objects either for yourself or for the person who possesses them.

3. Think about positive and valuable things you have that the envied person does not.

4. Compare yourself to those less fortunate than you rather than to those more fortunate than you.

5. Consider that the person you envy deserves the object or quality which he has as his just reward and that there may be good reasons why you do not.

6. Reflect upon the irrationality of your envy. It hurts you without improving your situation.

7. Think about the potential danger of your envy. It could lead you to do certain things which will harm others and yourself.

8. Consider that your envy is inconsistent with the kind of person you would really like to be.

9. Associate your envy with negative qualities.

10. Cultivate feelings and thoughts that are incompatible with envy and the emotions it evokes.

We recall that Frank quoted a fellow author and teacher with a novel suggestion: to help the author one envies become the best author possible (thus taking part in the other's success). Frank did not think much of this suggestion. Whether or not it works for writers, the same idea can be applied to other areas of accomplishment.

We can even generalize the idea to being a friend in other ways to those we envy, and this strategy can have a taming effect on our envy. Years ago when my son's misbehavior was causing me untold grief, he had a high school classmate who was headed for a certain prestigious physics program. Meanwhile, during that young man's last free summer and as a graduation gift from his parents, he was hiking on the Canadian tundra, during the glorious summer muskeg bloom—the kind of opportunity we wanted for our children, not as an unearned gift, but as a reward for achievement of the kind that my son also was fully capable of. I envied the other youth's mother, as I did the mother of the French major from the Ivy League college whom I treated—the anecdote with which I began this book. I realized that while I could not exorcise my envy for the physics student's mother, I could certainly control my behavior and act in a manner appropriate to my ego ideal. This young graduate's mother happened to like me, and we would sometimes meet by chance at the library and chat. I could have timed my library visits to avoid those meetings that caused me a recrudescence of my envy, but I refrained. Instead, I clipped the article from the local paper about her son's accomplishments, stowed it in my purse, and passed it along the next time I saw her, so she would have an extra copy for relatives. The value of this clipping was symbolic, not to her, but to me.

Penultimately, we cite a simple but profound antidote to envy, difficult advice to follow, a cliché of religious and secular authors over the centuries: to learn to replace envy with love. This requires learning to enjoy and share the other's advantage and to be grateful for what we have. All this requires ego strength, as well as a lifetime.

We look at one final important way to enrich our lives, with or without envy. Develop a sense of humor, specifically the ability to laugh not at others, but at oneself. Remember how Epstein poked fun at himself for having, as a young author, experienced envy for another author's success in another genre. He could see that this was ludicrous.

Dawidziak, a reporter on the Cleveland *Plain Dealer,* commented on how Tom Lehrer, the Harvard mathematics professor who, back in the mid-twentieth century, had composed humorous and satiric songs and performed them first at parties and then in nightclubs, had "expressed his amazement" about the people who can make you realize how little you have accomplished in life. "It's a sobering thought... that when Mozart was my age, he'd been dead for five years." The person who had that same effect on Dawidziak was Robert Louis Stevenson, for his prolific and diverse output despite his poor health, which required him to sleep with his arm strapped to his side to brace his chest lest he break a rib when coughing from tuberculosis. At Dawidziak's age RLS had been dead for two years.

And on this note we conclude our inquiry into coping with envy.

Notes

1. This guide was either not suffering from envy, or possibly concealed it as the guides mentioned above may have done, but I include his story because I admired him so much.

2. Just like the fictional character Jean Valjean who, in Victor Hugo's classic novel *Les Miserables,* spent eighteen years in the French galleys for stealing a loaf of bread for his sister's starving children.

3. I was aware of my own envy, particularly when, in another conversation, I learned from this man that the laureates are invited to gatherings at intervals, something like class reunions. Those must be marvelously stimulating.

4. Even this is not necessarily the case. A sizable contingent of the deaf wish their children to remain deaf so as to maintain a separate "culture" or sub-society, even though partial hearing can now be produced surgically with cochlear implants. (One raises the question of the role of a parent's envy of his child in this case.) Even if partial hearing does nothing else, it can make one safer in our environment of ever-increasing decibels from ever-increasing noise pollution. What about the entire world of music denied to the deaf, although I believe the hearing produced by cochlear implants is not yet of sufficient quality to enable the erstwhile deaf to appreciate music. (Only a few exceptional deaf people like Helen Keller and the percussionist Evelyn Glennie are able to experience music through their sense of touch, via vibrations.) The deaf promote, and some of our schools offer American Sign Language (which can admittedly convey nuanced ideas) as a "foreign" language, equivalent in academic credit to, e.g., French. One asks, "Should we give academic credit for studying a language without a literature?" Maybe, like "Conversational French".

5. In Clinton's first term, when Hillary Clinton was trying to reform the entire medical care system, at one time she included the idea that no one should be permitted to buy expensive kinds of care if they were not equally accessible through the system to those unable to afford them. This prohibition illustrates one classic feature of envy: the wish

for someone else not to have a certain advantage even though that does not give it to the envier.

6. There are several reasons for this. One reason I see is that at intervals in the Western world, going back to Greek times, inquiry into the workings of nature was tolerated and pursued. Thus persons with inquiring minds adopted the habit of observing and investigating systematically, and, slowly and laboriously, developed scientific method, permitting the application of scientific principles and mechanisms to the production of life's needs. Our forebears also developed a simple written language based on an alphabet (unlike syllabaries and whole-word written languages), making record-keeping and later reading accessible to a larger proportion of the population than just the professional literate scribes. A system of grouping and categorizing made possible a library system for retrieving information. Now our smallest branch library preserves more information than the best human brain can store for humankind's future, and that does not even take into consideration the problems of transmitting accurately from one generation's brains to the next. Peoples without a relatively simple written language of their own fulfill their daily needs with back-breaking labor unless they adopt someone else's (as peoples all over Asia Minor used Sumerian cuneiform) and adapt it to their situation.

7. Janet: "Feelings regulate action." Schopenhauer: "Will is primary over intellect."

8. I have never ceased to be amazed that the problems patients bring to therapy (not just envy but the entire gamut) are often best addressed by helping them step back and learn problem-solving techniques.

9. In the early part of the twentieth century women were considered more like chattel than they are now, even being identified not by their given name but as the wife of so-and-so, Mrs. John Doe. A woman's clothing, furs, and jewelry proclaimed the standing of the man she orbited around, like a satellite, and who defined her status.

10. When I was a child, I was taught the old strategy for handling anger

for any reason—we weren't even talking about envy. I should bite my tongue, and rather than respond, count silently to ten. This is how my mother helped me learn rational response over emotional, so as not to do or say something I would later regret, while I decided whether talking was the best way to handle this problem, and if so what was the best thing to say, or else what the best other response would be, such as leaving.

I have recently learned in William Bennett's *Children's Book of Virtues*, to credit Jefferson for "When angry, count to ten; when very angry, count to a hundred." I rather enjoy Mark Twain's amendment: "...when very angry, swear."

11. Envious or not, I believe there is no one in the world from whom we cannot learn something, if not by what they teach, then by watching what they do right, and what they do wrong. Montaigne opined, "Wise men have more to learn from fools than fools can learn from wise men."

12. I recall that when Oscar Wilde made the same comment as mine, his friend responded, "Don't worry; you will."

13. In his day and ours, life is hard on those with problems of birth, the underclass of society, those with physical and mental handicaps.

14. My husband told me that when he was going through college on full scholarship (awarded to one student in each county of his state each year), and stoking the furnace every morning at four for room and board, he made it a priority every week to read the library's copy of *Time* from cover to cover. Thus there wasn't much going on in the world that he hadn't at least heard about. This familiarity with world events made him not only an interesting conversationalist, but helped him become a championship debater. I learned many things from him. Another thing I learned from him was to scan every bulletin board I passed, for what they had to announce and offer, meetings, lectures, often in areas outside my own, where by listening I could broaden my perspective. In this way I found Great Books.

Chapter 16

The Evolution of Envy

As I have thought and read about envy over the past quarter century, I have come to recognize how our understanding of it has changed and evolved, mostly in the past hundred years, not by losing its former characteristics but by adding accretions, like recent layers in an archaeologic site.

Envy is as widespread as humankind and doubtless antedates recorded literature. Throughout history, most people have had to scramble constantly to get enough of the necessities to keep themselves and their families alive. When someone suffered hardship, which was much of the time, it was natural to question why others were better off, and to resent their advantages denied to him. When an individual experienced this universal phenomenon of envy, it was a private matter and usually directed at someone with marginally more of what was needed to sustain life. The privileged few, however, comfortably warm and well fed, could ratchet envy up to the next level, for life's plums, where envy would often coexist with greed, the combination Berke called "grenvy". In such cases, envy could also be stoked by pride, as in "I am as good as so-and-so, and so I should have what she has." The ancients even saw nothing strange in the concept of the gods envying a human or a hybrid human/god, as in the case of Prometheus. But on the whole, over most of time, the envy that people usually felt was for others who had whatever the envier more or less urgently needed, and the line was often blurred between envy and covetousness. Beyond the physical necessities, however, people then as now felt the need for and envied those with certain intangibles, more attention, status, recognition, and "love", also necessities, that follow closely on the heels of food and shelter. It was millennia before most people became accustomed (shall we say "programmed"?) to expect non-necessities. In general their envy was for those they saw daily, living close by, for family members, neighbors, and coworkers whose advantages were a daily reminder and source of irritation, not for persons with wealth and power at a distance. In the Judeo-Christian heritage, envy was seen as a "sin", the second worst of the "seven deadly sins", and the envious were warned to eliminate it by replacing it with love, but there was little concrete advice on how to do this. Envy of this private type has not changed over the millennia and is not likely to go away.

With the Enlightenment came ideas and hopes for freedom and opportunity in Europe and America, for many people hitherto condemned to lives of poverty and few choices, who became ambitious to better their lot. But the down side of those opportunities was that they were just that, opportunities to compete for a limited supply, not guarantees. For every success there were many partial successes and many more failures, followed by disappointment. Then, as now, there was not enough of anything for everyone to have all he wanted, as in the anthropologist Foster's "Image of the Limited Good". [See my anthropologic appendix.] The corollary of opportunity, ambition, and competition was disappointment and envy of those more successful. Alexis de Tocqueville, the French aristocrat traveling in the United States, observed that envy was much more in evidence in our infant federation than in societies like his own with little or no opportunity for persons not to the manor born.

As we moved from the late nineteenth to the early twentieth century, one large social change was increased visibility. People saw each other more, if not in person, then in print, including an increasing barrage of pictures, especially of "society" and its well-to-do. Films during the Great Depression sought to provide escape, often by way of observing the antics of the rich, dressed in gold lamé, giving viewers something to wish for beyond their humdrum lives of worry and scraping along. When these films were shipped around the world, citizens elsewhere got a distorted idea of life in America. Many developed envy for what they saw and resented America for having. This was despite the fact that the United States had played a major role in feeding the hungry in Europe after WW I (for which Herbert Hoover should always be remembered) and for rebuilding Europe, the defeated as well as the allies, sending Marshall Plan aid even to noncombatants such as Iceland, after WW II. The result of this generosity at a time of our increased visibility was not, as one might expect, appreciation, but envy.

Another reason for hope for improving the lot of many people was the fact that a large percentage of our population had moved from the country to the city, from farm work to industry, where they were struggling to increase income, with the help of unions. Changes including these encouraged envy by the have-nots for the haves. In this way a new kind of "group envy" evolved, with whole groups of people envying what other groups had and were often flaunting. In these ways, in addition to private envy, which continued unabated, envy was escalating from private to public, from micro to macro.

Formerly the chance of birth had determined which young men could be excused from wage-earning beyond early childhood, long enough to take advantage of our formal education system and perhaps even go on to professional education (most skills were acquired by some kind of apprenticeship). Fathers in business hoped that higher education would help their sons make important connections. This was a prime source of envy in the breasts of those who valued and yearned for education. As the twentieth century progressed, scholarships, grants, loans, and other forms of assistance[1] were developed to address this wish for equality of opportunity.

One place to look for explanations for psychologic phenomena such as envy is the psychoanalytic movement. However, in its early years envy did not attract much attention, except as Freud's handy explanation for much of women's overt and covert dissatisfaction. Alfred Adler, Freud's follower who later left the group, came closer to incorporating envy into a comprehensive system, in his stress on rivalry and competition in establishing one's place. Later child analysts also observed the roles of envy and jealousy in the development of children in learning to negotiate and accomplish their ends. By the mid-twentieth century, however, Freud's follower Melanie Klein evolved her own explanation of envy as a largely innate or "constitutional" component of hate, directed against the first available object, the mother or nourisher, whether she be good, bad, or somewhere in between, inevitably displaying flaws everyone human brings to parenthood—and to every other task. Klein did not see envy as "reactive" or a feeling engendered by the caregiver's ineptitude or gross neglect or incapacity in her role, but as an innate feeling, part of the hate spectrum. Most of Klein's followers agreed on the appearance of envy in infancy but disagreed, considering the hate/envy of infancy as a reaction to the inevitable offenses and lapses coming from the environment in the one-down mother/infant feeding configuration. They agreed that it is a phenomenon so early that it could not possibly have resulted from comparison with the advantaged other, on which we define and base mature envy. Adler and other later child analysts saw envy as a positive growth enhancer and a goad to devise ways to get for oneself the advantages one sees others enjoying. All psychoanalysts agree that envy "belongs" to the envier and is his responsibility to recognize and handle, using his experience constructively, learning which advantages are within reach, how to appreciate others' advantages that he cannot himself attain, and developing other ways to live, as St. Paul advised, "abundantly".

During the early years of the twentieth century a curious phenomenon occurred: a sudden silence fell on the subject of envy after millennia of open discussion and writing and preaching about it by commentators ranging from Christian theologians to literary allegorists to "God-is-dead" philosophers like Nietzsche. "Classical sociologists" such as Emil Durkheim and Raiga (who considered envy as contributing to "survival of the fittest") had discussed envy at length, but another sociologist, Schoeck, in the mid-century, noted that the word "envy" had for the most part dropped out of sociologic and anthropologic indices. Now, the word is used infrequently in ordinary speech, but when heard at all, it is in a trivialized sense. Taking its place has been concern for "justice" and "fairness". The two concepts, envy and justice-hunger, are easily distinguishable at the extremes, but on the intervening continuum the two are confused and muddied, with a failure to recognize the envy component in what people are demanding or what others are demanding for them and claiming as their "right". Those who work for fairness and justice deny that envy plays a part in the change they are pursuing; those who study envy say that those who are concerned with justice and fairness are blind to the role of envy, and, for that matter, to the positive features of envy, which should be used as a lever and a guide for what to strive for.

Whereas for centuries there has been virtual unanimity in condemning envy as something to be rooted out (although with an occasional breath of advice regarding emulating the envied one), more recently envy has been credited, particularly by Schoeck, as a force behind advances in evolving civilization, significant when people see something they envy and devise a better way to get it despite the omnipresent fear of retaliation by those who envy them. Society had to evolve, in some cases stumble upon, ways to protect those willing to take risks, to experiment, hoping to benefit themselves and those willing to adopt their improvements. In primitive and preliterate societies, both explanations for envy and protection therefrom centered on beliefs in magic, luck, "evil eye", etc., whereas now legal processes can be invoked where needed. Similarly, in early childhood as we just noted, Adler and more recent psychoanalysts have identified the role of envy as a driving force behind trying new strategies for achieving children's wishes.

We have been considering envy from the viewpoint of the envier, but there have always been persons who, when aware of being envied, have become uncomfortable, wished to remedy the inequality, and perhaps tried. Others who were envied have enjoyed and maximized their advantage. Another development has been an organized use of envy as a tool by third parties who, though not themselves the envied, had something to gain by the envy of one group for another, including votes and dollars. I refer to the advertisers, "packagers", and mind-manipulators. Sometimes their pitch is to offer to help you be the envied one. "Your neighbor will envy your new [fill in the blank]."

By early in the twentieth century, Sigmund Freud's nephew who lived in the United States, Edward Bernays, conceived the idea of capitalizing on Freud's ideas of the unconscious, i.e., how we think at various levels of consciousness simultaneously, and our thinking is not all rational and driven by logic. Freud himself rejected as unethical and beneath his consideration, inducements to capitalize on the unconscious, Over his vehement protests Bernays went to manufacturers of retail goods with proposals to exploit these unconscious feelings in the service of marketing. Whereas formerly advertisers had focused on attracting customers by showing how their products satisfied physical needs, with Bernays' help they began, instead, to devise ways to exploit psychologic needs, often unconscious, by encouraging them to imagine greater happiness if they obtained what they had no genuine need for and in many cases could not afford, but that the advertisers wanted to sell. Thus greed, another of the "seven deadlies", is at work on both sides, the greed of advertisers, the minions of industry, wanting to sell, preying on the greed of the consumers, wanting to have and to flaunt. We see this increasingly to this day, particularly in industries that do not address basic human needs, such as food, but, for women, in fashion, cosmetics, and weight loss (for beauty, lately increasingly for health) and, for men, for automobiles par excellence. As we moved through the twentieth century, with mass communication and, soon, a barrage of media pictures and exposure to the well-to-do whom we had never met face-to-face, we were nudged and pressured by the mind benders to envy them. The message was "Everyone else has it, and you deserve it too." "Deserve" in common parlance changed in implication from "You have earned it" to "I'm going to help you borrow it from the bank."

With the advent of mass marketing, opportunities expanded to play on people's envy in the aggregate, not just one at a time. It was not long until envy came to be exploited in the promotion not only of products but also the packaging of political causes and persons.[2] The motivation of politicians, like that of everyone else, is mixed, in their case mixed between what they think might be good in the long run for their constituency or the country and what might get them elected in the here and now. When votes are at stake, one way to get them is to promise whatever the voters think would be "fair" and represent "justice". As always, along all but the extremes of the envy/justice continuum, these issues are very muddied and debatable. Very few can see the legitimacy of claims by the other as well as his own.

In this way concern with envy (albeit not under that term with all its negative connotations) shifted to groups of likely enviers by those intent on stoking their envy.

The visual impact of Western television, exported to the Third World, has served to escalate envy and its attendant covetousness to a new level, and resentment followed in its wake: "Why shouldn't we have what they have in America?" The next thought was often "We hate them."

When we are displayed on the media to the rest of the world, envy (albeit not under that opprobrious term) has seized larger groups, even those we have tried to help.

Often when we have tried to help them move toward opportunities, instead of using such help as a launching platform, they react by expecting more help. As always, envious feelings for what we have and they don't are mixed with feelings of legitimate anger over our many shortcomings, such as how we are recklessly consuming resources far beyond our numbers and degrading the planet.

In these ways envy has expanded from personal affliction in the microcosm of the individual to a tool used by outsiders to stir up feelings in either persons or groups who see what others have and feel that life is passing them by, i.e., envy in the macrocosm. This expansion happened coincidentally with the sudden silence on the subject of envy that Schoeck drew attention to. Just at the same time that communication exploded in our age of mass communication and visibility, the new attitude to envy has become no longer to call envy by its name but to trivialize the genuine article, i.e., not to call envy "envy" but to confuse and fail to differentiate between envy and justice.

As envy has shed its "sin" classification of earlier centuries in favor of "emotion", another major change in how we have come to view envy has been from a former near-100%-negative view of envy as something "bad" and "evil" to something with features to be understood, appreciated, and turned to good. Throughout most of history the only advice we received from leaders, religious and secular, has been to stifle envy and replace it with love. Only recently a handful of authors have brought our attention to envy's positive possibilities. Towering over the others is the sociologist Schoeck, who asserts that throughout history, envy has been responsible for advances in civilization, by persons willing to risk the envy of their fellows when they try to do or create something better. From the viewpoint of the individual, envy can be a wake-up call that the time has come to investigate better strategies, such as emulating the envied one, or planning to shift direction so as to acquire other advantages within range, or even to reevaluate what we have been seduced into envying, analyzing it in the same way we analyze other propaganda (e.g., "Do I really want what they wish to sell or 'sell', or do I have my own agenda to promote?")

As my friend and critic Bill Cashman[3] pointed out, "Maybe you haven't gotten to the bottom of this envy thing yet. Maybe it's some kind of adjustment strategy gone awry. Maybe envy can save us from self-hate." I like his idea of "adjustment strategy". His reasoning for saving from self-hate went: "Why didn't I get that advantage instead of that lucky SOB? It could just as well have been assigned to me. There's nothing defective about me; my bad luck was just a whim of fate." If this is a more comfortable way of assessing the situation than thinking, for example, "The boss must not like my work", this is fine for this occasion, but it does not offer hope for achieving something similar in the future. I would hazard a further way of looking at it: Envy lies somewhere between overwhelmed abdication of a potential good and creative problem-solving.

As I have said, my take-home message is that envy has evolved in our thinking from a "sin" to an "emotion" to an opportunity for learning and enrichment, albeit often wasted. The lessons can be in true values, alternative possibilities, and new directions.

We should try to shift focus, to look at envy as an opportunity not to be missed, to bring into play our highest faculties to get a better match between our fantasies and what our talents and circumstances permit.

Shakespeare's character Prospero pointed out, "What's past is prologue."

And I add, "What's relevant is where we go from here."

Notes

1. Some claim (I think rightly) that the two most important acts of legislation in our history were Morell's Land Grant Act establishing land grant universities and the GI Bill, both of which made education accessible to citizens formerly shut out, and which enabled massive shakeup in social position and opportunity for advancement. Many men returned from Normandy or El Alamein or Anzio or Iwo Jima or Corregidor to pick up their education where the war had interrupted it or to pursue education beyond their wildest hopes before World War II. My late husband, for example, 4F from the sequellae of polio (the worst of it corrected in his childhood by the generosity and charity of the Shriners), with a Ph.D. in physiologic chemistry, talked the army into taking him as a chemist and microbiologist, performed nutrition research on Conscientious Objectors, served in the Sanitary Corps in the Occupation, mustered out rather than accept the offered rank of major, and returned to let the GI Bill put him through medical school. With his double doctorate he spent a lifetime in the research of the biochemistry of connective tissue diseases.

2. For a fascinating survey of the burgeoning of mass mind-manipulation in the twentieth century by advertisers of both goods and ideas, I recommend a hard-to-get DVD of four BBC television hours cobbled together, entitled *The Century of the Self*, coordinated by the cinematographer Adam Curtis, beginning with the exploitation of Freud's "unconscious" and ranging from selling cake mixes to "guilty" housewives to the manipulation of politics in Guatemala to the packaging of Bill Clinton and Tony Blair.

3. Another observations of Bill's: "Envy is under-recognized in the quagmire of love."

Anthropologic Addendum

One of the prime sources from which we learn of the strange customs and beliefs of, mainly, preliterate peoples is accounts by those who worked with them over months or years—colonial administrators, missionaries, both supplanted in recent years by anthropologists. One such account I found late in the preparation of this book, in the references of one of my other sources, a study by George M. Foster, *The Anatomy of Envy: A Study in Symbolic Behavior*. I was interested to note that Foster's comparative anthropology material cast light on yet other facets of our topic. Too late to pursue other anthropologists' views on envy, I nevertheless perused Foster's study for inclusion and encountered a manner of publication new to me. Before submitting his paper, Foster had sent it to a number of colleagues for comments, and he attached his harvest of responses to his paper, followed by his own final agreements or refutations. The result was a kind of paper debate.

He began by citing Schoeck's observation that "envy" had dropped off in anthropologic as well as sociologic indices prior to the publication of his book in the late sixties, then found, similarly, that in psychologic and psychiatric indices, the usual sequence jumped from "environment" to "epistemology".

Foster recognized that we often find in ourselves a wish for some advantage we see in others, or feel distress over being more fortunate than those around us. Yet we are reluctant to call these feelings by their name, "envy" or fear thereof. The length to which we go to deny and conceal envy from others and even from ourselves correlates with how reprehensible an emotion we find it to be.[1]

While admittedly oversimplifying, Foster delineated envy along two major axes: the competitive axis and the fear axis. He chose to ignore the competitive axis, with obvious, overt envy, which engenders manipulative behavior. For the present study he addresses the largely ignored fear axis, which is handled subliminally and is usually disguised in symbolic behavior. Foster notes that symbolic behavior is easier to recognize in exotic societies than in ours. An example he gives is a Spanish custom for a young man to throw a club with a knob on one end into a girl's house as a proposal of marriage. One of our customs whose symbolism struck me years ago is for proud new fathers to give out cigars.

Foster spent years studying the culture of a peasant village in Mexico with the delightful name of Tzintzuntzan. He refers to his own earlier "Image of the Limited Good", i.e., belief in economies of scarcity that there are not enough of the necessities for all, and life is played as a zero-sum game. (In many ways this is true, and not only in impoverished cultures, but, e.g., in business in our society.) One observation by Foster of a hundred schoolchildren eating a government-provided breakfast in complete silence sent him on the path of collecting examples of behavior that might be explained by envy or fear of it. Foster is one of the few (I include myself) who recognize that our reluctance to admit to envy is because such admission is tantamount to acknowledgment of inferiority.

> To overgeneralize for a moment, we can say that man fears being envied for what he has, and wishes to protect himself from the consequences of the envy of others; man also fears he will be accused of envying others, and he wishes to allay this suspicion; and finally, man fears to admit to himself that he is envious, so he searches for rationales

and devices to deny to himself his envy and to account for [envy] in terms other than personal responsibility, the conditions that place him in a position inferior to another.

In affluent societies the most envied items are wealth and power (identified by fine homes, clothing, cars, and travel) and prestige and status. In peasant societies Foster finds that the main objects of envy are food, health, and children. With the latter two one has a fighting chance to survive into the next generation. Most of his examples in this study are in the area of food.

In Foster's dozens of examples, he describes cases of hiding food and eating alone and in silence, as explained by wish to avoid envy by those without adequate food.[2] These peasants will pretend to be poor to avoid envy. When it is obvious someone is eating, he will "throw a sop" or give a little. The final mode of avoiding envy is true sharing. Foster cites fear of envy as the basis of feasts to acknowledge happy events, weddings, births, baptisms, etc., rather than risk the envy of others for the good fortune that prompted these celebrations. One component of our use of housewarming gifts and wedding and baby gifts may have originally been to allay the fear that the one whom fortune has blessed is envied.

Our practice of tipping, Foster sees not as a rationalization for part-payment of the underpaid server or for what is sometimes called its acronymic meaning, "To Insure Promptness". (How can it insure promptness after the fact?) He cites our emotional reluctance to leave without tipping even for abominable service, and he refers again to "throwing a sop" (that phrase Foster uses for a whole category of envy-avoidance behavior) to the server to minimize envy caused by his being outranked by the diner. He sees the fact that many languages with a word for "tip" (many other languages have no need for such a word) incorporate the word for "drink" *(pourboire, trinkgeld)* in an effort to buy off the server's envy. He suggests that our word "tip" derives from "tipple".

An obvious mechanism to avoid the envy of have-nots (along

with other reasons for its use) is the progressive income tax and even the negative income tax, both "given" grudgingly.

Paying compliments is another area rife with possibilities for hidden envy, at all levels of society. Foster noted that compliments were extremely rare in Tzintzuntzan, and one reason is that they suggest envy in the complimenter. I believe that compliments may be a way to disavow our own envy, as in the case of the journalist who sent the telegram.[3]

One area that Foster, but no one else, in my readings so far, has commented on, I found particularly interesting because of my own experience: travel. Foster writes:

> That travel may be a sensitive envy-provoking area is evident by the behavior of American academicians who are almost apologetic about travel not associated with research or other professional activities, which validate and thus justify—in fact, force upon one—travel. Academicians often are apologetic when forced to confess 'We were really just tourists.' The colleague to whom the confession is made must then hasten to assure the speaker that the role of the tourist can be an honorable one, that he himself has traveled as a tourist, thus reassuring the first speaker that he harbors him no grudge for his good luck in traveling.

This reaction may be particularly prominent in anthropologists because, in addition to the congresses that academics of all disciplines attend, they travel to field sites and may live there, as Foster did in Tzintzuntzan.

I had also explained to professional colleagues and to patients that my husband and I were going to a meeting at which he would present a paper and hide the "just tourists" part by passing over the fact that we would see as much as possible of that part of the world before and after the meeting. I had more than an inkling that it was from fear of envy.

One year when we visited Iguassu Falls in November (I hasten to add that it was in conjunction with my husband's congress in Buenos Aires), I hatched the idea that instead of regular Christmas cards, we would send postcards of the world's widest waterfall. Recipients commented favorably, and so I repeated that strategy for several years. Then I began to worry about the possibility of envy, and so I quit sending postcards from abroad. To my surprise, I received many complaints: "Where are our postcards this year?" I pointed out that I thought they must be tired of them, but then I resumed my practice to selected recipients.

Moving from Foster's many examples of behavior fascinating in their own right with or without envy, we consider alternative explanations offered by commentators. "Brøgger warns us that an author once possessed of a broad conceptual scheme finds it tempting to cram every possible bit of data into that scheme." Foster agrees and notes further that "examples I have given can be interpreted or explained at several levels, and in a variety of ways not necessarily mutually exclusive". Another critic compared the tendency to fit as much data as possible into one conceptual scheme to how persons dedicated to psychoanalytic principles are inclined to find much behavior a symbolic representation of sex.

Foster made a point similar to those of Raiga and de Tocqueville, to the effect that societies with "encapsulated" subgroups with equal rights and obligations have less need for envy than do open societies. When I first read Foster's point that caste systems have this advantage, "caste" being in his opinion a system that minimizes envy, I was appalled. One critic, however, agreed with Foster that this explanation is not "hopelessly far out". Apthorpe and Whiting point out that Foster's work is "not a scientifically testable model, but rather 'an essay in conceptualization', an 'essay rather than a scientific treatise'". Foster could not agree more. We are reminded of how Schoeck (and others) repeat that envy must be surmised and cannot be tested scientifically in real-life situations or "proven". Foster concludes: "The purpose of an essay like

'The Anatomy of Envy' is not to establish eternal scientific verities; it is to ask questions, to explore plausible lines of explanation, to afford new insight into old or forgotten problems."

Notes

1. My mother, a caring, sensitive, and intelligent woman, spotted envy in me as a child and tried to draw me out to help me deal with it. Still, I was ashamed for her to know because I wanted her respect.

2. Not in Foster's study but somewhere long ago I read of women in a protein-poor society who would hide their occasional scrap of meat in their vagina until they could eat alone.

3. I recall that as a teenager I was uncomfortable when complimented, and I assumed the reason was that I became flustered and didn't respond in what I considered a sophisticated manner. And so I trained myself, if I could think of nothing better, at least to acknowledge a compliment with a "Thank you". I had opportunities to practice because my mother, in contrast to the then widely held view that you should not praise a child because she (in this case) would get a "swelled head", held that if a child did well, she had earned recognition, just as she had similarly warranted rebuke or worse for wrongdoing. My mother was also clever enough to teach me to eschew the frequent, embarrassed reply in those days to a compliment on clothing, "Oh, this old rag!", since, among other things, it was an insult to the complimenter's taste. I don't believe that envy had any place in parent/child praise, usually for behavior. And I soon became adroit at reflecting back compliments in a way that made us both look good.

References

Adler, Alfred, *The Individual Psychology of Alfred Adler: A Systematic Presentation of Selections from His Writings*, tr. and ed. by Heinz L. and Rowena R. Ansbacher, New York, Torchbooks, Harper, 1964.

Aeschylus, *Prometheus Bound*, tr. by Robert Whitelaw, Oxford at The Clarendon Press, 1907.

Albom, Mitch, *Tuesdays with Morrie*, Doubleday, New York, 1997, p. 119.

Appleby, Louis, "Envy", Brit. Med. J. 313 (12/21–28):1592–3, 1996.

Aquinas, St. Thomas,"Of Envy", *The Summa Theologica II-II, 36*; in *Great Books of the Western World,* Robert Maynard, Ed.-in-Chief, Encyclopedia Britannica, Chicago, 1952.

Aristophanes, "Plutus (Wealth)", in *Aristophanes, the Complete Plays*, tr. by Paul Roche, New American Library, Penguin, New York, 2005.

Aristotle, *Nicomachaean Ethics*, tr. by D. P. Chase, J. M. Dent & Sons, London, 1910.

Au, Wilkie, and Noreen Cannon, *Urgings of the Heart: A Spirituality of Integration*, Paulist Press, New York, Mahwah, New Jersey, 1995.

Augustine, St., *The City of God*, tr. by Marcus Dods, intro. by Thomas Merton, Modern Library, New York, 1993.

Bacon, Sir Francis, "On Envy" in *Francis Bacon's Essays*, intro. by Oliphant Smeaton, Dent, London; Dutton, New York, 1906, 1966, 1993.

Balzac, Honoré, *Cousin Bette*, tr. by Katharine Prescott Wormeley, Roberts Brothers, Boston, 1888.

Bandow, Doug, *The Politics of Envy: Statism as Theology*, "The Conundrum of Capitalism and Christianity", Transaction Publishers, Piscataway, New Jersey, 1994.

Berke, Joseph H., *The Tyranny of Malice: Exploring the Dark Side of Character and Culture*, Summit Books, Simon & Schuster, New York, 1988.

Bion, W. R., H. Rosenfeld, H. Segal, and Melanie Klein, *Int. J. Psychoanal.* 42:4–8, 1961.

Bloomfield, Morton Wilfred, *The Seven Deadly Sins: An introduction to the history of a religious concept, with special reference to medieval English literature*, Michigan State College Press, East Lansing, 1952.

Boethius, Amicius Manlius Severinus, *The Consolation of Philosophy*, intro. and notes by P. G. Walsh, Oxford Univ. Press, New York, 1999.

Boris, Harold N., *Envy*, Jason Aronson, Northvale, New Jersey, London, 1994.

Brooke, Arthur, *Romeus and Juliet*, Originals and Analogues for Shakespeare Society, Part I, ed. by P. A. Daniel, N. Trubler & Co., London, 1875.

Bunyan, John, *The Pilgrim's Progress*, The Religious Tract Society, London, 1906.

Burke, N., "On the Domestication of Envy", *Psychoanal. Psychol.* 17:497–511, 2000.

Burton, Robert, *The Anatomy of Melancholy*, intro. by A. H. Bullen; ed. by Rev. A. R. Shilleto, George Bell and Sons, 1896.

Čapek, Karel, *War with the Newts*, Gregg Press, div. of G. K. Hall, Boston, 1975.

Catechism of the Catholic Church: www.usccd.org/catechism/text/pt3sect2chpt2art10.htm.

Chaucer, Geoffrey, *The Canterbury Tales,* "The Persones Tale", Thomas Wright, ed., Printed for The Percy Society, London, 1751.

Collette, "The Cat", in film *Les sept péchés capitaux.*

Curtis, Adam, ed. film *The Century of the Self,* Britain, 2002.

Dahl, E. Kirsten, "The Concept of Penis Envy Revisited: A child analyst listens to adult women", *Psychoanal. Study Child* 51:303–325, 1996.

Dante Alighieri, *The Divine Comedy,* tr., by Henry F. Cary, P. F. Collier & Son, 1909.

Dai, Sijie, *Balzac and the Little Chinese Seamstress,* Knopf, New York, 2001.

Dawidziak, Mark, *"Kidnapped* promises to sweep viewers away", [Cleveland, Ohio] *Plain Dealer,* 10/30/2005.

De Broca, Phillippe, and Claude Chabral, dir. film *Les sept péchés capitaux (The Seven Deadly Sins),* Envy portrayed as in "The Cat" by Collette.

Denis, Jean-Pierre, dir. film *Les Blessures Assasines (Murderous Maids),* France, 2002.

de Tocqueville, Alexis, *Democracy in America,* intro. by Alan Ryan, Alfred A. Knopf, New York, 1945, 1972.

Descartes, René, *Philosophical Writings,* Nelson, 1899.

(New) Dictionary of Thoughts: A Cyclopedia of Quotations from the Best Authors of the World Both Ancient and Modern, original compiled by Tryon Edwards, Standard Book Company, 1960.

Diderot, Denis, "Rameau's Nephew", from *Diderot and The Encyclopaedists,* by John Morley, Chapman & Hall, 1884.

Eccles, Mark, ed., *The Macro Plays,* The Castle of Perseverance, Oxford Univ. Press, London, 1969.

Elliott, G. P., "Buried Envy: The Last Dirty Little Secret", *Harper's,* July 1974, p. 12.

Elworthy, Frederick Thomas, *The Evil Eye: An Account of This Ancient and Widespread Superstition,* Julian Press, 1895, 1958; 1986.

Epstein, Joseph, *Envy,* New York Public Library and Oxford University Press, 2003.

Erasmus, Desiderius, *The Praise of Folly*, Clarendon Press, Oxford, 1913.

Etchegoyen, R. Horatio, Benito M.Lopez, and Moses Rahib, "On Envy and How to Interpret It", *Int. J. Psychoanal.* 68:49–61, 1987.

Evans, William R., "The Eye of Jealousy and Envy", *Psychoanal. Rev.* 62, No. 3, 481–492, 1975.

Fairlie, Henry, *The Seven Deadly Sins Today*, Chapter 2, "Envy or Invidia", Simon & Schuster, New York, New Republic Books, Washington, D.C., 1978.

Feldman, Eliahu (Tel Aviv), and Heitor De Paola, (Rio de Janiero), "An Investigation into the Psychoanalytic Concept of Envy", *Int. J. Psychoanal.* 75:217–234, 1994.

Fincher, David, dir. *Se7en*, 1995.

Fisher, Antwone Quenton, *Finding Fish: A Memoir*, Morrow, New York, 2001.

Fleming, Ian, foreword in *The Seven Deadly Sins*, Wm. Morrow, New York, 1962.

Fontaine, Anne, dir. film *How I Killed My Father,* France, 2002.

Foster, George M., "The Anatomy of Envy: A Study in Symbolic Behavior", *Current Anthropol.* 13:165–201, 1972.

Frank, Joan, "Visiting Envy", *The Writer's Chronicle* (George Mason University), May/Summer, vol. 32, no. 6, pp. 19–22, 2000.

Frankel, Steven, and Ivan Sherick, "Observations on the Development of Normal Envy", *Psychoanal. Study Child* 32:257–281, 1977.

Freud, Sigmund, "The Rat Man", in the *Standard Ed. of the Complete Psychological Works*, xviii, Vol. X, tr. James Strachey, the Hogarth Press and the Institute of Psycho-Analysis, London, 1909, 1951.

Gardner, John, and John Maier, tr. *Gilgamesh Epic,* Sîn-Leqi-Unninī Version, Knopf, New York, 1984.

Gay, John, *The Poetical Works of John Gay,* Houghton, Mifflin and Company, 1880.

Giles, Molly, "The Blessed Among Us", in *Creek Walk and Other Stories*, Anchor Books, Doubleday, Garden City, New York, 1960, 1967.

Gilgamesh—see Gardner.

Gorman, Ed, "The Eye of the Beholder", in *Such a Good Girl and Other Crime Stories*, Five Star, Unity, Maine, 2001, pp. 190–222.

Gower, John, *Mirour de l'Omme*, tr. as *The Mirror of Mankind* by William Burton Wilson, revised by Nancy Wilson Van Baak, foreword by R. F. Yeager, East Lansing (Michigan) Colleagues Press, 1992.

Greenleaf, Victoria, *Fighting the Good Fight: One Family's Struggle against Adolescent Alcoholism*, Cypress House, Fort Bragg, Calif., 2002.

Greenleaf, Victoria, *A Handful of Ashes: One Mother's Tragedy*, Cypress House, Fort Bragg, Calif., 2001.

Harris, Adrienne, "Aggression, Envy, and Ambition: Circulating Tensions in Women's Psychic Life", *Gender and Psychoanal.* 2:291–325, 1997.

Harris, Judith Rich, *The Nurture Assumption: why children turn out the way they do; parents matter less than you think and peers matter more*, Free Press, New York, London, etc., 1998.

Hartley, L. P., *Facial Justice*, Doubleday, Garden City, New York, 1961.

Hazlitt, William, *Characteristics in the Manner of Rochefoucault's Maxims*, intro. by R. H. Horne, J. Templeman, London, 1837.

Herdt, Gilbert H., *Guardians of the Flutes: Idioms of Masculinity*, McGraw-Hill, New York, 1981.

Hermann, Fabio, and Heitor De Paolo, discussion moderators, "Envy, Jealousy, and Shame", *Int. J. Psychoanal.* 82:381–384, 2001.

Herzog, Don, "Envy: Poisoning the Banquet They Cannot Taste" chapter in Solomon, Robert C., *Wicked Pleasures,* Lanham, MD, Rowman and Littlefield, 1999.

Hume, David, "Justice and Injustice", in Book 3, Part 2, of Morals, *A Treatise of Human Nature*, [ed. David Fate Norton and Mary J. Norton], Oxford University Press, New York, 2005.

Hume, David, *A Treatise of Human Nature: Being an attempt to Introduce the Experimental Method of Reasoning into Moral Subjects*, Vol. 2, Of the Passions, ed. by John Noon, 1739, reprinted by Thoemmes Press, Bristol, England, 2001.

Hurd, Michael J., "Envy", in 2/14/99 *Living Resources Newsletter.* www.drhurd.com/.

Hutson, Peggy B., "*Envy* by Harold N. Boris" a review in *Psychoanal. Q.* 67:182–183, 1998.

Inge, William, *Picnic: A Summer Romance*, Dramatists Play Service, New York, 1955.

Jacob's Well, ed. Arthur Brandeis; rare book collection, Cleveland Public Library.

Jannett, Andrew F., "Wisdom's Way", Vantage Press, New York, 2004.

Joffe, Walter G., "A Critical Review of the Status of the Envy Concept", *Int. J. Psychoanal.* 50:533–545, 1969.

Johnson, Samuel, *Rasselas, A Tale*, Longman, Green, Longman and Roberts, 1860.

Kant, Immanuel, *The Geneology of Morals*, Bobbs Merrill, Indianapolis, Ind., The Metaphysics of Morals, Part I, "The Metaphysical Elements of Justice", 1965, and Part II, "The Metaphysical Principles of Virtue", Bobbs-Merrill, 1964.

King James Version, Protestant Bible, Old and New Testaments.

Klein, Melanie, *Envy and Gratitude*, London, Tavistock Publications, 1957.

Kurosawa, dir. film *Ikura* (*Living: To Live*), Japan, 1952.

Lahr, John, "Prisoners of Envy: Donald Margulies and David Rabe on the Not-so-Sweet Smell of Success", review of *Brooklyn Boy* by Margulies in *The New Yorker*, Feb. 14 and 21: 256–8, 2005.

Langland, William, *The Vision of Piers Plowman*, edited by The Rev. Walter W. Skeat, M. A., Clarendon Press, 1869.

La Rochefoucauld—see under R.

Lax, R. F., "Aspects of primary and secondary Genital Feelings and Anxieties in Girls during the Preoedipal and Early Oedipal Phases", *Psychoanal. Q.* 63:271–296, 1994.

——, "Freud's View and the Changing Perspective on Femaleness and Femininity: What My Female Analysands Taught Me", *Psychoanal. Psychol.* 12:393–406, 1995.

——, "Boys' Envy of Mother and the Consequences of This Narcissistic Mortification", *Psychoanal. Study Child* 52:118–139, 1997.

Levinson, Barry, film dir. *Envy*, 2004.

Lopez–Corvo, Rafael E. (Caracas), "Self-Envy and Intrapsychic Interpretation of Self-Envy", *Psychoanal Q.* 68:209–219, 1999.

——, *Self-Envy: Therapy of the Divided Internal World*, Aronson, Northvale, New Jersey, 1994.

MacLeod, Wendy, *Sin*, Dramatists Play Service, New York, 1997.

Macro plays, ed. Mark Eccles, Oxford Univ. Press, London, 1969.

Maizels, Neil, "Self-Envy, the Womb, and the Nature of Goodness: A Reappraisal of the Death Instinct", *Int. J. Psychoanal.* 66:185, 1985.

Margulies, Donald, *Brooklyn Boy*, Theatre Communications Group, New York, 2005.

Marlowe, Christopher, *The Tragicall History of the Life and Death of Doctor Faustus*, ed. Israel Gollancz, J. M. Dent and Company, London, 1897.

McGovern, George S., *Terry: My Daughter's Life-and-Death Struggle with Alcoholism*, Villard Books, New York, 1996.

Melville, Herman, *Billy Budd, Sailor: (An Inside Narrative)*, Everyman's Library, 1919.

Menotti, Gian Carlo, *Amahl and the Night Visitors*, Video Arts Int./ World Vision Enterprises, New York, 1979.

Milton, John, *Paradise Lost*, edited with intro. and notes by Albert S. Cook, Leach, Shewell & Sanborn, 1896.

Mortimer, Raymond, in *The Seven Deadly Sins*, see Fleming.

New Jerusalem Bible (including Wisdom of Solomon in the Apocrypha), Doubleday, New York, 1990.

Neubauer, P. B., "Rivalry, Envy, and Jealousy", *Psychoanal. St. Child* 37:121–142, 1982.

Nietzsche, Friedrich, "The Flies in the Marketplace", in *Also Sprach Zarathustra*, tr. by Alexander Tille, Macmillan & Company, New York, 1896.

——, *Beyond Good and Evil*

——, *The Birth of Tragedy & The Geneology of Morals*, tr. by Francis Golffing, Anchor, Random House, New York, 1956.

Olesha, Yuri, *Envy and Other Works*, in Russian, 1927, tr. by Andrew R. MacAndrew, Anchor Books, Doubleday, Garden City, New York, 1960 and 1967.

O'Neill, Eugene, *Beyond the Horizon*, Boni and Liveright, New York, 1920.

——, *Long Day's Journey into Night*, Yale Univ. Press, New Haven, 1956, 1989.

Ovid, *The Metamorphoses* 2:779–781, Book 2 tr. and intro. by Horace Gregory, Mentor, Penguin, London, 1958.

Ozick, Cynthia, "Envy; or, Yiddish in America", in Kauvar, Elaine M., ed., *A Cynthia Ozick Reader*, Indiana Univ. Press, Bloomington and Indianapolis, 1996.

Parrott, W. Gerrod, "The Emotional Experiences of Envy and Jealousy", in Salovey, pp. 3–30.

Patton, Thomas, Ill Will: "On Matters of Envy, Resentment, and Schadenfreude", first chapter on Internet, 6/10/2006.

Petrarch, Francesca, *Remedies for Fortune Fair and Foul* (Book 2, Vol. 3, Fortune Foul), tr. and intro. by Conrad H. Rawski, Indiana Univ. Press, Bloomington and Indianapolis, 1991.

Piers, Gerhard, and Benjamin B. Singer, 1952.

Plato, "Symposium", from *The Dialogues of Plato*, tr. by Benjamin Jowett, Scribner, Armstrong & Co., 1873.

Pope, Alexander, *The Rape of The Lock And An Essay On Man*: *Eclectic English Classics*, American Book Company,1898.

Potter, Stephen, *The Complete Upmanship (including Gamesmanship, Lifemanship, One-Upmanship, and Supermanship)*, New American Library, New York, 1958.

Powell, Dawn, *The Golden Spur*, in *Novels, 1930–1942, and Novels, 1942–1965*, ed. Tim Page, Library of America, Steerforth Press, Vt, 1962, 1997.

Prudentius, Aurelius, *The Psychomachia of Prudentius*, tr. as *The Fight for Mansoul* by H. J. Thomas, Harvard Univ. Press, Loeb Classical Library, Cambridge, Mass, 1953.

Pushkin, Alexander, "Mozart and Salieri", in *The Little Tragedies*, tr. by Antony Wood, fwd. by Elaine Feinstein, Angel, London, 1982, 1987.

Raiga, *L'Envie: Son rôle social,* Librairie Felix Alcan, Paris, 1932.

La Rochefoucauld, *Moral Reflections, Sentences and Maxims of Francis, Duc De La Rochefoucauld*, William Gowans, New York, 1851.

Rodgers, Janet, "Women and the Fear of Being Envied", *Nursing Outlook*, June: 344–347, 1982.

Rosenblatt, Allan D., "Envy, Identification, and Pride: Analysis of eight related emotions", *Psychoanal. Q.* 56:57–71, 1988.

Rosenfeld, Herbert, "A Clinical Theory of the Life and Death Instincts: An Investigation into the Aggressive Aspects of Narcissism", *Int. J. Psychoanal.* 52:169–178, 1971.

Rousseau, Jean-Jacques, *A Discourse on Inequality*, tr. by G.D.H. Cole, The Academy of Dijon, 1754.

Russell, Bertrand, *On Education*, Allen & Unwit, London, 1926.

——, "The Aims of Education", *Education And The Good Life*, Boni & Liveright, New York, 1926.

Salovey, Peter, and Alexander J. Rothman, "Envy and Jealousy: Self and Society" in Salovey, pp. 271–286.

——, *The Psychology of Jealousy and Envy*, Guilford Press, New York, 1991.

Sandell, Rolf (Stockholm), "Envy and Admiration", *Int. J. Psychoanal.* 74:1213–1221, 1993.

Schimmel, Solomon, *The Seven Deadly Sins: Jewish, Christian, and Classical Reflections on Human Nature*, The Free Press, Macmillan, New York, 1962.

Schoeck, Helmut, *Envy: A Theory of Social Behavior*, orig. in German, Harcourt, Brace & World, 1969; tr. by Martin Secker, Warburg Limited, Liberty Press, Indianapolis, 1987.

Schopenhauer, Arthur, *The Wisdom of Life and Counsels and Maxims*, tr. by T. Bailey Saunders, Allen and Unwin, 1890 (reprinted by Prometheus Books, 1995).

Segal, Hanna, *Introduction to the Work of Melanie Klein*, Hogarth Press, London, 1975, 2004; 2nd ed. Basic Books, Harper Collins, New York, 1964, 1974.

——, "Melanie Klein's Technique", in Benjamin B.Wolman, *Psychoanalytic Techniques: A Handbook for the Practicing Psychoanalyst*, Basic Books, New York, 1967.

Sennet, Richard, and Jonathan Cobb, *The Hidden Injuries of Class*, Knopf, New York, 1972.

Serling, Rod, dir. television film "The Eye of the Beholder", described in Zicree.

Dr. Seuss, "Gertrude McFuzz" in *Yertle the Turtle and Other Stories*, Random House, New York, 1958.

Shaffer, Peter, *Peter Shaffer's Amadeus*, Harper & Row, New York, 1981.

Shakespeare, William, *The Tragedie of Othello, the Moor.*

Shengold, Leonard, "Envy and Malignant Envy", *Psychoanal. Quart.* 63:615–640, 1994.

Shepard, Sam, *True West*, Samuel French, New York, 1981.

Shioya, Nobi, "7S: An Olfactory Instillation of the Seven Deadly Sins", traveling art exhibit at Cleveland State University, Jan.–March, 2003.

Smith, Adam, *A Theory of Moral Sentiments*, ed. D. D. Raphael and A. L. Macfie, Clarendon Press, Oxford, 1976.

Smith, Richard H., "Envy and the Sense of Injustice" in Salovey.

Smith, Vivien, and Margaret Whitfield, "The Constructive Uses of Envy", *Can. J. Psychiat.* 28:14–17, Feb., 1983.

Sobel, Dana, *Galileo's Daughter*, Walker & Co., New York, 1999.

Solomon, Robert C., ed. *Wicked Pleasures: Meditations on the Seven "Deadly" Sins*, Rowan C. Littlefield Publishers, Lanham, Md.; Boulder, Col.; Oxford, New York, 1999.

Sorge, Bob, *Envy: The Enemy Within*, Regal, Ventura, Calif., 2003.

Spenser, Edmund, *The Faerie Queene: Book One*, intro. by Martha Hale Shackford, Houghton, Mifflin and Company, 1905.

Spielman, P. M., "Envy and Jealousy: An Attempt at Clarification", *Psychoanal. Q.* 40:59–82, 1971.

Spillius, Elizabeth Bott, "Varieties of Envious Experiences", *Int. J. Psychoanal.* 74:1199–1212, 1993.

Spinoza, Benedict, *Ethics*, Dent and Dutton, 1916.

St. John, Warren, "Sorrow So Sweet: A Guilty Pleasure in Another's Woe", *New York Times,* 8/24/02, p. 7+.

Sue, Eugène, *Frederick Bastien: Envy*, in *The Works of Eugène Sue*, Brainard, Boston, New York, 1900.

Sullivan, Harry Stack, *The Collected works of Harry Stack Sullivan; Clinical Studies in Psychiatry,* ed. Helen Switch Perry, Mary Ladd Garvel, and Martha Gibbon, foreword by Dexter M. Bullard, M.D., ch. 6, "Envy and Jealousy as Precipitating Factors in the Major Mental Disorders", W. W. Norton, New York, 1956.

Tarkovsky, Andrei, dir. film *Andrei Rublev*, Russia, 1969.

Thomson, James, *The Poetical Works of James Thomson*, D. Appleton & Co., 1854.

Tocqueville, see de T.

Torsti, Marita, "The Feminine Self and Penis Envy", *Int. J. Psychoanal.* 75:469–478, 1994.

Updike, John, "Late Work: Writers and Artists Confronting the End", *The New Yorker* vol. 80, no. 24, pp. 64–71, 8/7/2006.

Van Leeuwen, Kate, "Pregnancy Envy in the Male", *Int. J. Psychoanal.* 47:319–324, 1966.

Veblen, Thorstein, *The Theory of the Leisure Class*, Prometheus Books, Amherst, New York, 1998.

Vonnegut, Kurt, "Harrison Bergeron" in *Welcome to the Monkey House*, Delacourt, New York, 1968.

——, *The Sirens of Titan*, Laurel, Dell, Bantam, Doubleday, New York, 1959.

Wahba, Rachel, "Envy in the Transference: A Specific Selfobject Disruption Progress in the Self", *Psychol.* 7:137–154, 1991.

Waska, Robert T., "Oral Deprivation, Envy, and the Sadistic Aspects of the Ego", *Canad. J. Psychoanal.* 7:97–110, 1999.

Webster's Elementary School Dictionary, University of Michigan, 1914.

Webster's New World Dictionary of the American Language, David B. Guralnik, Ed.-in-Chief, World Publishing, New York, Cleveland, 1970.

Welt, Sheila Rouslin, "Envy and Its Consequences", *Arch. Nursing* 1987:322–333.

——, and Wm, G. Herron, Ch. 12, "Envy and Its Consequences" in *Narcissism and the Psychotherapist*, Guilford Press, New York, 1990, pp. 258–276.

Whitman, Roy M. and James Alexander, "On Gloating", *Int. J. Psychoanal,* 49: 732–738, 1968.

Whitman, Roy M. and Ellin L. Bloch, "Therapist Envy", *Bull. Menninger Clinic* 54 (4): 478–487, Fall, 1990.

Wideman, John Edgar, *Fatheralong*, Vintage, Random House, New York, 1995.

Wilkinson, Sallye M., "Penis Envy: Libidinal Metaphor and Experiential Metonym", *Int. J. Psychoanal.* 72:335–346, 1991.

Wilson, Angus, "Envy", chapter in *The Seven Deadly Sins*, foreword by Ian Fleming, 1962.

Wisdom of Solomon, in New Jerusalem Bible.

Zicree, Marc Scott, "The Eye of the Beholder" by Rod Serling in *The Twilight Zone Companion*, Silman-James Press, Los Angeles, 1965, pp. 144–149.

Index

vitality, 204n13
Voltaire, 211, 277
Vonnegut, Kurt, 175–76, 314

W

Wahba, Rachel, 262
War with the Newts (Čapek), 297
Waska, Robert T., 261
weakness, 276
wealth
    Bandow on, 295
    and conspicuous consumption, 45n1
    in literature, 146–47, 148
    Morey-Kyrle's categorization of, 263–64
    Rousseau on, 277, 278
    Schoeck on, 291
    Tocqueville on, 283
Wealth (Aristophanes), 300n11
The Wealth of Nations (Smith), 275
Websters's Elementary School Dictionary,
    xxi, 10
Websters's Third International Dictionary,
    10
wedding gifts, 343
Welt, Sheila Rouslin, 51, 166
Whitelaw, Robert, 78–79
Whitfield, Margaret, 260–61, 321
Whiting, Beatrice Blyth, 345
Whitman, Roy, 305
*Wicked Pleasures: Meditations on the
    Seven "Deadly Sins"* (Solomon), 219
Wideman, John, 65–68
Williams, Tennessee, 192
Williams, William Carlos, 182
Willkinson, Sallye M., 258
"will to power," 235
Wilson, Angus, 212, 213–14
Wilson, William Burton, 120
wisdom, 276
Wisdom's Way (Jannett), 176–77
withdrawal, 218, 244, 253
Wolman, Benjamin B., 244
women
    and beauty, 29–30, 31
    competitiveness of, 258
    devaluation of, 259

    in literature, 227–28
    and long-term contentment, 57–58
    and mother/daughter relationships, 258
    as objects of envy, 243, 256–57, 259
    and primitive societies, 45n4
    and reproductive envy, 47, 49, 259
    who have lost children, 255 (*see also*
        mothers)
women's psychology, 232
work settings, 40–41
worthlessness, 251, 263
wrath, 123
"writer's disease," 201, 202, 322. *See also*
    authors and authorship
written language, 80

X

Xerxes, 297

Y

youth, 36–37, 40, 87, 173, 226

Z

zero-sum approach to relationships, 223,
    342
Zeus, 142n9

About the Author

One of the most important things I learned from my father was to recognize and seize opportunities. Therefore the articles and books I have written as a psychiatrist/author reflect the opportunities life has given me.

When I was an interne uncertain about my future route in medicine, I noticed that the psychiatric residents several years ahead of me were usually reading good classic literature such as *Anna Karenina* and *Madame Bovary*. This appealed to me as a fringe benefit of a life in psychiatry, because I have always been an avid reader of significant literature (both fiction and nonfiction). Later I became a member and leader of a Great Books Discussion Group. This feature that drew me to a life in psychiatry is the fact that it interfaces between science and the humanities.

From the start of my career in psychiatry, I knew that I would be writing at least journal articles in psychiatry, and I have done so. They began with studies of my patients with special teaching features. My husband helped me with ideas for papers. ("That patient who consulted you because he takes enemas for sexual pleasure—take good notes and write him up, and if the condition doesn't have a name, give it one," he suggested. And I did, both, contributing the word "klismaphilia" to the psychiatric terminology.) Already a mature and seasoned scientist, a biochemist first and a physician, my husband also helped me learn to write in the format of medical journals. I have never had a paper rejected by the first journal to which I submitted it.

Even before I began practice, while in training at the University of Michigan, an opportunity offered there was a special degree, an M.S. in psychiatry (after the M.D.). Candidates for that degree had to write term papers for the seminars all residents attended anyway, and we had to accumulate credit hours in cognates—psychology, sociology, anthropology, history of science, and others. When the Women's Medical Association branch I belonged to agreed to edit an issue of the journal and called for papers, I was able to offer, from my sociology term paper and a presentation I had made at the residents' journal club, the lead article on mental illness in primitive peoples.

But for my M.S., my dissertation remained. Good fortune was with me in assigning me a patient brought in for seizures and mental deterioration. When I examined her, I saw that the slightest touch on her face and neck resulted in tetanic spasms, which (from the chemistry studies I ordered) I identified as resulting from a failure of the tiny parathyroid glands in the neck beside the thyroid. (These glands function so well that usually no one thinks to question their failure unless the patient has had thyroid surgery and they were injured or removed accidentally.) Receiving proper treatment, within two days this woman was playing Ping-Pong on the ward.

The case caused excitement through the medical school, and I was asked to present the patient's history and physical at the weekly grand rounds that psychiatry did not usually attend. After I began my presentation, a friend of my husband's sat down beside him and whispered, "Who's that girl presenting the case?"

With his quick wit, he adapted the old joke and replied, "Why, that's no girl; that's my wife!"

The opportunity offered to me by the fortuitous arrival of this patient was to parlay the question of psychiatric symptoms in idiopathic hypoparathyroidism into my needed dissertation. In days before Internet and databases, and with the generous help of interested and enthusiastic librarians, I searched the world literature for other cases of the idiopathic condition, to inquire about psychiatric symptoms, and found only a hundred such reported cases. My paper completed the requirements for my M.S., and another version under my name and that of my chief, Rudolf Kaelbling, was accepted as a monograph supplement to a psychiatric journal, hence as a freestanding publication, my first "book".

My husband brought to my attention another opportunity. In the Sunday newspaper appeared an article about a new organization, the Mensa Society, membership in which required a documented IQ in the upper 2 percent. The line that attracted me was that members were willing to be studied by "qualified researchers". What a marvelous gift, I thought, to have a population (adults with high IQ) already identified and willing to be studied. My husband and I joined and enjoyed the association with people in careers other than medicine. And I did my questionnaire study on members of two chapters, resulting in my second book, *Through The Keyhole at Gifted Men and Women: A Study of 159 Members of the Mensa Society*.

As my life unrolled as a new mother, I noticed charming, jewel-like incidents in the mother/child relationship that I considered poetry-worthy. To me it seemed strange that mothers rarely wrote about these, but I determined to try my hand. I was encouraged when my first such effort won my only first prize in an all-Ohio contest, and the judge was kind enough to write me a note encouraging me to continue my efforts, which I have done. Many years later, when painful, tragic events rounded out my experiences as a mother, I embedded those also in poetry and collected the mother/child poems in *Into a Mirror and Through a Lens*, a title intended to suggest scrutiny by a trained observer who was also a mother.

Those tragedies in our family offered insights for other parents with similar problems. For this reason I wrote a book about each of them: *A Handful of Ashes* and *Fighting the Good Fight*. To protect identities, I went to a pen name and have used it subsequently to keep my oeuvre under one name.

Finally, my interest in nature led to a collection of nature poems, *Interlink*.

And now, *Envy*.

My current work is a collection of vignettes by anyone ancestral to my grandchildren including their other grandparents, my late husband, myself, our sons, and their wives, on our life experiences that we want not to be forgotten after the death of my entire generation. This book will be of interest primarily to family members and will be under my own name, Joanne D. Denko.

Victoria C. G. Greenleaf, M.D., M.S.
2009